Building Agentic AI Systems

Create intelligent, autonomous AI agents that can reason, plan, and adapt

Anjanava Biswas

Wrick Talukdar

Building Agentic AI Systems

Copyright © 2025 Packt Publishing

The author acknowledges the use of cutting-edge AI, such as ChatGPT, with the sole aim of enhancing the language and clarity within the book, thereby ensuring a smooth reading experience for readers. It's important to note that the content itself has been crafted by the author and edited by a professional publishing team.

Every effort has been made in the preparation of this book to ensure the accuracy of the information presented. However, the information contained in this book is sold without warranty, either express or implied. Neither the authors, nor Packt Publishing or its dealers and distributors, will be held liable for any damages caused or alleged to have been caused directly or indirectly by this book.

Packt Publishing has endeavored to provide trademark information about all of the companies and products mentioned in this book by the appropriate use of capitals. However, Packt Publishing cannot guarantee the accuracy of this information.

Portfolio Director: Gebin George

Relationship Lead: Ali Abidi

Project Manager: Prajakta Naik

Content Engineer: Aditi Chatterjee

Technical Editor: Irfa Ansari

Copy Editor: Safis Editing

Proofreader: Aditi Chatterjee

Indexer: Pratik Shirodkar

Production Designer: Pranit Padwal and Vijay Kamble

Growth Lead: Kunal Sawant

First published: April 2025

Production reference: 404125

Published by Packt Publishing Ltd.
Grosvenor House
11 St Paul's Square
Birmingham
B3 1RB, UK.

ISBN 978-1-80323-875-3

www.packtpub.com

*In loving memory of my father, whose guiding influence shapes every challenge I embrace.
To my mother, my wife, and my son—this book exists because of your love and constant support.
To my mentors and colleagues—thank you for lighting the way through this AI frontier. It's been
a privilege to learn from you and to share that journey.*

– Anjanava Biswas

*I dedicate this book to my parents, my son, my wife, and all my well-wishers—whose unwavering
support and constant encouragement have been the foundation of my journey. Their belief in me
has turned challenges into opportunities and dreams into accomplishments, making every milestone
along the way all the more meaningful.*

– Wrick Talukdar

Foreword

Artificial intelligence has always been driven by a profound aspiration: creating systems that not only perform predefined tasks but can also reason, adapt, and act with autonomy. With the rise of Generative AI and agentic systems, we are witnessing a transformative moment, one where artificial agents can reflect upon their experiences, strategize effectively, and collaborate seamlessly. This book arrives precisely at this pivotal juncture, offering a comprehensive exploration of this emerging and impactful field.

As someone with decades of experience in AI, spanning core research and product development as a technical leader at Microsoft Research and VC-backed AI startups, I've been deeply involved in high-impact AI research and the deployment of large-scale AI products that serve millions of users across both consumer and enterprise domains. My involvement in the IEEE in various AI leadership roles has also provided me with a unique perspective on the critical importance of ethical and responsible AI advancement.

I first met the authors, Wrick Talukdar and Anjanava Biswas, through our collaborative work on global IEEE AI initiatives. Their extensive expertise, demonstrated through their high-impact technical roles at AWS, work on AI and ML, as well as their scholarly AI research, is very impressive. Both Anjanava and Wrick are recognized leaders in Generative AI, bringing world-class expertise, dedication, and deep insights from architecting, developing and deploying cutting-edge AI platforms on a global scale. Their rich understanding of the technical complexities and ethical considerations uniquely qualifies them to author this important book.

Organized into three parts, the book initially lays a solid theoretical foundation by clearly defining and demystifying Generative AI and the essential characteristics of agentic systems. Readers are guided through core concepts, from Variational Autoencoders and Generative Adversarial Networks to sophisticated agent architectures, enabling both newcomers and seasoned professionals to navigate this complex landscape confidently.

In its second part, the book shifts focus to practical techniques necessary for developing intelligent agents capable of self-awareness, adaptability, and collaborative decision-making. The chapters on reflection, introspection, planning, and multi-agent collaboration provide invaluable methodologies and insights, empowering practitioners to design systems that dynamically learn and continuously improve.

The final section thoughtfully addresses the broader implications of deploying generative agentic systems in real-world contexts. By emphasizing transparency, explainability, safety, and ethical governance, this book underscores the essential responsibilities associated with advanced AI technologies. It provides a critical framework for fostering trust and ensuring these powerful tools align with societal values and ethical standards.

More than a technical reference, this book serves as an essential guide for shaping the future of Generative AI and intelligent agents. It invites researchers, industry leaders, and innovators to actively participate in crafting the next chapter of AI, one that responsibly advances technological boundaries while enriching society.

I wholeheartedly endorse this timely and insightful work. I encourage you to delve deep into the chapters that follow, embracing your role as an active contributor to the exciting and evolving frontier in artificial intelligence.

Matthew R. Scott,

Chief Technology Officer, Minset.ai

Spring 2025

Foreword 2

The world was caught by surprise when ChatGPT first launched in November 2022. It was an aha moment—suddenly, it felt like you were conversing with a real person. The responses weren't just fluent; they were informative and useful. Since then, the technology has evolved at an astonishing pace, with hundreds of millions of people using ChatGPT and similar systems as writing assistants or to find answers that aren't easily discoverable through traditional web searches.

However, when you ask a human assistant to book travel, they don't just talk about it—they actually book the flights and hotel. This is the essence of agentic systems. **Large language models** (**LLMs**), like those used in ChatGPT, can be repurposed not just to generate text but to act—executing tasks by generating code, calling APIs, and interacting with web services. Just as the World Wide Web transitioned from serving static content to enabling interactive applications, agentic systems are poised to revolutionize how we interact with AI.

Unlike other books that focus primarily on the theory behind agentic systems, this book emphasizes real-world implementation. The authors provide hands-on code examples, practical use cases, and step-by-step guidance on integrating agentic workflows into organizations to solve real business challenges. This book serves as an accessible yet comprehensive resource for software developers, ML engineers, technical leads, directors, and other decision-makers looking to get up to speed on agentic systems.

Those who have used AI assistants like ChatGPT understand their value as writing and coding assistants, where users validate the output before taking action. However, AI can sometimes generate incorrect answers with such confidence that users may mistakenly trust them. Unlike humans, who often hedge their statements with phrases like "I'm not sure, but I think…", AI systems lack built-in uncertainty indicators. We want to trust that our AI agents will take the correct actions and ask us when in doubt. This book delves into the crucial issues of trust, transparency, explainability, and reliability, as well as ethical considerations such as bias and safety. It describes how agentic systems can be personalized and made context aware, and how they can plan and react to the results of their actions.

As somebody that has been working on artificial intelligence for decades, I believe this book will be a great resource for students, researchers, and professionals alike, charting a clear path forward in an era profoundly influenced by intelligent systems. I first met Wrick Talukdar at an IEEE conference panel, and I was immediately impressed by his ability to bridge the gap between theory and practice. In *Building Agentic AI Systems*, he and Anjanava Biswas do just that—offering a practical guide to the future of AI-driven automation.

Dr. Alex Acero,

Member of the National Academy of Engineering,

IEEE Fellow

Contributors

About the authors

Anjanava Biswas is an award-winning senior AI specialist solutions architect with over 17 years of industry experience. Specializing in machine learning, generative AI, natural language processing, deep learning, data analytics, and cloud architecture, he partners with large enterprises to build and scale advanced AI systems in the cloud. Anjanava is widely recognized for his contributions to the field of applied AI. He has published research in multiple scientific journals and actively contributes to open-source AI/ML projects. His professional accolades include Fellowships with BCS (UK), the IET (UK), IETE (India), and he is a senior IEEE member. A frequent public speaker, Anjanava has held key positions at industry giants like IBM and Oracle Corp. Originally from India, he now resides in San Diego, CA, with his wife and son, where he continues to innovate and inspire within the tech community.

I would like to express my heartfelt gratitude to everyone who has accompanied me on this generative AI journey. To my colleagues, both past and present, who challenged my thinking and shared in the excitement of this rapidly evolving field—your collaboration has been invaluable. To my mentors, who saw potential in my ideas and guided me with wisdom and patience—your belief in me made this book possible.

To my remarkable son, whose eleven-year-old imagination reminds me daily that the future belongs to those who can dream it. Your questions force me to distill complexity into clarity—perhaps the most valuable skill in understanding generative AI. And to my wife, my steadfast companion through late nights and breakthrough moments—your patience has been the silent foundation upon which these ideas have been built.

To my mother, whose wisdom transcends technology and whose encouragement knows no bounds. And to my father, whose absence is felt deeply but whose influence remains in every challenge I choose to accept. I know you would have turned these pages with pride.

As Ada Lovelace once observed, "The Analytical Engine weaves algebraic patterns, just as the Jacquard loom weaves flowers and leaves." Today's generative AI continues this beautiful interplay between human creativity and computational possibility—a dance I have been privileged to document.

For everyone who believes that technology should elevate our humanity rather than diminish it— this book is for you.

– Anjanava Biswas

Wrick Talukdar is a visionary technology leader in generative **artificial intelligence (AI)** at Amazon, with over two decades of global experience in AI, cloud computing, and product leadership. A pioneer in AI-driven transformation, he has led large-scale modernization initiatives that drive enterprise growth and impact millions worldwide. He has spearheaded the productization of award-winning AI/ML technologies, now deployed at scale for Fortune 500 companies, shaping real-world AI applications.

A recognized figure in AI research, Wrick's work in generative AI, multimodality, natural language processing, and computer vision is widely cited and referenced in the field. As a senior IEEE member, Chair, and panelist in multiple industry forums, he advises global committees like CTSoc Industry Forums and NIC, setting industry standards and shaping AI's role for the future. He frequently presents his innovations at premier conferences such as World Technology Summit, IEEE HKN, ICCE, CERAWeek, and ADIPEC, bridging cutting-edge research with real-world AI applications to accelerate industry-wide innovation.

Deeply rooted in his computer science background, he co-chairs IEEE NIC to empower young professionals. As an author and thought leader, he continues to push AI's boundaries, inspiring future innovators. Wrick lives in California with his family.

In the words of Marian Wright Edelman, "Education is for improving the lives of others and for leaving your community and world better than you found it."

I am profoundly grateful to everyone who has supported, guided, and inspired me throughout this journey.

To my family—my parents, my son, and my wife—your unwavering belief in me has been the bedrock of my strength.

To my son, whose endless curiosity about "what Dad is working on" reminded me every day why discovery matters—your wonder and questions sparked ideas when I needed them most, and your imagination reminded me of the limitless possibilities this work can unlock. You've taught me that inspiration often comes in the form of a simple question from someone who believes you can explain the universe.

To my parents, whose unwavering support, confidence, and hunger to understand a rapidly evolving world reminds me that knowledge is meant to be shared, not stored. Your belief in lifelong learning has been my moral compass, and your pride in my work has been one of my greatest motivators.

And to my wife, whose quiet strength, patience, and constant encouragement made this journey not only possible, but meaningful. Your presence through long nights, your unwavering faith through every obstacle, and your calming reassurance gave me the clarity to finish what I started. You've been my anchor and my inspiration.

To the AI research community—your relentless pursuit of innovation continues to inspire and humble me. After years of writing research papers, technical articles, and blogs, authoring my first book has been a transformative experience—one that challenged me to translate complexity into clarity and ideas into impact.

And to my friends and well-wishers—your presence through every challenge turned obstacles into milestones. Whether through a kind word, a shared insight, or simply showing up when it mattered most, you reminded me that no journey is ever truly walked alone.

This book is a tribute to each of you. You've walked with me, believed in my vision, and helped shape every word on these pages.

– Wrick Talukdar

About the reviewers

Manjit Chakraborty is a seasoned technology leader with extensive experience in driving digital transformation in the financial services sector. As an enterprise solutions architect at **Amazon Web Services (AWS)**, he spearheads initiatives to modernize legacy systems and design innovative cloud-native solutions for the largest financial institutions across the globe. With a proven track record in business and technical architecture, Manjit excels in delivering actionable insights through data-driven analysis. His expertise spans diverse areas, including cloud migration, mainframe modernization strategies, system integrations, hybrid deployments, data analytics, and business intelligence. Manjit is a sought-after public speaker, having delivered presentations at numerous prestigious technical forums. He is an accomplished author and has also contributed to various technology publications, sharing his knowledge and insights with the broader tech community. Manjit is a distinguished reviewer, critically evaluating industry submissions and scholarly research papers on a regular basis, significantly influencing technological advancements and academic discourse. He is based out of the Sunshine State, Florida, in the United States.

Martin Yanev is a highly accomplished software engineer with nearly a decade of experience across diverse industries, including aerospace and medical technology. Over his illustrious career, Martin has carved a niche for himself in developing and integrating cutting-edge software solutions for critical domains such as air traffic control and chromatography systems. Renowned as an esteemed instructor and computer science professor at Fitchburg State University, he possesses a deep understanding of the full spectrum of OpenAI APIs and exhibits mastery in constructing, training, and fine-tuning AI systems. As a widely recognized author, Martin has shared his expertise to help others navigate the complexities of AI development. With his exceptional track record and multifaceted skill set, Martin continues to propel innovation and drive transformative advancements in the field of software engineering.

Join our communities on Discord and Reddit

Have questions about the book or want to contribute to discussions on Generative AI and LLMs? Join our Discord server at `https://packt.link/z8ivB` and our Reddit channel at `https://packt.link/0rExL` to connect, share, and collaborate with like-minded enthusiasts.

Table of Contents

3

Essential Components of Intelligent Agents   51

Part 2: Designing and Implementing Generative AI-Based Agents   75

4

Reflection and Introspection in Agents   77

5

Enabling Tool Use and Planning in Agents   107

6

Exploring the Coordinator, Worker, and Delegator Approach   137

7

Effective Agentic System Design Techniques   161

Part 3: Trust, Safety, Ethics, and Applications   187

8

Building Trust in Generative AI Systems   189

9

Managing Safety and Ethical Considerations   205

10

Common Use Cases and Applications   221

11

Conclusion and Future Outlook   239

12

Unlock Your Exclusive Benefits   249

Index   253

Other Books You May Enjoy   264

Preface

Building Agentic AI Systems is designed to provide both a theoretical foundation and practical guidance on generative AI and agent-based intelligence. Generative AI and agentic systems are at the forefront of the next wave of AI, driving automation, creativity, and decision-making in ways that were previously unimaginable. By enabling machines to generate text, images, and even strategic plans while reasoning and adapting autonomously, these technologies are transforming industries such as healthcare, finance, and robotics.

The book begins by introducing generative AI, covering key models such as **Variational Autoencoders (VAEs)**, **Generative Adversarial Networks (GANs)**, and autoregressive models. We explore their applications in content creation, design, and scientific research while addressing the limitations and challenges of these models.

Next, we dive into the world of agentic systems, defining concepts such as agency, autonomy, and multi-agent collaboration. We analyze different agent architectures—deliberative, reactive, and hybrid—and explore how multiple agents can interact, cooperate, and coordinate toward common goals.

Once the foundations are established, we move into practical implementation. We explore how agents can reflect on their own reasoning processes, plan, and use external tools effectively. This includes hands-on techniques for meta-reasoning, self-explanation, strategic planning, and multi-agent coordination. The book also introduces best practices for designing intelligent, trustworthy AI agents, balancing autonomy with control, and ensuring ethical and responsible AI development.

To conclude, we examine real-world use cases and applications across multiple domains, from NLP and robotics to decision support and optimization. We also explore trust, transparency, bias mitigation, and AI safety—key elements for ensuring the reliability of AI-driven systems.

Throughout this book, you will find code examples, practical exercises, and implementation strategies to help bridge the gap between theory and real-world application. Whether you are an AI practitioner, researcher, engineer, or technology leader, this book will equip you with the skills and knowledge to build autonomous, adaptive, and intelligent AI agents that can reason, collaborate, and evolve.

Let's embark on this journey together, shaping the future of intelligent systems—one agent at a time.

Who this book is for

This book is intended for AI practitioners, developers, researchers, engineers, and technology leaders who want to understand and build AI-driven agents that exhibit autonomy, adaptability, and intelligence. Whether you are a developer looking to integrate generative models into intelligent systems or an AI architect exploring advanced agentic capabilities, this book will equip you with both theoretical foundations and hands-on implementation strategies.

What this book covers

Chapter 1, Fundamentals of Generative AI, introduces generative AI, explaining its core concepts, various model types—including VAEs, GANs, and autoregressive models—real-world applications, and challenges such as bias, limitations, and ethical concerns.

Chapter 2, Principles of Agentic Systems, defines agentic systems, covering agency, autonomy, and the essential characteristics of intelligent agents, including reactivity, proactiveness, and social ability. It also explores different agent architectures and multi-agent collaboration.

Chapter 3, Essential Components of Intelligent Agents, details key elements of intelligent agents, including knowledge representation, reasoning, learning mechanisms, decision-making, and the role of Generative AI in enhancing agent capabilities.

Chapter 4, Reflection and Introspection in Agents, explores how intelligent agents analyze their reasoning, learn from experience, and improve decision-making using techniques such as meta-reasoning, self-explanation, and self-modeling.

Chapter 5, Enabling Tool Use and Planning in Agents, discusses how agents leverage external tools, implement planning algorithms, and integrate tool use with strategic decision-making to improve efficiency and goal achievement.

Chapter 6, Exploring the Coordinator, Worker, and Delegator Approach, introduces the CWD model for multi-agent collaboration, explaining how agents take on specialized roles—coordinator, worker, or delegator—to optimize task execution and resource allocation.

Chapter 7, Effective Agentic System Design Techniques, covers best practices for designing intelligent agents, including focused instructions, setting guardrails and constraints, balancing autonomy and control, and ensuring transparency and accountability.

Chapter 8, Building Trust in Generative AI Systems, examines techniques for fostering trust in AI, including transparency, explainability, handling uncertainty and bias, and designing AI systems that are reliable and interpretable.

Chapter 9, Managing Safety and Ethical Considerations, addresses the risks and challenges of generative AI, strategies for ensuring responsible AI development, ethical guidelines, and privacy and security considerations for AI deployments.

Chapter 10, Common Use Cases and Applications, showcases real-world applications of Generative AI, covering areas such as creative content generation, conversational AI, robotics, and decision-support systems.

Chapter 11, Conclusion and Future Outlook, summarizes key concepts covered in the book, explores emerging trends in generative AI and agentic intelligence, discusses **artificial general intelligence (AGI)**, and highlights future challenges and opportunities in the field.

To get the most out of this book

Following along will be a bit easier if you have the following:

- **Familiarity with AI and machine learning concepts**: While the book covers foundational principles, prior knowledge of AI/ML, deep learning, and Python programming will help you understand the more advanced topics.

- **Hands-on practice**: Experiment with the provided code examples and frameworks for building Generative AI and agentic systems. Setting up a local or cloud-based development environment will enhance your learning experience.

- **Think critically about AI ethics and safety**: As you explore Generative AI and autonomous agents, consider the implications of trust, bias, and responsible AI design to build intelligent systems that align with ethical guidelines.

Software/hardware covered in the book	Operating system requirements
Python, Jupyter Notebooks, and CrewAI	Windows, macOS, Linux

Download the example code files

The code bundle for the book is hosted on GitHub at `https://github.com/PacktPublishing/Building-Agentic-AI-Systems`. We also have other code bundles from our rich catalog of books and videos available at `https://github.com/PacktPublishing`. Check them out!

Disclaimer on images

Some images in this title are presented for contextual purposes, and the readability of the graphic is not crucial to the discussion. Please refer to our free graphic bundle to download the images. You can download the images from `https://packt.link/gbp/9781803238753`

Conventions used

There are a number of text conventions used throughout this book.

Bold: Indicates a new term, an important word, or words that you see onscreen. For instance, words in menus or dialog boxes appear in bold. Here is an example: "**Customized onboarding plan**: Based on the goals and needs identified, create a bespoke onboarding plan that outlines the steps, milestones, and timelines toward achieving the set objectives."

> **Tips or important notes**
> Appear like this.

Get in touch

Newsletter: To keep up with the latest developments in the fields of Generative AI and LLMs, subscribe to our weekly newsletter, AI_Distilled, at `https://packt.link/Q5UyU`.

Feedback from our readers is always welcome.

General feedback: If you have questions about any aspect of this book, email us at `customercare@packtpub.com` and mention the book title in the subject of your message.

Errata: Although we have taken every care to ensure the accuracy of our content, mistakes do happen. If you have found a mistake in this book, we would be grateful if you would report this to us. Please visit `www.packtpub.com/support/errata` and fill in the form.

Piracy: If you come across any illegal copies of our works in any form on the internet, we would be grateful if you would provide us with the location address or website name. Please contact us at `copyright@packt.com` with a link to the material.

If you are interested in becoming an author: If there is a topic that you have expertise in and you are interested in either writing or contributing to a book, please visit `authors.packtpub.com`.

Share Your Thoughts

Once you've read *Building Agentic AI Systems*, we'd love to hear your thoughts! Scan the QR code below to go straight to the Amazon review page for this book and share your feedback.

https://packt.link/r/1803238755

Your review is important to us and the tech community and will help us make sure we're delivering excellent quality content.

Free Benefits with Your Book

This book comes with free benefits to support your learning. Activate them now for instant access (see the "*How to Unlock*" section for instructions).

Here's a quick overview of what you can instantly unlock with your purchase:

PDF and ePub Copies

Next-Gen Web-Based Reader

Access a DRM-free PDF copy of this book to read anywhere, on any device.

Use a DRM-free ePub version with your favorite e-reader.

Multi-device progress sync: Pick up where you left off, on any device.

Highlighting and notetaking: Capture ideas and turn reading into lasting knowledge.

Bookmarking: Save and revisit key sections whenever you need them.

Dark mode: Reduce eye strain by switching to dark or sepia themes

How to Unlock

UNLOCK NOW

Scan the QR code (or go to `packtpub.com/unlock`). Search for this book by name, confirm the edition, and then follow the steps on the page.

Note: Keep your invoice handly. Purchase made directly from packt don't require one.

Part 1: Foundations of Generative AI and Agentic Systems

This part establishes the fundamental concepts of generative AI and agentic systems, providing you with a solid theoretical foundation for understanding and developing intelligent, autonomous agents.

This part contains the following chapters:

- *Chapter 1, Fundamentals of Generative AI*
- *Chapter 2, Principles of Agentic Systems*
- *Chapter 3, Essential Components of Intelligent Agents*

1

Fundamentals of Generative AI

Generative AI has quickly become a transformative technology in the field of **artificial intelligence** (**AI**) and machine learning, revolutionizing creative processes and problem-solving across diverse industries and use cases. It is pushing the boundaries of autonomy in agent-based intelligent systems. In this chapter, we will cover the basics of generative AI. We will explore what generative AI is along with a brief history of generative AI models. We will then discuss the different types of generative models, which include **variational autoencoders** (**VAEs**), **generative adversarial networks** (**GANs**), autoregressive, and Transformer models. Next, we will delve into the applications of generative AI and wrap up the chapter with a brief discussion of some of the limitations and challenges related to generative AI.

We will cover the following topics in this introductory chapter that will help set the foundations of generative AI as we explore further the capabilities of autonomous intelligent agents powered by generative AI:

- Introduction to generative AI

- Types of generative AI models

- Applications of generative AI

- Challenges and limitations of generative AI

By the end of this chapter, you will have gained a comprehensive understanding of generative AI, including its fundamental concepts, diverse applications, and current challenges. You will also learn about the technology's potential and limitations, with a particular focus on its critical role in advancing intelligent agents and agentic systems.

Free Benefits with Your Book

Your purchase includes a free PDF copy of this book along with other exclusive benefits. Check the *Free Benefits with Your Book* section in the Preface to unlock them instantly and maximize your learning experience.

Introduction to generative AI

Generative AI refers to a class of AI technologies that is capable of generating various forms of content, including but not limited to text, images, audio, and video. These AI systems can generate new content, based on their training data and input parameters, which usually include text prompts but can also involve other forms of input such as images. The recent buzz around generative AI comes from the simplicity with which new user interfaces powered by this AI technology can create high-quality text, graphics, and videos in seconds.

In very simple terms, generative AI is about making new data that looks like the data from which it has been trained. In other words, learning the underlying patterns, structures, and distributions of input data enables a procedure within the model allowing it to generate new data in a similar way. For instance, if trained on a dataset of human faces, a generative AI model will be able to create completely new faces of people that don't actually exist in real life but are very realistic. In essence, generative AI models work by learning the probability distribution of a dataset and then sampling from that distribution to create new instances. This approach is different from discriminative models, whose goal is to learn how to tell classes of data apart. For example, a discriminative model could be trained to separate pictures of cats and dogs, but a generative model would be trained to make up completely new pictures of cats or dogs.

The concept of generative AI goes a long way back; in fact, it dates back to the time when machine learning was in its cradle. However, it is only recently that this field has come under the limelight due to neural networks and drastic improvements in computing power over the last 10 years. In the early attempts at generative modeling—Gaussian mixture models and hidden Markov models—many simpler statistical techniques were involved. Methods of modeling arbitrary complex data distributions have much higher potential compatibility with the kinds of methods that were previously dominant but have recently been overcome by deep learning. Deep learning was therefore a watershed development for the field of generative AI. Models, such as VAEs, which started appearing around the beginning of the 2010s, were able to leverage deep neural networks to model more complex data distributions. Around that same period, GANs were proposed; for the first time, they offered a new way for two neural networks to work together to create data, using principles from game theory. In a general sense, these breakthroughs took leaps toward the possibilities of making real, high-quality, realistic creation of data.

This can lead to innovation in most fields across industries, such as healthcare, finance, education, travel and hospitality, manufacturing, and more. Generative AI in creative industries helps artists and designers think outside the box, helping with the conception of new and innovative content. It opens ways for new routes of drug discovery and personalized medicine in health. In the business world, generative AI works by providing efficient and effective customer engagement through personalized content and experiences. The other point involves questioning one's own stance regarding creativity and originality: when machines are able to pump out very similar material, one is automatically forced to think about what creativity is, who the artist really is, and what the ethical parameters should be for AI-created content.

Having understood what generative AI is and its brief history, let's explore the different types of generative AI models.

Types of generative AI models

Generative AI is an exciting domain of AI that deals with the generation of new, synthetic data by learning patterns from existing datasets, aiming to generate outputs that share similar statistical properties and characteristics with the training data. Here is a broad overview of some of the most prominent types of generative models: VAEs, GANs, and autoregressive models.

VAEs

One of the most popular generative models is the VAE. The core idea behind VAE consists of learning a probabilistic mapping between data and a latent space, and vice versa. This means learning how to convert real data into a simplified representation (such as a compressed form) and then back again into data that looks real. VAEs are designed to ensure a high likelihood of the data while preserving a well-structured latent space to enable the generation of new data samples similar to the training data. Some of the most common flavors of VAE are as follows:

- **VAE**: The basic model that compresses and reconstructs data. It gives a framework for generating new samples out of the learned latent space. The VAE is a generative model that learns to compress and reconstruct data while also learning a probability distribution of the latent space. In simpler terms, a VAE is like a clever algorithm that learns to understand and recreate data. Imagine it as a skilled artist who can compress a detailed painting into a simple sketch (encoding) and then recreate the full painting from that sketch (decoding). What makes VAEs special is that they don't just copy data but also learn the essence of it, allowing them to create new, similar data. This is like an artist learning not just to copy specific paintings but also to understand the style so well that they can paint new, original works in that style. In real life, VAEs have been used in many creative ways. For instance, in drug discovery, VAEs have been used to generate novel molecular structures. Researchers at AstraZeneca used VAEs to explore chemical space and propose new drug-like molecules with desired properties, potentially accelerating the drug development process [1].

- **Beta-VAE**: An extension of VAE that introduces a hyperparameter to control explicitly the trade-off between the reconstruction quality and the disentanglement of the latent space. The model undertakes the creation of more interpretable disentangled representations. In simpler terms, Beta-VAE is like a more flexible version of the original VAE. It allows researchers to adjust how much the model focuses on recreating exact details versus understanding the underlying features of the data. This is similar to teaching an art student to not just copy a painting but also to understand and separate the key elements such as color, shape, and style. This ability to *disentangle* features makes Beta-VAE particularly useful in fields such as computer vision and robotics. For example, researchers have used Beta-VAE to teach robots to understand objects better. By learning to separate features such as size, color, and position, robots can more easily recognize and manipulate objects in different situations, making them more adaptable and efficient in various tasks [2].

- **Conditional variational autoencoder (CVAE)**: A variant that conditions the generation process on some extra information, typically class labels, producing not just data similar to the training set but also samples that can then be drawn from specific classes . Think of CVAE as a more controlled version of VAE, like an artist who can paint in different styles on demand. Instead of just creating random new paintings, this artist can be told to *"Paint a landscape"* or *"Paint a portrait"* and they'll create new art in that specific category. This added control makes CVAE very useful in practical applications. For instance, in the field of computer games, CVAE has been used for game development and procedural content generation with the generation of game elements such as character design, level layouts, music and sound effects, and so on. By providing different conditions such as *"Create a forest level"* or *"Create a desert level,"* the CVAE can produce a wide variety of game environments, saving time for designers and enhancing the player's experience with more diverse and interesting game worlds [3].

GANs

A GAN is basically formed by two neural networks: a **generator** and a **discriminator**. The generator generates synthetic data samples; the other trained neural network should then be able to tell the difference between real and created samples. While training these networks, they are trained together antagonistically: the generator tries to fool the discriminator, while the discriminator tries rightly to classify real versus fake data. In this competition, the generator gets better and better at faking data. The following are some of the different types of GANs:

- **GAN**: The basic model in which the generator and discriminator are trained adversarially; it is the root model for most innovations in generative modeling. As explained earlier, you can imagine GAN as a game between two players—a counterfeiter (generator) trying to create fake money, and a detective (discriminator) trying to identify the fakes. As they compete, they both get better at their jobs, which means that the counterfeiter gets increasingly better at creating fake money. This clever setup allows GANs to create incredibly realistic fake data, such as images or sounds [4].

- **Deep convolutional GAN (DCGAN)**: This is a refinement of the base GAN model with deep convolutional neural networks; at the moment, it is one of the best architectures for generating images of high quality. Think of DCGAN as a more sophisticated artist compared to the basic GAN. It's like upgrading from simple sketching tools to a full digital art studio, allowing for the creation of much more detailed and realistic images. DCGANs are particularly good at understanding and recreating complex patterns in images [5].

- **Wasserstein GAN (WGAN)**: This proposes a different loss function with the Wasserstein distance. This removes problems while training with a GAN, hence making training more stable and improving sample quality. This helps measure the distance between two probability distributions better. WGAN is like giving the artist (generator) and critic (discriminator) in a GAN a better way to communicate and evaluate each other's work. Instead of just saying *"good"* or *"bad,"* they can now give more nuanced feedback, such as *"You're getting warmer"* or *"You're way off."* This leads to more consistent improvement and high-quality results. In practical applications, WGANs have been used in medical imaging to generate synthetic medical images for training purposes. This helps in creating larger, more diverse datasets for training diagnostic AI systems, potentially improving their accuracy in detecting diseases from scans and X-rays [6].

- **StyleGAN**: This generates high-quality realistic images. The model is especially good at handling style and content separately. Progressions offered by the introductions of StyleGAN2 and StyleGAN3 are still aimed at improving image fidelity and realism. Think of StyleGAN as an advanced digital artist that can not only create realistic images but also mix and match different styles and contents. It's like having a painter who can take the style of Van Gogh and apply it to a modern cityscape. This flexibility makes StyleGAN incredibly versatile [7].

Autoregressive models and Transformer architecture

Autoregressive models generate their data points one at a time, conditioning each of its data points on the previous one. Surprisingly, this ultimately proves very useful in tasks in which the sequence or structure of data is relevant, such as text generation and image generation. The Transformer architecture, introduced in the *Attention Is All You Need* paper [8], is a model architecture that has revolutionized many sequential data tasks, especially in **natural language processing (NLP)**. Its key components are demonstrated in *Figure 1.1*:

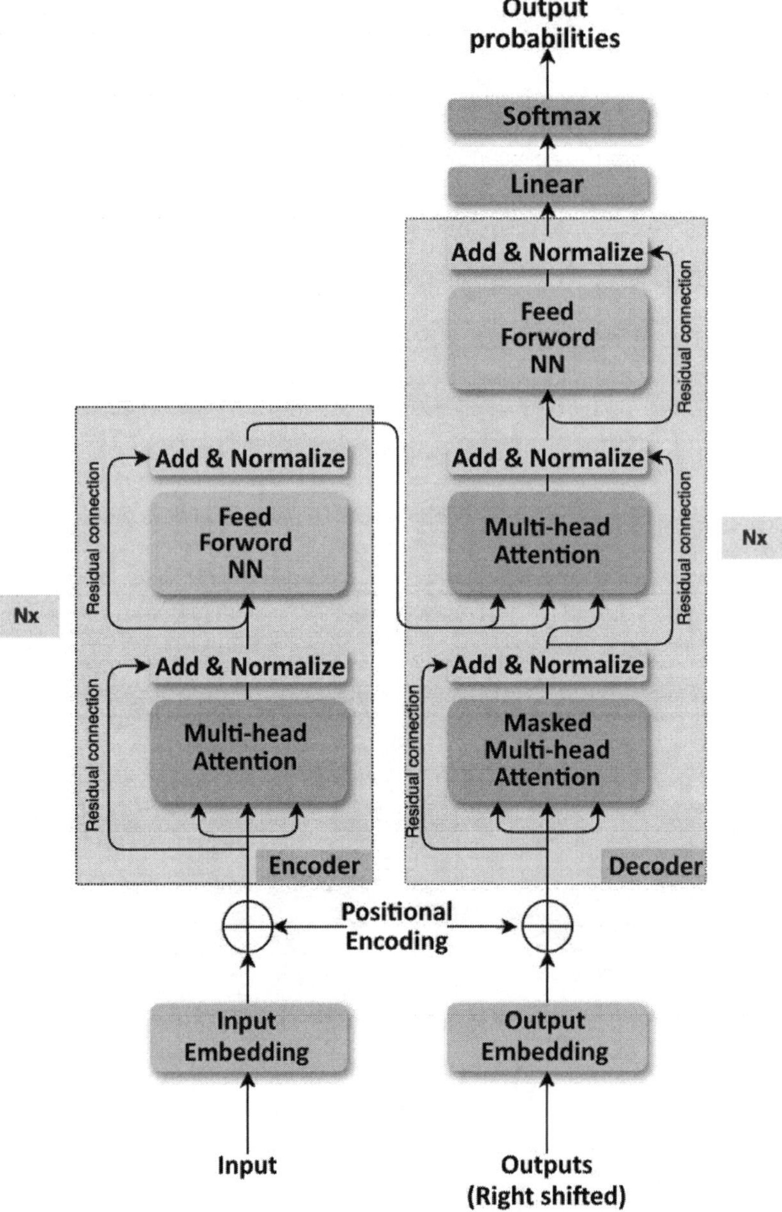

Figure 1.1 – The Transformer architecture

These key components include the following:

- **Self-attention mechanism**: A computational technique that allows the model to dynamically focus on different parts of the input when processing each element

- **Multi-head attention**: Multiple attention mechanisms running in parallel, allowing the model to focus on different aspects of the input simultaneously

- **Positional encoding**: Adds information about the position of each element in the sequence

- **Feed-forward neural networks**: Process the output of the attention layers

- **Layer normalization and residual connections**: Enhance training stability and information flow

Transformers can be used in both autoregressive and non-autoregressive configurations, making them versatile for various tasks. The following are some examples:

- **PixelCNN**: Autoregressively generates images pixel by pixel, conditioning each pixel on the previously generated ones. This model works very well in generating high-quality images with fine details [9].

- **PixelSNAIL**: A refinement over PixelCNN that adds attention mechanisms into the model to capture strong dependencies between pixels, and hence, a better quality of an image [10].

- **GPT**: Standing for **Generative Pre-trained Transformer**, it is a line of models specializing in text generation—namely, predicting which words should come next. Among them are GPT-2, GPT-3, and GPT-4, making a huge leap in generating coherent and contextually relevant text [11] [12].

- **BERT**: Unlike GPT, BERT, which stands for **Bidirectional Encoder Representations from Transformers**, is designed to understand the context from both directions in text. It uses the encoder part of the Transformer and is typically used for tasks that require an understanding of the entire input at once, rather than generating text autoregressively [13].

- **Text-To-Text Transfer Transformer** (T5): This model frames all NLP tasks in a text-to-text format. It uses the full Transformer architecture (both encoder and decoder) and can handle various text generation tasks [14].

Although it depends on the task, these models demonstrate how the Transformer architecture can be adapted for both autoregressive (such as GPT) and non-autoregressive (such as BERT) tasks, showcasing its versatility in handling sequential data. Strengths differ across generative models. This class of models goes from generating photorealistic images to coherent text to totally new data samples.

Building upon the success of models such as GPT, researchers have scaled up these architectures to create **large language models (LLMs)**. These models, often trained on vast amounts of open web text and other freely available text data, have demonstrated exceptional proficiency in understanding and generating human-like text across diverse applications, showcasing their versatility and advanced linguistic abilities. Examples of LLMs include GPT-3, GPT-4, PaLM, and BERT-large. These models have pushed the boundaries of what's possible in NLP, showing proficiency in tasks ranging from question-answering and summarization to creative writing and code generation. The following is an overview of the common types of LLMs:

- **Autoregressive LLMs**: These language models are typically capable of generating text sequentially, that is, one token at a time. Some of the common tasks that these types of models are used for include text generation, text completion tasks, and creative writing. Some popular examples of autoregressive LLMs are the GPT series (GPT-3, GPT-4), and PaLM.

- **Encoder-only LLMs**: These models specialize in **natural language understanding** (**NLU**) tasks, which involve analyzing and comprehending input text without generating new text. Encoder-only LLMs, such as BERT and its variants including RoBERTa, focus on understanding the context and meaning of input text. These models process the entire input sequence simultaneously, allowing them to capture the context helping with tasks such as text classification, **named entity recognition** (**NER**), and sentiment analysis.

- **Encoder-decoder LLMs**: This is a combination of encoder and decoder architecture where the models can not only understand the context of the input text (NLU) but are also capable of generating textual output. The T5 model discussed earlier is a very popular example of an encoder-decoder LLM, along with models such as BERT. These models are capable of language translation, summarization, and question-answering.

- **Multimodal LLMs**: Multimodality is a concept where an AI model can not only handle text but also other modalities such as image, video, and audio. Multimodal LLMs can process and generate content in various modalities such as text, image, audio, video, and any combination thereof. These models are rather novel in nature and recent advancements in compute have made it possible to train multimodal LLMs. Some of the well-known multimodal LLMs are DALL-E, Stable Diffusion, Flamingo, GPT-4, and LlaVa.

- **Instruction-tuned LLMs**: LLMs are often trained on a large corpus of openly available web or other text. As such, in certain scenarios, these models may not perform effectively for tasks that use data that the model has never seen before and thus may fail to follow the user intent. For example, a manufacturing manual for a proprietary instrument may contain domain-specific proprietary language, which the model may not have been exposed to during training. In such cases, LLMs can be fine-tuned using the domain-specific data to follow specific instructions and prompts (that is, text input to the model). This special fine-tuning enables the model to perform domain-specific tasks on which the model was fine-tuned, in addition to its other capabilities. Think of this as localizing a personal copy of a model to be good at performing a task that is meaningful for your use case. One of the common examples of such a model is InstructGPT, where researchers fine-tuned the GPT-3 model on specific instructions. These types of models are used in a multitude of different tasks such as chatbots, virtual assistants, and task-specific applications.

- **Domain-specific LLMs**: As mentioned earlier, while LLMs are often trained on a large set of open, generally available, web data, they may not perform very well in domain-specific environments. While instruction-tuned LLMs are an avenue to make these general-purpose models work for domain-specific tasks, researchers have innovated on training domain-specific LLMs from the ground up. This means that these models were pre-trained on highly specialized, domain knowledge. For example, the BioBERT model is trained on hyper-specialized medical data, whereas LegalBERT is trained on legal documents. These models are useful for specialized tasks in specific fields such as medicine, law, and finance.

LLM-powered AI agents

Each of the previously discussed LLM types has its own strengths and weaknesses and is well-suited for different applications. However, our focus in this book would be to dive deeper into LLM agent capabilities and explore how advanced systems can be built utilizing them. It is important to note that LLM agents do not fit neatly into a single category, as they represent an advanced application of LLM technology rather than a specific type of model architecture. Agents are typically built using instruction-tuned LLMs as their foundation, often combined with additional components and capabilities as you will learn further in this book.

Let us take a look at a simple example to demonstrate the capabilities of an agentic system powered by an LLM. Our example is a travel website that has a **Flight Booking Assistant** chatbot that is a conversational interface built with an LLM. It can help customers book travel tickets via human-like conversations. In the backend, the chatbot can perform various tasks as the conversation progresses. Here's what a sample conversation may look like for a customer who is looking to book a flight ticket:

Flight Booking Assistant	
	Hi, I want to book a flight.
	Hello! I'd be happy to help you book a flight. To get started, could you please tell me your departure city and destination?
	I want to go from San Diego to SFO.
	Great, thank you for providing that information. You're looking to fly from San Diego (SAN) to San Francisco International Airport (SFO). To help you find the best flight options, I'll need a few more details. 1. What is your preferred travel date? 2. Is this a one-way trip or a round trip? 3. How many passengers will be traveling?

I want to go next Friday and come back on Sunday. Just me traveling.

Thank you for the additional information. Let me summarize what I have so far:

- Departure: San Diego (SAN) to San Francisco (SFO)

- Outbound Date: Next Friday – 08/23/2024

- Return Date: Sunday – 08/25/2024

- Passengers: 1 adult

Before I search for flights, I have a few more questions:

1. Do you have a preferred time of day for your flights (morning, afternoon, or evening)?

2. Do you have a preferred airline or are you open to all airlines?

3. What class of service would you prefer (Economy, Premium Economy, Business, or First Class)?

I prefer morning flights. No airline preference. Economy is fine.

Thank you for those details. I'll search for morning flights in Economy class across all airlines for your trip. Give me a moment to find the best options for you.

[searching flights...please stand by....]

I've found a few options for your trip. Here are the best morning flights:

Outbound (SAN to SFO) - Next Friday:

1. United Airlines UA1234: Depart 7:15 AM, Arrive 8:45 AM

2. Alaska Airlines AS5678: Depart 8:30 AM, Arrive 10:00 AM

Return (SFO to SAN) - Sunday:

1. Delta Air Lines DL9876: Depart 9:00 AM, Arrive 10:30 AM

2. Southwest Airlines WN5432: Depart 10:15 AM, Arrive 11:45 AM

The total price for the round trip, including taxes and fees, is:

- Option 1 (United/Alaska): $325

- Option 2 (Delta/Southwest): $310

Which option would you prefer? Or would you like me to look for different flights?

The second option looks good. Can you book that for me?

Certainly! I'd be happy to book the second option for you. Just to confirm, I'll be booking the following itinerary:

Outbound: Alaska Airlines AS5678

- Date: 08/23/2024

- Depart San Diego at 8:30 AM, Arrive in SFO at 10:00 AM

Return: Southwest Airlines WN5432

- Date: 08/25/2024

- Depart SFO at 10:15 AM, Arrive in San Diego at 11:45 AM

Total price: $310

To proceed with the booking, I'll need some additional information:

1. Your full name as it appears on your government-issued ID

2. Your date of birth

3. Your email address (for sending the confirmation)

4. Your phone number

5. Any special requests (for example, meal preferences, seat preferences)

Also, please note that you'll need to provide a form of payment to complete the booking. Are you ready to proceed with this information?

Yes, I'm ready. My name is John Smith, born on 05/15/1985. My email is john.smith@email.com and my phone number is 555-123-4567. No special requests.

Thank you for providing that information, Mr. Smith. I've entered your details into the booking system. Here's a summary of the information I have:

- Name: John Smith

- Date of Birth: 05/15/1985

- Email: john.smith@email.com

- Phone: 555-123-4567

- Special Requests: None

The final step is to process the payment of $310 for your flights. For security reasons, I can't accept credit card information directly in this chat. Instead, I'll send a secure payment link to your email address (john.smith@email.com).

Once you receive the email, please follow the link to complete the payment process. After the payment is successfully processed, you'll receive another email with your flight confirmation and e-tickets.

Is it okay to proceed with sending the payment link to your email?

Yes, that's fine. Please send the payment link.

Excellent, Mr. Smith. I've initiated the process to send the secure payment link to your email address (john.smith@email.com). You should receive it within the next few minutes. Please check your inbox and spam folder if you don't see it right away.

Once you complete the payment, the system will automatically process your booking and send your confirmation email with the e-tickets. This email will include important information such as:

1. Booking confirmation number

2. Detailed flight itinerary

3. Check-in instructions

4. Baggage allowance information

5. Airline contact information

After you receive your confirmation email, please review all the details to ensure everything is correct. If you notice any issues or have any questions, please don't hesitate to contact us.

Is there anything else you need assistance with regarding your trip or the booking process?

	No, that's all. Thank you for your help!
	You're welcome, Mr. Smith! I'm glad I could assist you with booking your flights from San Diego to San Francisco. If you need any further assistance with this booking or have any questions about your trip, please don't hesitate to reach out. We're here to help 24/7. Have a great trip to San Francisco next week!

On the surface, this example looks pretty straightforward. However, there are a number of things that are happening in the background. Firstly, the customer starts with a vague request to book a flight. The AI assistant understands that in order to proceed with this request, it needs a few more pieces of information to look up available flights, such as departure/arrival city, dates of travel, and so on.

As the conversation progresses, the AI assistant requests further pieces of information to be able to successfully complete the booking. The information it gathers at each step is used as a parameter value to call flight booking-related APIs in the backend; for example, city/travel dates/number of passengers are required to look up available flight information using a (fictitious) API named **flightLookup**, customer name/phone/email are required to actually make the booking using an API named **bookFlight**, and so on. *Figure 1.2* gives an overview of the decisions that the model makes, the flow of the interaction, and the tools (API functions) it calls to complete each step:

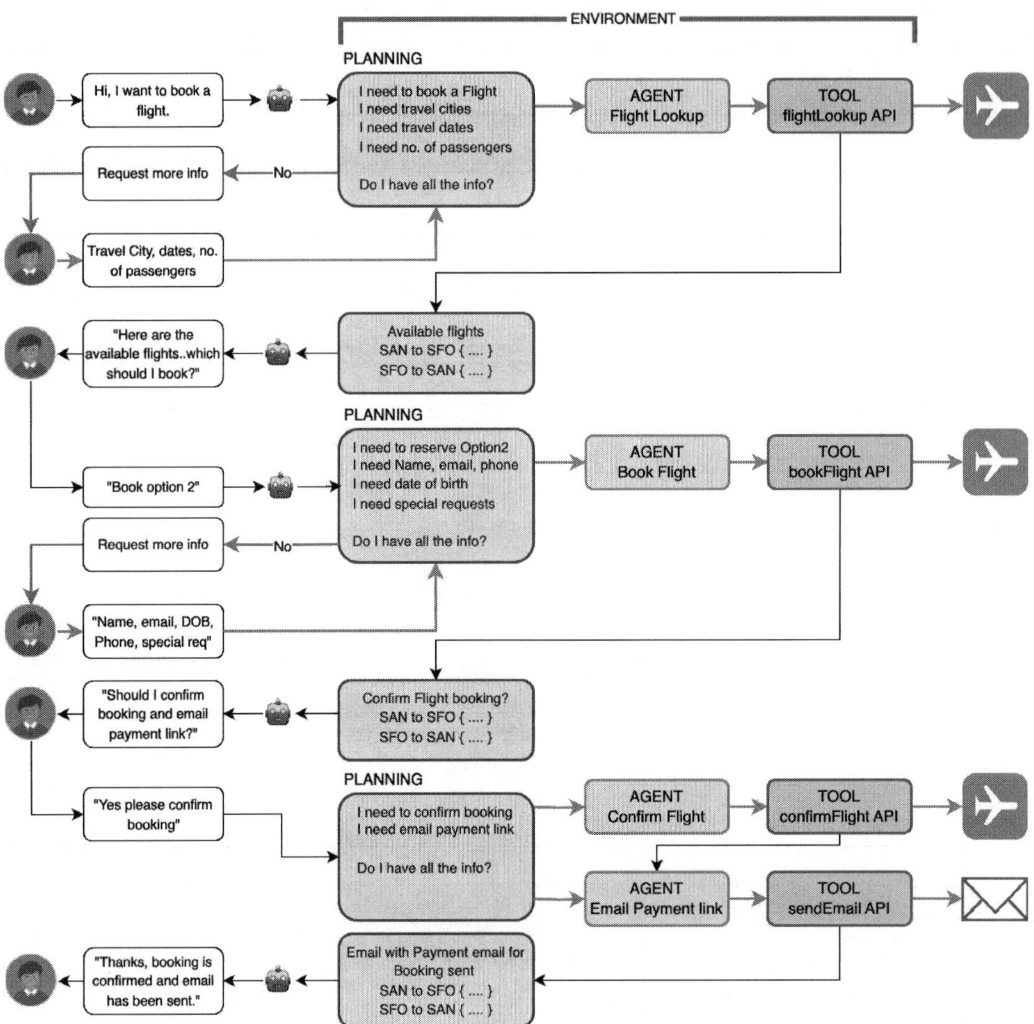

Figure 1.2 – Flight Booking Assistant chatbot with LLM-powered multi-agents

In addition to just tool calling, you will also notice that the model does a bit of introspection, also known as **chain of thought** (**CoT**), at the beginning of the conversation. This means the model in the backend crafts a step-by-step approach to complete the task but identifies some missing information. It then responds back to the customer with a request to provide the required information. Subsequently, based on the input from the customer, it makes certain decisions autonomously to call specific tools using the agent and completes the task.

In addition to the external tools and APIs, there are a number of other things to consider when designing such a system. We will cover the fundamentals of each of these components in detail in the subsequent chapters. For now, it is sufficient to know that agents are an advanced application of LLMs (such as this travel booking AI assistant) and represent an emerging field that combines aspects of various LLM types with additional AI techniques such as reinforcement learning, planning, and tool use. As you learn more in subsequent chapters, you will notice that agents are designed to be more interactive, adaptable, and capable of completing complex, multi-step tasks compared to standard LLMs, which makes them suitable for a variety of different complex tasks and workflows.

But before we dive deeper into the details of agentic systems, let us review some of the applications of generative AI.

Applications of generative AI

Generative AI has innovation capabilities that cover a diverse set of fields. As discussed earlier, industries such as healthcare, finance, education, media and entertainment, marketing, manufacturing, retail, and so on all have the potential to benefit from generative AI capabilities. The following is a survey of only a few of the primary applications of generative AI:

- **Generation of images and videos**: Multimodal generative models (that is, LLMs that can handle images, text, audio, and videos) are making it possible to generate realistic audio/visuals through various platforms and tools. For example, in media and entertainment, generative AI can help in generating visual effects, designing avatars, and developing virtual reality content. In the fashion and design industry, it is being used to conceptualize new clothing designs, prepare virtual fashion shows, and make fashion trend predictions. In marketing ads and promotion space, generative AI is being used to generate tailor-made advertisements, campaigns, marketing communications, and other marketing materials creatives such as images and logos.

- **Text and content generation**: Generative AI has made significant strides when it comes to text-based tasks. For instance, content writing such as rapid and hassle-free generation of articles, blog posts, marketing, and product copies are already some of the most common use cases. Chatbots and virtual assistants are providing customer support in a very humanlike manner to information-related inquiries. Generative AI is also assisting in text translation, document summarization, and content localization for increased accessibility of content for platforms such as online learning and specialized search engines.

- **Music and audio generation**: Creating original music, sound effects, and voice synthesis is yet another paradigm of multi-media content generation that is being powered by generative AI. Practically, contents such as these are being used in the gaming and entertainment industry to create audio-assisted training materials, automated call center assistants, and IoT devices such as Amazon Alexa, or Google Next that can take audio commands and use voice responses to complete automated tasks.

- **Healthcare and drug discovery**: Generative AI finds space in health care. For example, the design of new drugs and the prediction of their capability to treat diseases or other conditions; personalized medicine, whereby treatment plans are tailored individually on a patient-by-patient basis; and medical imaging, whereby image quality is refined and synthetic images generated for research purposes.

- **Code generation**: Code generation is an emerging LLM feature that is helping developers in software development. These models can often generate accurate code snippets, or sometimes an entire function based on text prompts. Advanced implementation of generative AI in code generation includes plugins created for various **integrated development environments (IDEs)**, such as **Visual Studio Code (VS Code)**, that can understand the entire context of the code base, identify errors, create code documentation, and generate unit test scripts. Another implementation of code generation is text-to-query use cases where a natural language prompt is converted into a SQL query, which can then be executed against a database to get the desired results. However, this is one of the areas where special caution must be taken, especially before executing the code generated by an LLM, to prevent risks of malicious code execution. Often, in these situations, the code generated by the LLM is executed in a sandbox and sanitized to check whether the code is safe and appropriate for execution in an autonomous environment.

- **Autonomous workflows and robotics**: As we briefly discussed earlier, LLM-powered AI agents are an advanced implementation of generative AI with LLMs serving as their foundations. These agents can perform several tasks in various use cases. For example, a travel booking website with a virtual assistant chatbot can implement agents to automate the travel and hotel booking process for the customer. In these cases, the agent-based system can act on specific tasks using tools (such as calling a flight booking API) simply by understanding the context of the conversation that the customer is having with the chatbot. More advanced agent-based systems often come into play when discussing robotics, where a robot's actions are primarily controlled by agents. The robotic agent essentially determines what decisions to make based on its environment or the specific task it is assigned to perform. It uses agents to execute actions that an LLM would otherwise be unable to perform; for example, an agent can turn on or off the limb actuators of a robot. AI in robotics is a novel and open field of research, with numerous innovations emerging in the industry, particularly targeted toward manufacturing applications.

These are just some of the common examples of the uses of generative AI with LLMs. Other specific examples include uses in fashion and design, synthetic data generation, personalized educational content, financial modeling and forecasting, and predictive maintenance. The following is a brief list of examples of commercial and open source tools that use generative AI for the number of use cases we discussed:

Use case	Commercial tools	Open source tools
Visual effects and avatar design	• **Unreal Engine's MetaHuman Creator**: Allows for the creation of highly realistic digital humans for games and films • **NVIDIA Omniverse**: A platform for 3D design collaboration and simulation, useful for creating visual effects	• **DeepFaceLab**: Used for face swapping and creating digital avatars • **StyleGAN**: Capable of generating highly realistic faces and can be adapted for avatar creation
Virtual reality content development	• **Unity**: While not exclusively for VR, it has robust VR development capabilities • **Adobe Aero**: Allows for the creation of AR experiences	• **A-Frame**: A web framework for building virtual reality experiences • **Godot**: An open source game engine with VR support
Clothing design and virtual fashion shows	• **CLO3D**: A 3D garment design software that can create virtual fashion shows • **Browzwear**: Offers 3D design solutions for the fashion industry	• **Blender**: While primarily a 3D modeling tool, it can be used for fashion design and virtual shows
Fashion trend predictions	• **WGSN**: Uses AI for trend forecasting in fashion • **Heuritech**: Provides AI-powered trend forecasting	• None

Use case	Commercial tools	Open source tools
Marketing – ad generation and campaign creation	• **Jasper**: An AI writing assistant that can help create marketing copy • **Midjourney**: An AI image generation tool useful for creating marketing visuals	• **GPT-J**: An open source language model that can be fine-tuned for marketing content generation • **Stable Diffusion**:An open source image generation model that can create marketing visuals.
Logo and image creation	• **DALL-E 2**: Can generate unique images and logos based on text descriptions • **Canva**: While not fully AI-powered, it incorporates AI features for design assistance	• **Stable Diffusion**: Can be used for logo and image generation • **Craiyon (formerly DALL-E mini)**: An open source alternative to DALL-E
Text and content generation	• ChatGPT by OpenAI • Claude AI by Anthropic • Jasper • Copy.ai • Anyword • Writer • WriteSonic And many more…	• **Mistral 7B**: An open source LLM known for its efficiency and precision in text generation tasks • **LLaMA**: A collection of open source pre-trained and fine-tuned generative text models, offering versions with different parameter sizes • **BLOOM Language Model**: A large open-access AI model developed by over 1,000 AI researchers, known for its robustness and versatility in text generation And many more…

Use case	Commercial tools	Open source tools
Code generation	- GitHub Copilot - Amazon Q for Developers - Tabnine - OpenAI Codex And many more…	- **Code T5**: An open source AI model trained for code-related tasks. It can generate code snippets, complete code, and even translate between programming languages. - **Polycoder**: An open source alternative to commercial code generators. It's trained on a large code base spanning multiple programming languages and can generate code for various tasks.
Autonomous workflows and robotics	- **UiPath** incorporates generative AI into its **robotic process automation (RPA)** platform. It uses AI to discover automation opportunities and enhance tasks such as document understanding and communications mining. - **Automation Anywhere** integrates generative AI into its automation platform. It offers features such as Automation Co-Pilot for Automators, which uses generative AI to accelerate developer productivity. - **NVIDIA** provides AI workflows that leverage their AI frameworks, including generative AI capabilities, for developing innovative solutions in robotics and autonomous systems.	- **OpenAI Gym** provides a toolkit for developing and comparing reinforcement learning algorithms, which can be combined with LLMs for more advanced robotics applications. - **Hugging Face** offers open source libraries that can be used to implement LLMs in robotics and autonomous workflow applications. - **LangChain** is an open source Python library used for developing applications using LLMs, which can be applied to create more intelligent autonomous workflows and robotic systems.

Table 1.1 – Examples of commercial and open source tools that use generative AI

This is in no way an exhaustive list of commercial and open source tools available in the market at the moment and the landscape is changing every day. We are witnessing a host of new start-ups providing new and innovative ways of solving real-life use cases with generative AI, and we are also witnessing new model providers developing state-of-the-art LLMs that are more capable than the previous ones and are much cheaper to operate. This just goes to show you how dynamic and exciting the field of generative AI is.

Challenges and limitations of generative AI

Though generative AI has immense benefits, it is not without its own set of challenges and limitations. Some of these challenges and limitations need to be taken into account with a lot of caution while considering a generative AI technology for any particular use case. Here's a brief discussion of some of the most common caveats related to LLMs and some of the ways to mitigate them.

Quality of data and bias

The generative models are largely aided by the quality and diversity of data in the training dataset. Any model trained with biased or unrepresentative data will reproduce outputs with the same kind of bias, hence solidifying existing biases or allowing marginalization of one or several groups in case of bias in the training data.

One way this challenge can be dealt with is by ensuring richness in diversity, good quality data, and so on for a wide array of perspectives within the dataset itself used for training. As with any machine learning problem, analysis of the data and knowing the data distribution across features is often helpful. Data analysis can reveal imbalances that can introduce bias in the model. There are several algorithmic ways of mitigating bias in training data (for instance, using oversampling or undersampling), but each of these methods has its own advantages and disadvantages. For example, consider two classes of data in a training dataset that contains more instances of *Class 0* data than *Class 1* data, causing a natural imbalance in the dataset. When a model is trained with such a dataset, the model would "overfit" on the *Class 0* type of data and would become more proficient in or even memorize data that belongs to *Class 0* and may not perform well for data belonging to *Class 1* This inherently causes the model to perform poorly and demonstrate heavy bias. The following figure demonstrates the effect of oversampling and undersampling on such a dataset to mitigate bias:

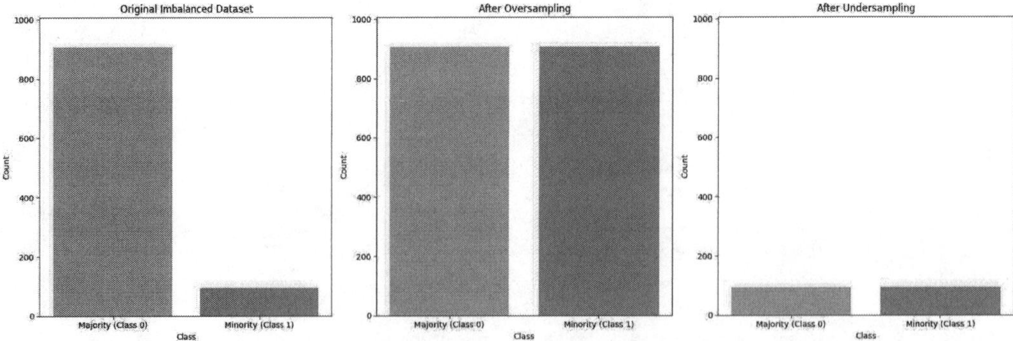

Figure 1.3 – Imbalanced data distribution and effects of oversampling and undersampling

Data privacy

Multiple experiments and researchers have proven that LLMs have a propensity to leak data they are trained on. This is especially problematic if the models are trained on large amounts of private or proprietary information. Special techniques and styles of prompting LLMs have shown that it is sufficient to coerce the model to generate data that includes verbatim text from its training dataset. These prompting techniques are not sophisticated and often make it a very easy, cost-effective attack vector to get a model to leak information. For example, as discussed in the paper named *Scalable Extraction of Training Data from (Production) Language Models* [15], researchers were able to spend only $200 worth of API calls to OpenAI's GPT-3.5 model and use prompt injection techniques to coerce the model to leak private information. The leaked information includes people's names, email and physical addresses, and phone numbers that were inadvertently present in the model's training dataset. While some of these issues are actively being addressed by model providers such as OpenAI, it can still be problematic for organizations that choose to train their own models in-house.

Some of the common mechanisms to mitigate this is to perform data anonymization or pseudonymization on the training data to remove or obscure personal, private, and or proprietary information, even before training the model. Both of these techniques involved using smaller, cheaper, and faster AI models to perform classification and entity detection to identify the presence of personal or private data in the training dataset. Once identified, the private information can be obscured, masked, or entirely removed from the training dataset. Note that there could be several implications to doing this depending on your use case, so special analysis must be performed to ensure that it doesn't impact the model's performance.

Computational resources

Training sophisticated generative models is very resource-intensive and requires high computational power; this often makes it economically cost-prohibitive and energy-consuming to train large language models. Although there have been several hardware breakthroughs that make it possible to train such models, access to these hardware assets still remains expensive, privileged, and limited. For example, **graphics processing units (GPUs)**, initially designed for rendering high-fidelity graphics, have become crucial for AI model training, fine-tuning, and computations. NVIDIA's CUDA architecture, introduced in 2006, allowed GPUs to be used for general-purpose computing, and modern GPUs such as NVIDIA's A100 and H100 have since been specifically optimized for AI workloads. However, these high-end GPUs can often cost tens of thousands of dollars per unit.

Training large models such as GPT-3 is estimated to cost millions of dollars in compute resources alone. The exact cost depends on factors such as model size, training duration, and hardware efficiency. For example, training GPT-3 was estimated to cost around $4–5 million in compute resources, and more recent models such as GPT-4 and PaLM are likely even more expensive to train. Beyond the hardware itself, there are significant infrastructure costs related to power consumption, cooling, and data center space. Due to the high costs, training large language models is primarily done by large tech companies or well-funded research institutions. Cloud services now offer access to pre-trained models and fine-tuning capabilities, making some level of LLM work more accessible to smaller organizations and the general public. A way to overcome this challenge can be found in recent innovations with **small language models (SLMs)**, which are much smaller generative AI models that can be trained to achieve specific tasks. Even though these models are limited to a very narrow set of domain-specific tasks, it is much more economical to train these models since they require far fewer computational resources.

Ethical and social implications

The range of issues in ethics and society exposed by strides in technological generative AI opened up the following many-headed issues, which is far from an exhaustive list:

- **Deepfakes and misinformation**: It is able to produce very realistic synthetically generated content. If that were to happen, it would yield deepfakes or even misinformation, which could be a threat to privacy, security, or even public trust.

- **Intellectual property**: The process of developing comparable content to existing ones brings forth issues with copyright and intellectual property rights. The legal complexity attached to the very originality of the creation and correct ownership can be most perplexing.

- **Job displacement**: Economists often downplay concerns about significant job losses in content generation and other automated task sectors. Of concern is the fact that resultant effects are expected to be paralleled with studies on ways of reskilling and adjustment strategies that can help the affected workers, as well as entrepreneurial opportunities.

When it comes to mitigating social and ethical implications, the question is more philosophical than technical. While some measures such as deepfake AI image detection and private and personal data detection methods are common strategies, the societal implications are a larger question in the context of AI's benefit to society and any existing or impending government regulations.

Generalization and creativity

One of the big problems with these generative AI models is that their generalization ability turns out to be very poor. More concretely, they seldom generate content that is strikingly different from the training data. That is, they are brilliant at copying the repeating patterns but fail really to create something original or novel. As a consequence, their potential for capital *C* creativity stays very limited.

As generative AI continues to evolve in novel ways, it is bound to introduce novel challenges, as we are witnessing the barrage of new research and efforts to ensure sensible and responsible use of this technology.

Summary

Generative AI is a rather rapidly growing area, having huge disruptive potential for industries and changing areas of our lives. In contrast, applications of generative AI include very realistic image generation and generation of text, accelerated drug discovery, and enriched creative expression.

One of the key points regarding this is an understanding of the different generative models, such as VAEs, GANs, and autoregressive models, that provide insight into how technologies work and where they can be applied. It would also, however, be important to state the many problems and limitations generative AI faces, including data quality, computational resources, ethical considerations, and even creativity.

In the next chapter, we will learn about the principles of agentic systems, which include the concepts of agency and autonomy, the characteristics of intelligent agents, various architectures of intelligent systems, and multi-agent systems.

Questions

1. Generative AI models can only take text data as input. True or false?
2. What are the different types of generative AI models?
3. What are some of the ethical and social implications of generative AI?
4. What are some of the methods to mitigate bias in training data?
5. What are some of the text and content generation open source LLMs?

Answers

1. False. Generative AI models can take text as well as image, video, and audio data as inputs.
2. VAEs, GANs, and autoregressive models.
3. Deepfakes, misinformation, issues with copyright or intellectual property, and job displacements are some of the social and ethical implications of generative AI.
4. Some of the common methods to address bias in training data are oversampling or undersampling.
5. Mistral, LLaMA, and Bloom are some of the open source text and content generation LLMs.

Further reading

- *Mastering Machine Learning Algorithms – Second Edition* by Giuseppe Bonaccorso
- *Machine Learning for Imbalanced Data* by Kumar Abhishek and Dr. Mounir Abdelaziz
- *Generative AI with Python and TensorFlow 2* by Joseph Babcock and Raghav Bali

References

1. *Auto-Encoding Variational Bayes*: https://arxiv.org/abs/1312.6114

2. *beta-VAE: Learning Basic Visual Concepts with a Constrained Variational Framework*: https://openreview.net/forum?id=Sy2fzU9gl

3. *Learning Structured Output Representation using Deep Conditional Generative Models*: https://papers.nips.cc/paper_files/paper/2015/hash/8d55a249e6baa5c0677 2297520da2051-Abstract.html

4. *Generative Adversarial Networks*: https://arxiv.org/abs/1406.2661

5. *Unsupervised Representation Learning with Deep Convolutional Generative Adversarial Networks*: https://arxiv.org/abs/1511.06434

6. *Wasserstein GAN*: https://arxiv.org/abs/1701.07875

7. *A Style-Based Generator Architecture for Generative Adversarial Networks*: https://ieeexplore.ieee.org/document/8953766

8. *Attention Is All You Need*: https://arxiv.org/abs/1706.03762

9. *Conditional Image Generation with PixelCNN Decoders*: https://arxiv.org/abs/1606.05328

10. *PixelSNAIL: An Improved Autoregressive Generative Model*: https://www.researchgate.net/publication/322114155_PixelSNAIL_An_Improved_Autoregressive_Generative_Model

11. *Language Models are Few-Shot Learners*: https://arxiv.org/abs/2005.14165

12. *GPT-4 Technical Report*: https://arxiv.org/abs/2303.08774

13. *BERT: Pre-training of Deep Bidirectional Transformers for Language Understanding*: https://arxiv.org/abs/1810.04805

14. *Exploring the Limits of Transfer Learning with a Unified Text-to-Text Transformer*: https://arxiv.org/abs/1910.10683

15. *Scalable Extraction of Training Data from (Production) Language Models*: https://arxiv.org/abs/2311.17035

2

Principles of Agentic Systems

In the previous chapter, we introduced the basics of generative AI, learned about types of generative AI models, and briefly discussed LLM-powered AI agents. In this chapter, we will discuss the basic principles of agentic systems, starting with a brief discussion about the concept of agency and autonomy, followed by a discussion about intelligent agents and their characteristics. We will also discuss various agentic system architectures as well as multi-agent systems through the lens of the travel booking assistant example that we discussed in the previous chapter.

The main topics discussed in this chapter are as follows:

- Understanding self-governance, agency, and autonomy
- Reviewing intelligent agents and their characteristics
- Exploring the architecture of agentic systems
- Understanding multi-agent systems

By the end of this chapter, you will have an overview of the basics of intelligent agents and the most critical aspects of agentic system architecture that must be considered while building an intelligent agentic system.

Technical requirements

You can find the code files for this chapter at `https://github.com/PacktPublishing/Building-Agentic-AI-Systems` and follow the README file in the repository to set up your development environment.

Understanding self-governance, agency, and autonomy

The captivating aspect of **agentic systems** lies in the intricate decision-making processes they employ, which provide valuable insights into how choices are optimized within specific contexts. These systems often challenge our conventional understanding of accountability and responsibility.

Agentic systems act as the driving force behind innovation and technological advancements in various fields, including robotics, AI, and systems engineering. The development and deployment of these systems have catalyzed the exploration and creation of new forms of automation and intelligent behaviors. Let's discuss some of the areas where agentic systems are making headway:

- **Robotics**: In the field of robotics, agentic systems have paved the way for the design and implementation of autonomous robots capable of navigating complex environments, performing intricate tasks, and adapting to changing conditions. These robots, equipped with decision-making capabilities and agency, have found applications in areas such as manufacturing, exploration, search and rescue operations, and healthcare. For instance, robots with agentic behavior can autonomously navigate through disaster zones, assess potential risks, and make decisions to assist in rescue efforts, demonstrating intelligent and adaptive behavior.

- **AI**: In AI, agentic systems have been instrumental in the development of intelligent agents and decision support systems. These systems leverage advanced algorithms, machine learning techniques, and knowledge representation methods to analyze data, reason about complex scenarios, and provide intelligent recommendations or automated decision-making capabilities. Agentic AI systems have been applied in domains such as finance, healthcare, transportation, and marketing, enabling more efficient and effective decision-making processes.

- **Systems engineering**: In the field of systems engineering, agentic systems have facilitated the design and implementation of complex, distributed, and adaptive systems. These systems often consist of multiple interacting components or subsystems, each exhibiting agentic behavior and decision-making capabilities. Such systems are found in areas such as power grids, transportation networks, and cyber-physical systems, where intelligent and autonomous decision-making is crucial for efficient operation, resource allocation, and fault tolerance.

Central to the idea of agentic systems are the concepts of self-governance, agency, and autonomy. Let's discuss each of these concepts in the subsequent sections to understand what they are and explore the critical role they play within an agentic system architecture.

Self-governance

Agentic systems are artificial and human systems that possess self-governance, adaptability, and interaction. Self-governance refers to the ability of a system or entity to govern or control itself autonomously, without external direction or control. In the context of agentic systems, self-governance implies that the system can make its own decisions, set its own goals, and regulate its behavior based on its internal rules, models, and decision-making algorithms. Basically, they operate according to their rules and internal states, and execute a change of behavior, if necessary, due to a change of the environment or the objectives. Such systems interact with the environment or other systems in a way that is meaningful to them and, through these interactions, become influenced.

Some key aspects of self-governance in agentic systems are as follows:

- **Self-organization**: The ability to organize and structure its own internal processes, resources, and behavior without external intervention

- **Self-regulation**: The capability to monitor and adjust its own actions and outputs based on feedback from the environment or internal states, to ensure it operates within desired parameters or constraints

- **Self-adaptation**: The ability to modify its behavior, strategies, or decision-making processes in response to changes in the environment or its own internal conditions, to achieve its goals more effectively

- **Self-optimization**: The ability to continuously improve its performance, efficiency, or decision-making capabilities through learning, experience, or evolutionary processes

- **Self-determination**: The ability to set its own objectives, priorities, and courses of action based on its internal decision-making processes, without being entirely controlled by external forces

Self-governance in agentic systems is often enabled by the integration of various technologies, frameworks, and methodologies such as machine learning, knowledge representation, reasoning, and decision-making algorithms. These allow the system to process information, learn from data and experiences, and make autonomous decisions based on its acquired knowledge and the current context.

Agency

Agency is described as the capability of an individual, or any other entity, to act independently and make choices. In the context of human and artificial systems, agency encompasses the following key elements:

- **Decisional authority**: This refers to the power or ability to act and perform actions according to a chosen alternative or course of action. Systems with agency possess the autonomy to evaluate different options and select the most appropriate action based on their internal decision-making processes, rather than being solely driven by external forces or predetermined rules.

- **Intentionality**: Agency implies the existence of intentions, goals, or objectives that guide the actions and behavior of the system. Agentic systems are not merely reactive; they have a sense of purpose and can pursue specific objectives, adjusting their actions and strategies as necessary to achieve those goals.

- **Responsibility**: Agency is closely tied to the concept of responsibility, which is the answerability or accountability for the outcomes and consequences of one's actions. Systems with agency are considered responsible for their decisions and the impact of their actions on the environment or other entities they interact with.

In most cases, AI agency involves the system's ability to make decisions autonomously based on its internal programs, models, and the data it processes. These decisions can have a significant impact on the functioning of the system itself or its interactions with the environment.

Let's go back to our travel booking assistant example from the previous chapter, which is responsible for booking flight tickets and perhaps even making hotel reservations. In this case, the system would exhibit agency by analyzing various factors, such as the availability of flights between two cities, the price of the tickets, and any other restrictions given by the user such as preferred seat class and so on, and then making decisions on how to optimally look for flights and hotels that meet those criteria so that it minimizes the overall cost of travel for the customer. The system would be responsible for the outcome of its decisions, which would impact the overall travel plan and the cost of travel for the customer.

Autonomy

Autonomy is closely related to the concept of agency but focuses more specifically on the degree of independence an entity or system possesses. It can be broken down into several aspects:

- **Operational autonomy**: This refers to the ability of a system to perform a specific task or set of tasks without direct human intervention or control. A system with operational autonomy can execute its functions independently, relying on its own internal processes, decision-making algorithms, and environmental sensing capabilities.

- **Functional autonomy**: This aspect of autonomy involves the system's ability to make choices and take action to achieve set targets or objectives, modulated by the environment or context in which it operates. Functionally autonomous systems can adapt their behavior and decision-making processes in response to changing conditions or stimuli, enabling them to pursue their goals more effectively.

- **Hierarchical autonomy**: This aspect relates to the amount of decisional authority or decision-making power awarded to a system within a larger framework or organizational structure. Systems with higher hierarchical autonomy have greater latitude in making decisions that impact their subsystems or broader operations, while systems with lower hierarchical autonomy may have more constraints or oversight from higher-level entities.

In AI and robotics, autonomy is a key concept that refers to the extent to which a system can perform tasks and make decisions without the need for continuous human intervention.

In our travel booking assistant example, the system would have operational autonomy to carry out tasks such as booking flights or hotels, managing reminders, and retrieving travel information with little or no human input. It would also possess functional autonomy, allowing it to interpret user commands, adapt to individual preferences, and make decisions that align with the user's goals and context. The level of hierarchical autonomy granted to such a system might depend on factors such as user privacy preferences or the system's access to sensitive data and resources.

Note that autonomy in AI and robotic systems does not necessarily imply a complete absence of human oversight or control. Often, these systems operate within well-defined boundaries and constraints set by their designers or operators, while still exhibiting a significant degree of autonomy. In our travel booking example, the chatbot requests additional information, such as travel dates, locations, name, and address, from the user to make flight bookings. It then cross-references this data with available flights, suggesting options that match the user's preferences. If any detail is missing or unclear, the chatbot prompts the user for clarification, ensuring accuracy while still operating autonomously within the boundaries set by its programming.

The concepts of self-governance, agency, and autonomy in AI systems are often accompanied by ethical considerations, particularly regarding the level of autonomy granted to these systems and the potential risks and implications of their decisions. As AI systems become more advanced and capable of independent decision-making, ensuring their alignment with human values and ethical principles becomes crucial.

Example of agency and autonomy in agents

Let's illustrate the concept of agency and autonomy with a simple algorithm for the travel booking assistant. Note that this algorithm doesn't necessarily use AI just yet, but it would help understand the concepts. Our travel booking assistant algorithm may look as follows.

Algorithm 1: Travel booking assistant algorithm with agency and autonomy

Require: Agent name N

Ensure: Initialized TravelAgent object A with agency and autonomy

1: Initialize A ← CreateTravelAgent(N)

2: Initialize A.goals ← empty list

3: Initialize A.knowledge_base ← empty dictionary

// Agency: Ability to act on behalf of a user

4: function SetGoal(G)

5: A.goals.Append(G) // Agency: Defining objectives

6: function UpdateKnowledge(K, V)

7: A.knowledge_base[K] ← V // Agency: Acquiring information from an API, and scoring

// Autonomy: Ability to operate independently

8: function MakeDecision(Options)

9: best_option ← max(Options, key =score) // Autonomy: Independent decision-making

10: return best_option

11: function BookTravel(Departure, Destination)

12: Output "Agent A.name is booking travel to Destination"

// Agency: Execute action on behalf of user

13: SetGoal("Book flight from Departure to Destination")

14: UpdateKnowledge({Departure, Destination})

// Autonomy: Book travel independently by finding best flight

15: MakeDecision()

// Implement booking logic here and store into A

16: Output A

Here is how the algorithm works, demonstrating the abilities of agency and autonomy:

1. We start by naming our agent; we call it `TripPlanner`.

2. Next, we initialize a new `TravelAgent` object with the name `N = "TripPlanner"`; this represents the creation of an entity capable of both agency and autonomy.

3. We then set up a list to store the goals for the agent. This relates to agency, as goals represent the intentions or desired outcomes the agent will work towards on behalf of the user. This is indicated by `A.goals ← empty list`.

4. Next, we initialize an empty dictionary (also known as a map or key-value pairs) to store the agent's knowledge. This is crucial for both agency (acting on behalf of users) and autonomy (independent operation), as it will contain information the agent uses to make decisions.

5. Steps *4* and *5* in the algorithm indicate the definition of a function that adds a new goal G to the agent's list of goals. This is akin to the agent taking on objectives on behalf of the user. This is indicated by `A.goals.Append(G)`. Think of this as the piece of code that will receive the user's chat message, such as *"Book me a flight from San Diego to Seattle."* Here, the goal is to book a flight from San Diego to Seattle.

6. Steps *6* and *7* in the algorithm indicate the definition of a function that updates the agent's knowledge base with a new key-value pair (map or dictionary). This represents agency through the acquisition of information that will be used to act on behalf of the user. It also supports autonomy by providing the agent with information it can use to make independent decisions. This operation is represented as `A.knowledge_base[K] ← V`. In our case, this function uses several travel-related APIs (in theory) to get flight options between two cities, thus forming the knowledge into a knowledge base. This is also a place where each of these flight options will be scored; for example, late flights get low scores, and early flights get higher scores.

7. Steps *8* through *10* define a function that does a few different things. It takes a list of options and selects the best one based on some scoring criteria. This is an example of autonomy in the algorithm since the agent independently evaluates options and makes a decision without direct human intervention.

8. Finally, steps *10* through *15* demonstrate how all of these components work together, starting from setting the goal of flight booking using the departure and destination cities, updating the knowledge base using a flight lookup API, and then scoring the available flights. Subsequently, it uses the `MakeDecision` function to find the best possible flight as per the highest score and performs the flight booking for the user.

A Python implementation of the `BookTravel` function from the algorithm is shown in the following code snippet:

```python
1 def book_travel(departure: str, destination: str):
2     self.set_goal(f"Book flight from {departure} to {destination}")
3     self.update_knowledge(departure, destination)
4
```

```
 5        try:
 6            best_flight = self.make_decision()
 7            booking_confirmation = f"BOOKING_#12345"
 8            self.knowledge_base['booking_confirmation'] = \
 9                            booking_confirmation
10            print(f"Booking confirmed: {booking_confirmation}")
11        except Exception as e:
12            print(f"Booking failed: {str(e)}")
13
14 if __name__ == "__main__":
15     agent = TravelAgent("TripPlanner")
16     agent.book_travel("SAN", "SEA")
17     print("\n----------- Final Agent State: -----------")
18     print(f"Name: {agent.name}")
19     print(f"Goals: {agent.goals}")
20     if 'booking_confirmation' in agent.knowledge_base:
21         print(f"Booking Confirmation: \
22         {agent.knowledge_base['booking_confirmation']}")
```

The output of this code when the agent is initialized to book a flight from SAN (San Diego) to SEA (Seattle) looks as follows:

```
1 Agent TripPlanner is booking travel from SAN to SEA
2 Goal set: Book flight from SAN to SEA
3 Knowledge updated with 3 flight options
4 Decision made: Selected flight JetBlue
5 Booking confirmed: BOOK-JetBlue-TRIPPLANNER
6 ----------- Final Agent State: -----------
7 Name: TripPlanner
8 Goals: ['Book flight from SAN to SEA']
9 Booking Confirmation: BOOK-JetBlue-TRIPPLANNER
```

For the full implementation of the trip planner agent, refer to the `Chapter_02.ipynb` Python notebook in the GitHub repository.

In this code snippet, the `book_travel` function takes a departure city code (such as SAN or SEA, which are airport codes) and subsequently calls other functions to set the goal, update its knowledge base, and then make a decision on which flight to choose and book that flight. Note that our agent, although has some functionality of agency and autonomy, is not intelligent. It cannot take plain text messages from a user and decipher what the user intends to do to set its goals, update its knowledge base, and then perform the actions; rather, it needs the airport codes. However, as we saw in our example, a user (or customer) may simply express their intentions in plain language such as *Book me a flight from San Diego to Seattle*.

In its current form, given any such user input (message), the agent is incapable of determining what the departure and destination cities are, what the user is asking for, or even what the string of input text even means. This is where generative AI steps in, as we will see in the subsequent chapters. For now, let's continue with our discussion by looking at the characteristics of agents.

Reviewing intelligent agents and their characteristics

An intelligent agent is a complex, self-governed entity that perceives its environment and takes action to achieve certain goals or objectives. These agents can range from basic systems that strictly adhere to a predefined set of rules to highly advanced systems with the ability to learn and adapt from experience. Intelligent agents are characterized by several key attributes:

- **Reactivity**: Reactive agents respond to changes and events occurring in their environment in real time. They continuously monitor their surroundings and adjust their behavior accordingly. This reactivity allows agents to adapt to dynamic conditions and respond appropriately to stimuli, ensuring their actions remain relevant and effective.

- **Proactiveness**: An ideal intelligent agent should not merely react to events but also exhibit proactive behavior. Proactive agents anticipate future needs, challenges, or opportunities, and take the initiative to plan and act accordingly. They are goal-oriented and actively pursue strategies to achieve their objectives, rather than simply reacting to circumstances as they arise.

- **Social ability**: Many intelligent agents operate in multi-agent systems, where they interact and cooperate with other agents or humans to achieve common goals that require collaborative effort. Social ability encompasses communication, coordination, and negotiation skills, enabling agents to work together effectively and leverage collective intelligence or resources.

With these key characteristics, intelligent agents demonstrate remarkable versatility and efficiency across a wide spectrum of domains and scenarios. Their capabilities enable them to excel in tasks ranging from simple, automated processes to highly complex, dynamic decision-making situations that demand real-time adaptation and environmental responsiveness. In addition to these core characteristics, intelligent agents may possess other advanced capabilities:

- **Learning and adaptation**: Intelligent agents have the ability to learn from experience and adapt their behavior over time. They can acquire new knowledge, refine their decision-making processes, and improve their performance through techniques such as machine learning, reinforcement learning, or evolutionary algorithms.

- **Reasoning and planning**: Intelligent agents may employ reasoning and planning capabilities to analyze complex situations, formulate strategies, and make informed decisions. They can leverage techniques such as knowledge representation, logical inference, and planning algorithms to navigate through intricate problem spaces and determine optimal courses of action.

- **Autonomy and self-governance**: Intelligent agents often exhibit a degree of autonomy and self-governance, allowing them to make decisions and take actions independently without constant human intervention or supervision. This autonomy enables agents to operate efficiently in dynamic environments or scenarios where continuous human control is impractical or impossible.

With these characteristics, intelligent agents can be versatile and efficient in a wide range of domains, from simple, automated tasks to highly complex, dynamic decision-making situations. They find applications in areas such as robotics, decision support systems, virtual assistants, gaming, and simulations, among others.

Exploring the architecture of agentic systems

Agentic systems, designed for executing complex goals in an autonomous way, can be implemented using a good variety of architectural patterns. In general, these patterns define the structure and the behavior that allows the system to perceive, reason, learn, and act upon the environment in an effective way. Three main architectural patterns for agentic systems are deliberative, reactive, and hybrid architectures. Let's discuss them in detail.

Deliberative architectures

Also known as *knowledge-based* or *symbolic* architectures, rely on the use of explicit representations of knowledge and reasoning mechanisms to reach decisions. They typically follow a *sense-plan-act* cycle, where they first perceive information about the environment, then make a plan of action according to that perception and the knowledge base, and finally execute such plans of action.

The key advantage of deliberative architectures is their ability to handle tasks that involve complex reasoning, such as planning, problem-solving, and decision-making. These architectures leverage techniques such as rule-based reasoning, constraint satisfaction, and heuristic search to navigate through intricate problem spaces and formulate appropriate courses of action.

One of the critical components of a deliberative architecture is the knowledge base that stores symbolic representations of the environment, goals, constraints, and domain-specific knowledge. This knowledge base is typically encoded using formal language or logic, enabling the system to perform logical inference and reasoning. The *sense-plan-act* cycle in deliberative architectures typically involves the following steps:

1. **Sensing**: The agent perceives and acquires information about the environment through various sensors or input mechanisms.

2. **Knowledge updating**: The perceived information is used to update the agent's internal knowledge base, ensuring that it maintains an accurate representation of the current state of the environment.

3. **Planning and reasoning**: Based on the updated knowledge base, the agent employs reasoning techniques and algorithms to formulate plans and make decisions. This may involve techniques such as constraint satisfaction, logical inference, search algorithms, or heuristic-based planning.

4. **Plan execution**: Once a plan or course of action has been determined, the agent executes the corresponding actions in the environment, potentially modifying the environment or achieving specific goals.

The following figure depicts a deliberative architecture of an agentic system with a sense-plan-act cycle:

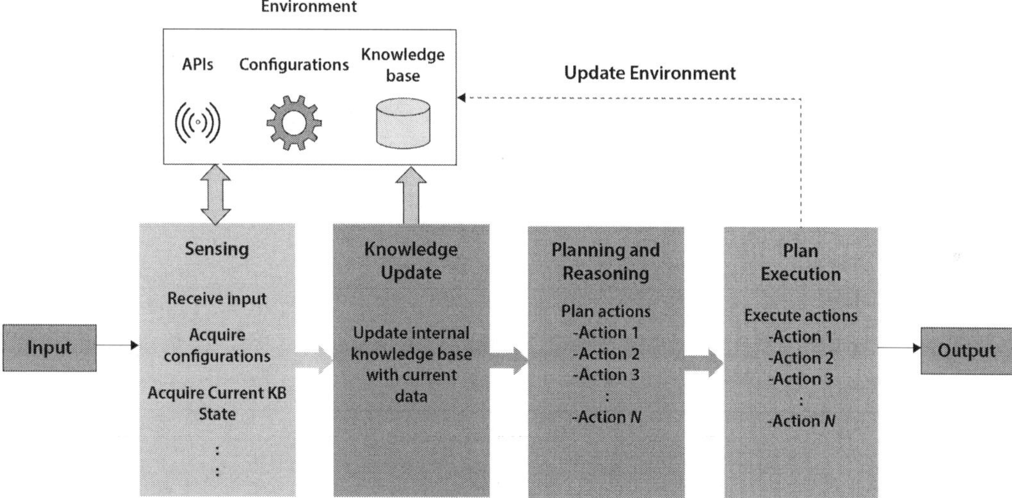

Figure 2.1 – Deliberative architecture of an agentic system

Deliberative architectures excel in handling tasks that require complex reasoning, planning, and decision-making in well-defined environments. They can effectively handle uncertainty and ambiguity through techniques such as probabilistic reasoning, fuzzy logic, or belief revision mechanisms.

However, deliberative architectures also have some disadvantages. One significant challenge is the computational cost associated with maintaining and reasoning over complex knowledge bases, which can limit real-time responsiveness in dynamic environments. Additionally, the explicit representation of knowledge can be challenging in domains where knowledge is difficult to formalize or constantly evolving.

To address these limitations, deliberative architectures are often combined with reactive or behavior-based components in hybrid architectures, allowing both complex reasoning and rapid response to environmental changes.

Despite their limitations, deliberative architectures remain a crucial component in many intelligent systems, particularly in domains where complex decision-making, planning, and reasoning are essential, such as robotics, decision support systems, and intelligent tutoring systems.

Reactive architectures

Reactive architectures, also known as *behavior-based* or *stimulus-response* architectures, aim to provide immediate responses to stimuli from the environment. Unlike deliberative architectures, reactive architectures do not rely on explicit models of the world or complex reasoning processes. Instead, these systems directly map perceptions onto actions, typically using simple condition-action rules or neural networks as depicted in the following figure:

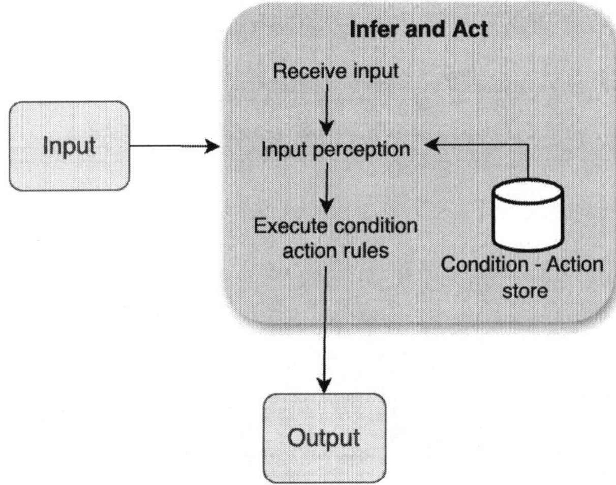

Figure 2.2 – Reactive architecture of an agentic system

Some of the key properties and characteristics of reactive architectures include the following:

- **Speed and responsiveness**: Reactive architectures are designed to react rapidly to changes in the environment. By directly coupling perceptions to actions, they can bypass time-consuming deliberative reasoning processes, enabling swift and timely responses.

- **Robustness and fault tolerance**: These architectures are generally robust and less susceptible to noise or incomplete information. Their simple, standalone nature makes them less prone to catastrophic failures, as individual components or behaviors can compensate for or mitigate the effects of faulty or missing input, especially when used within a deliberative architecture.

- **Handling uncertainty**: Reactive architectures can effectively handle uncertainty in dynamic environments. Their ability to respond directly to environmental stimuli allows them to adapt and adjust their actions based on the current situation, without relying on precise or complete models of the entire world.

- **Parallel and distributed processing**: Reactive architectures often employ parallel and distributed processing using multiple reactive modules, where multiple modules operate simultaneously and independently. This decentralized approach enables efficient handling of complex tasks and provides inherent scalability and modularity.

- **Emergence of complex behavior**: Despite the simplicity of individual behaviors or rules, the interaction and coordination of multiple reactive components can lead to the emergence of complex, intelligent-like behavior at the system level.

While reactive architectures offer advantages in terms of speed, robustness, and handling uncertainty, they also have limitations as highlighted:

- **Lack of long-term planning**: Reactive architectures generally lack the ability to plan ahead or reason about long-term consequences. Their focus is on immediate responses to environmental stimuli, making it difficult to pursue complex, multi-step goals or strategies.

- **Limited reasoning and abstraction**: These architectures may struggle with tasks that require abstract reasoning, generalization, or the manipulation of symbolic representations. They are primarily designed to operate at a lower, stimulus-response level.

- **Limited learning capabilities**: Many reactive architectures lack the ability to learn from experience or adapt their behavior over time. Their fixed set of rules or behaviors may not be suitable for dynamic environments or tasks that require continuous learning and adaptation.

Despite these limitations, reactive architectures are widely used in applications where real-time responsiveness, robustness, and ability to handle uncertainty are essential, such as in robotics, video games built with AI, and control systems. Additionally, reactive architectures often serve as components within more complex hybrid architectures, complementing deliberative or learning-based systems to achieve desired levels of performance and adaptability.

Hybrid architectures

Researchers have recognized the strengths and limitations of both deliberative and reactive architectures, leading to the development of hybrid architectures that aim to exploit the advantages of both approaches. Such hybrid architectures typically employ a layered structure, consisting of the following:

- A **reactive layer** for fast and low-level responses. The reactive layer is responsible for handling real-time interactions with the environment, providing rapid and situationally appropriate responses to external stimuli. This layer is designed to be highly responsive, fault-tolerant, and capable of handling uncertainty, leveraging the strengths of reactive architectures.

- A **deliberative layer** for high-level reasoning and planning. The deliberative layer is dedicated to higher-level reasoning, planning, and decision-making processes. This layer can maintain a more comprehensive representation of the environment, goals, and constraints, enabling it to formulate complex strategies, reason about abstract concepts, and plan long-term courses of action.

The interaction between these two layers is crucial for enabling agentic systems to respond effectively to dynamic environmental contexts while maintaining the capability to plan actions and reason about them. The reactive layer can provide real-time feedback and situational awareness to the deliberative layer, informing its decision-making processes. Conversely, the deliberative layer can guide and influence the reactive layer's behavior by providing high-level plans, goals, and constraints.

To achieve complex goals and leverage the strengths of both layers, hybrid architectures often employ the following techniques:

- **Task decomposition**: Break down complex tasks into subtasks that can be handled by the appropriate layer, with the reactive layer handling low-level, time-critical tasks and the deliberative layer focusing on higher-level planning and coordination

- **Multiplan selection**: The deliberative layer can generate multiple potential plans or strategies, and the reactive layer can dynamically select and execute the most suitable plan based on the current environmental conditions

- **Planning with external modules**: The deliberative layer can incorporate external modules or specialized algorithms for tasks such as path planning, resource allocation, or scheduling, leveraging domain-specific knowledge and techniques

- **Reflection and refinement**: The deliberative layer can reflect on the outcomes of executed plans, learn from experience, and refine its reasoning and planning processes accordingly, enabling continuous improvement and adaptation

- **Memory-augmented planning**: The deliberative layer can maintain a memory or history of past experiences, decisions, and outcomes, enabling it to leverage this knowledge in future planning and reasoning processes

By combining the strengths of both deliberative and reactive approaches, hybrid architectures seek to balance responsiveness and reasoning, enabling the development of more robust, autonomous, and adaptable agentic systems. These architectures leverage the power of both approaches, providing the ability to respond rapidly to dynamic environments while maintaining the capability for complex planning, reasoning, and decision-making.

The design and implementation of effective hybrid architectures remain an active area of research, as researchers strive to develop architectures that can seamlessly integrate and coordinate the deliberative and reactive components, enabling the creation of highly capable and intelligent agentic systems.

Selecting the appropriate architectural pattern for an agentic system is contingent upon the specific requirements of the application, encompassing factors such as task complexity, environmental uncertainty, and the necessity for real-time responsiveness. Deliberative architectures excel in scenarios that demand intricate reasoning and decision-making processes, while reactive architectures thrive in dynamic environments that necessitate swift and adaptive responses. Hybrid architectures strike a harmonious balance by judiciously leveraging the strengths of both paradigms, resulting in the development of more capable and adaptable agentic systems that can seamlessly navigate the complexities of their operating environments.

Understanding multi-agent systems

Multi-agent systems (MASs) represent an important subfield of the broader area of distributed artificial intelligence. They consist of several intelligent agents that interact, cooperate, and coordinate with each other to execute tasks and achieve collective goals. Each agent in a MAS is typically autonomous, capable of perceiving its environment through sensors, possessing a reasoning mechanism to make decisions, and acting upon those decisions to meet its design objectives. The collective behavior and interactions of these agents enable MASs to tackle complex problems that single-agent systems struggle with due to the inherent limitations of individual agents.

Examples of MASs can be found in various domains, demonstrating their applicability and effectiveness in solving complex problems:

- **Supply chain management and logistics**: MASs can be used to optimize supply chain operations by coordinating the activities of different agents representing suppliers, manufacturers, distributors, and retailers. Each agent can make decisions based on its local knowledge and constraints, while collaborating with other agents to ensure efficient resource allocation, inventory management, and transportation planning.

- **Traffic control and transportation systems**: MASs have been employed in managing traffic flow and optimizing transportation networks. Agents can represent individual vehicles, traffic lights, or traffic management centers, working together to reduce congestion, coordinate traffic signals, and find optimal routes for vehicles based on real-time traffic conditions.

- **Robotics and manufacturing**: In manufacturing environments, MASs can coordinate the activities of multiple robots or automated systems. Each robot or agent can be responsible for specific tasks, such as assembly, welding, or material handling, while communicating and coordinating with other agents to ensure efficient and synchronized operations.

- **Environmental monitoring and resource management**: MASs can be used for monitoring and managing natural resources, such as water distribution networks, forestry management, or wildlife habitat conservation. Agents can represent different stakeholders, environmental sensors, or decision-making entities, collaborating to make informed decisions about resource allocation, conservation efforts, or mitigation strategies.

- **Distributed sensor networks**: MASs are well suited for applications involving distributed sensor networks, such as environmental monitoring, surveillance, or disaster response. Each sensor node can be represented as an agent, collecting and processing local data, while coordinating with other agents to fuse information and provide a comprehensive understanding of the monitored area or phenomenon.

- **Intelligent virtual environments and simulations**: MASs can be used to create intelligent virtual environments and simulations, where agents represent various entities or actors within the simulated world. These agents can interact, make decisions, and exhibit complex behaviors, enabling realistic simulations of social systems, economic models, or military operations, among others.

The key advantages of MASs lie in their ability to distribute problem-solving capabilities, leverage the collective intelligence and specialization of individual agents, and exhibit robustness and fault tolerance through decentralized decision-making. Additionally, MASs can facilitate the integration of heterogeneous components, enabling the development of flexible and scalable systems capable of addressing complex, dynamic problems that would be challenging for monolithic, centralized approaches.

Definition and characteristics of MASs

A MAS is a system comprising multiple autonomous agents that can interact, collaborate, and cooperate to achieve shared goals. These agents can be software programs, robots, or even humans equipped with specialized capabilities and goals. Interaction among agents is a necessary component, enabling them to work together efficiently, share information, and divide tasks based on their strengths and areas of expertise. Key characteristics of MASs include the following:

- **Autonomy**: Each agent within a MAS is self-governing, making self-contained decisions based on its perception of the environment and its objectives. Agents operate independently without centralized control, exhibiting autonomous behavior.

- **Interaction**: Agents in a MAS communicate with each other through defined protocols, enabling them to share information, negotiate tasks, and coordinate their actions. This interaction can take various forms, such as cooperation, coordination, or competition, depending on the nature of the problem and the agents' goals.

- **Adaptability**: MASs possess the flexibility to adapt and change their behavior in response to changes in the environment or changes in the individual agents' goals. This adaptability makes MAS capable of handling dynamic situations, making them flexible and robust during operation.

- **Distributed control**: Unlike centralized systems, MASs employ distributed control, where decision-making and control are distributed among the individual agents. This distributed control contributes to the system's resilience, as failures or malfunctions in one agent do not necessarily affect the entire system's functionality.

- **Scalability**: MAS architectures are inherently scalable, allowing for the addition or removal of agents as needed. This scalability enables the system to grow or shrink in complexity and capabilities, making it suitable for a wide range of applications.

- **Heterogeneity**: Agents within a MAS can be heterogeneous, meaning they can have different architectures, capabilities, and goals. This heterogeneity allows the integration of diverse components and the leveraging of specialized expertise, contributing to the overall system's effectiveness.

- **Decentralized data and knowledge**: In a MAS, data and knowledge are decentralized and distributed among the individual agents. This decentralization enhances robustness, as there is no single point of failure, and agents can operate based on their local knowledge and perceptions.

A MAS's ability to distribute problem-solving capabilities, leverage collective intelligence, exhibit robustness, and integrate heterogeneous components makes them well suited for addressing complex, dynamic problems that are challenging for traditional, centralized approaches.

Interaction mechanisms in MASs

Interaction mechanisms in MASs play a crucial role in enabling effective communication, collaboration, and coordination among the agents within the system. The general classification of the basic interaction mechanisms in a MAS can be presented into three main types:

- **Cooperation**: Cooperation can be defined as agents working together towards a common goal or objective. It is particularly important in situations where no single agent, acting alone, can accomplish the objective.

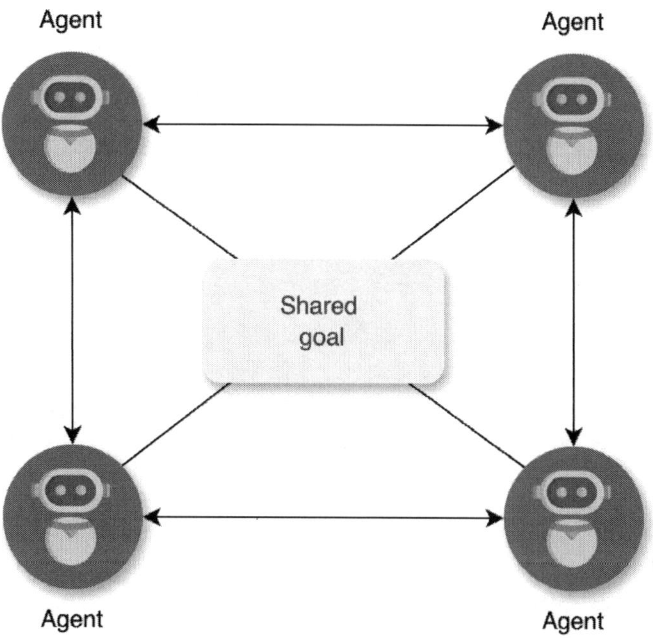

Figure 2.3 – Cooperation in a MAS

A prime example of cooperation in MAS is disaster rescue operations, where multiple drones, robotic agents, and humans need to cooperate and collaborate to locate and rescue victims effectively. A MAS relies on agents cooperating by pooling their knowledge, resources, and efforts to accomplish tasks that are too complex for one agent. Agents may cooperate by dividing tasks, combining their specialized expertise, or complementing each other's abilities to tackle complex problems more efficiently.

- **Coordination**: Coordination deals with managing interdependencies that arise from the actions and activities of agents within the system. Coordination is essential when agents share resources and have overlapping responsibilities or conflicting actions.

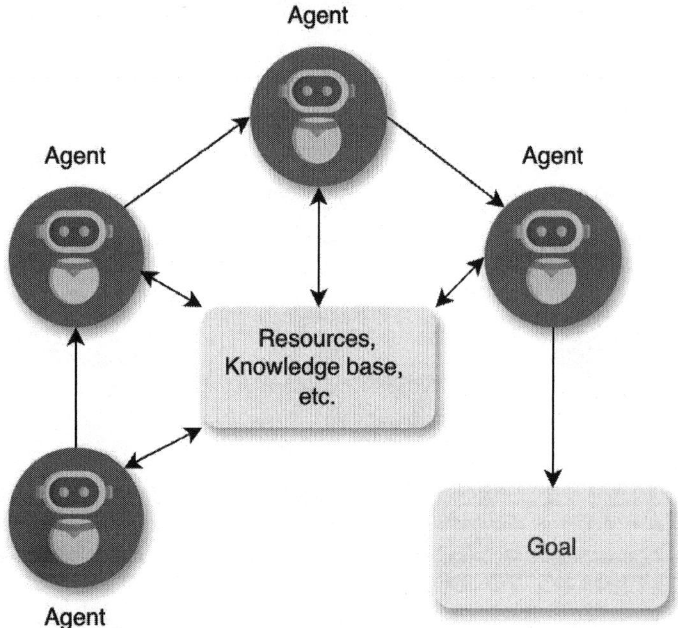

Figure 2.4 – Coordination in a MAS

Coordination mechanisms in MAS may include strategies such as task scheduling, resource allocation management, and conflict resolution. For example, in a manufacturing setting, agents representing different robots on production lines may need to coordinate their actions to ensure efficient use of shared resources, prevent interference, and maintain overall production efficiency.

- **Negotiation**: Negotiation is the process through which agents reach agreements on how to share resources, divide tasks, or resolve conflicts. It involves agents making offers, counteroffers, and compromises, even when their interests may initially conflict.

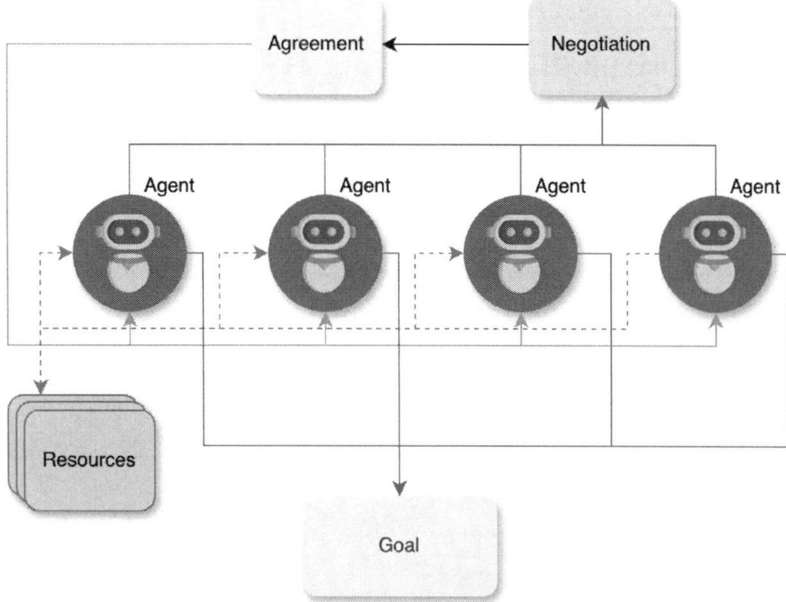

Figure 2.5 – Negotiation in a MAS

Negotiation mechanisms in MAS enable agents to find mutually beneficial solutions by exchanging proposals, evaluating alternatives, and reaching consensus. This is particularly useful in situations where agents have limited or conflicting resources, different preferences, or competing goals. Negotiation can involve various techniques, such as auctions, voting protocols, bargaining strategies, or game-theoretic approaches, depending on the specific requirements and constraints of the problem domain.

These interaction mechanisms – cooperation, coordination, and negotiation – are fundamental to the effective functioning of MAS. They enable agents to work together, leverage their collective capabilities, and resolve conflicts or interdependencies that may arise during their interactions. The choice and design of appropriate interaction mechanisms are crucial for enabling efficient and robust multi-agent systems that can tackle complex problems and adapt to dynamic environments.

In the context of our travel assistant example, MASs can play a vital role in facilitating efficient coordination and negotiation among various entities involved in the travel industry network. In such a scenario, agents can represent different stakeholders, such as airlines, hotels, car rental companies, tour operators, or travel agencies, and utilize negotiation mechanisms to optimize various aspects of the travel booking operations.

For example, consider a MAS where agents represent airlines, hotels, and other relevant parties involved in the travel industry. These agents can engage in negotiation processes to determine flight schedules, room availability, pricing, and other travel-related decisions, aiming to achieve the highest efficiency for the overall travel booking operations.

The negotiation process can unfold as follows:

1. Agents representing airlines can propose available seats, flight schedules, and pricing for their routes.

2. Agents representing hotels can evaluate these proposals based on their room availability, expected occupancy rates, and demand forecasts, and negotiate with the airline agents for the most suitable flight schedules that align with their check-in and check-out times.

3. Travel agency agents can then negotiate with both airline and hotel agents, taking into account customer preferences, budget constraints, and their specific requirements for travel dates and accommodations.

4. Transportation agents (for example, car rental companies or shuttle services) can also participate in the negotiation process, offering ground transportation services and proposing pickup/drop-off schedules and associated costs to the other agents involved.

Throughout the negotiation process, agents can utilize various strategies and algorithms to evaluate proposals, generate counteroffers, and find mutually acceptable agreements. These strategies may involve techniques such as auctions, bargaining protocols, game-theoretic approaches, or optimization algorithms tailored for travel industry operations. For example, agents may employ multi-attribute utility functions that consider factors such as travel time, cost, comfort, and customer preferences to evaluate and rank various proposals. They can then engage in iterative negotiations, adjusting their offers and counter offers based on their respective utility functions and constraints.

Moreover, the distributed nature of MAS allows decentralized decision-making, where each agent can make decisions based on its local knowledge and constraints, while still collaborating and coordinating with other agents to achieve global optimization goals. The negotiation mechanisms in MAS for our travel and hospitality example not only facilitate efficient coordination among various entities but also provide the flexibility and adaptability to handle dynamic changes in demand, supply, pricing changes, or other operational factors, ultimately leading to a more resilient and responsive system that caters to customer demands.

To illustrate a MAS for our travel booking assistant example, we will introduce some new functionalities. In addition to booking flights, we now want our system to find hotels at the destination and create an appropriate travel package for the customer. The algorithm for such a MAS system could look like the following:

Algorithm 2: Multi-agent system for travel booking assistant

Require: Sets of Airline Agents A = {A1, A2, ..., An} and Hotel Agents H = {H1, H2, ..., Hm}

Ensure: Initialized TravelBookingSystem S with Travel Agency Agent TA

1: Initialize S with A, H, and TA

2: function RequestTravelPackage(departure, destination, dates)

3:    for each Ai in A do

Algorithm 2: Multi-agent system for travel booking assistant

4:    available_flights ← Ai.GetAvailableFlights(departure, destination, dates)

5:   for each Hj in H do

6:      available_rooms ← Hj.GetAvailableRooms(destination, dates)

7:   packages ← TA.CompilePackages(available_flights, available_rooms)

8:   return packages

9: function BookTravel(selected_package)

10:   flight_booking ← selected_package.airline.BookFlight()

11:   room_booking ← selected_package.hotel.BookRoom()

12:   if flight_booking and room_booking are successful then

13:     return CreateBooking(flight_booking, room_booking)

14:   else

15:     return FailureNotification()

16: function UpdateDynamicPricing()

17:   for each Ai in A do

18:     Ai.UpdateFlightPrices()

19:   for each Hj in H do

20:     Hj.UpdateRoomPrices()

21: while True do

22:   if NewTravelRequest() then

23:     request ← GetTravelRequest()

24:     packages ← RequestTravelPackage(request.departure, request.destination, request.dates)

25:     selected_package ← TA.PresentOptionsToCustomer(packages)

26:     if selected_package is not null then

27:       booking ← BookTravel(selected_package)

28:       if booking is successful then

29:         NotifyCustomer(booking, "Booking confirmed")

30:       else

31:         NotifyCustomer("Booking failed")

32:   if TimeToUpdatePricing() then

33:     UpdateDynamicPricing()

34: Output S

Here is a breakdown of the key components of this algorithm:

1. The first step is to clearly define a set of agents: in this case a flight agent, a hotel agent, and a travel agency agent. The flight and hotel agents are responsible for airlines and hotel-related actions, and the travel agency agent is responsible for creating travel packages based on the best options available.

2. Steps *2* through *8* show how the travel agent interacts with multiple airline and hotel agents to compile travel packages. It finds appropriate flight schedules and hotel availability in the destination city and subsequently uses that data to create packages.

3. Steps *9* through *15* demonstrate the coordination between the selected airline and hotel agents to confirm the flight and hotel booking according to the chosen package.

4. Steps *16* through *20* show how each airline and hotel agent independently updates its pricing.

5. The main loop from steps *21* through *33* ties everything together, showing how the system handles travel requests and periodically updates pricing across all agents.

This example algorithm demonstrates a combination of coordination and cooperation between agents:

- Cooperation, since all the agents work towards a common goal of booking the travel itinerary for the user

- Coordination, since the travel agency agent needs input from both the flight agent and the hotel agent to build a travel package, and then subsequently book the best travel package

The full Python code related to this algorithm can be found in the `Chapter_02.ipynb` Python notebook in GitHub repository. Keep in mind, just like before, our MAS is not very intelligent since it still needs discreet input, that is, departure city code and arrival city code, to operate successfully, and lacks the ability to comprehend or infer values and actions from user messages or text.

Summary

In this chapter, we explored the intriguing world of agentic systems and intelligent agents, delving into the core concepts of agency, autonomy, and the characteristics that define an ideal agent. We studied various architectural patterns for designing and implementing such systems, including deliberative, reactive, and hybrid approaches. Additionally, we examined MASs, where multiple agents collaborate and coordinate to achieve collective goals through mechanisms such as cooperation, coordination, and negotiation.

The knowledge gained from this chapter provides a solid foundation for developing intelligent and autonomous systems capable of operating effectively in complex, unpredictable environments. You should now be able to decide which agentic system architecture best suits any particular use case, and be able to craft a mental model of a MAS that gives you the foundation of your agentic system. In the next chapter, we will dive deeper into the essentials of an agentic system, further strengthening our ability to build efficient systems.

Questions

1. What are the key characteristics of intelligent agents?

2. What are the main types of architectural patterns for intelligent agents?

3. How do deliberative and reactive architectures differ in their strengths and weaknesses?

4. What is a **multi-agent system** (**MAS**) and what are its key characteristics?

5. What are the main interaction mechanisms in MASs?

6. In what domains are MASs commonly applied?

Answers

1. Key characteristics of intelligent agents include reactivity, proactiveness, social ability, autonomy, and the capability to learn and adapt.

2. The main architectural patterns for intelligent agents are deliberative (knowledge-based), reactive (behavior-based), and hybrid architectures.

3. Deliberative architectures excel in complex reasoning and planning but may struggle with real-time responsiveness in dynamic environments. Reactive architectures are well suited for dynamic environments requiring rapid responses but lack long-term planning and abstract reasoning capabilities.

4. A **multi-agent system** (**MAS**) consists of multiple intelligent agents that interact, cooperate, and coordinate to achieve collective goals. Key characteristics include autonomy, interaction, adaptability, distributed control, scalability, heterogeneity, and decentralized data and knowledge.

5. The main interaction mechanisms in MASs are cooperation (working towards a common goal), coordination (managing interdependencies), and negotiation (reaching agreements).

6. MASs find applications in domains such as supply chain management, traffic control, robotics, environmental monitoring, distributed sensor networks, and intelligent virtual environments.

Subscribe to AI_Distilled, the go-to newsletter for AI professionals

To keep up with the latest developments in the fields of Generative AI and LLMs, subscribe to our weekly newsletter, AI_Distilled, at `https://packt.link/8Oz6Y`.

3

Essential Components of Intelligent Agents

In this chapter, we'll dive into the essential components that make up the core of intelligent agents. Just as the human body has a skeleton that provides structure and support, intelligent agents have certain fundamental elements that allow them to adapt, act independently, and pursue goals in complex environments.

We'll look at the important pieces that bring agents to life – how they represent and store knowledge, the reasoning processes that guide their decision-making, the algorithms that help them learn and grow, and the mechanisms for choosing the right actions to take. You'll also see how the exciting field of generative AI can supercharge these components, giving agents more powerful abilities to understand their surroundings, learn from experiences, and interact meaningfully with the world around them.

In this chapter, we're going to cover the following main topics:

- Knowledge representation in intelligent agents

- Reasoning in intelligent agents

- Learning mechanisms for adaptive agents

- Decision-making and planning in agentic systems

- Enhancing agent capabilities with generative AI

By the end of this chapter, you'll understand knowledge representation methods in intelligent agents, reasoning and learning mechanisms, decision-making, and planning techniques, as well as having explored a generative AI-powered enhanced agent example.

Technical requirements

You can find the code files for this chapter on GitHub at `https://github.com/PacktPublishing/Building-Agentic-AI-Systems`.

Knowledge representation in intelligent agents

The ability to store and manipulate information is fundamental for any intelligent agent. Knowledge representation provides the mechanisms for encoding an agent's understanding of its environment into formats amenable to reasoning and decision-making processes. It is the most basic way to enable an intelligent agent to build a model of its surroundings.

Knowledge representation can be formally defined as the method of structuring and organizing data in such a way that an agent can effectively utilize that information for tasks such as drawing inferences, solving problems, and determining a course of action. There are several well-established approaches to knowledge representation, each with its own strengths and ideal applications, which we will discuss next.

Semantic networks

Semantic networks provide one of the most intuitive and flexible approaches for representing knowledge within intelligent agents. At their core, semantic networks are graph-based structures composed of nodes that represent concepts, entities, events, or states in the world. These nodes are connected by labeled edges that explicitly define the semantic relationships between the represented concepts.

The simplicity yet expressiveness of semantic networks allows them to naturally capture the rich, diverse relationships and interconnections that exist in our complex world. For example, a node representing the concept of "*dog*" could be connected to the "*animal*" node via an "*is-a*" relation edge, indicating that dogs are a type of animal. That same "*dog*" node may also be connected to nodes for "*mammal*," "*domesticated*," "*canine*," and "*pet*" via other typed relationship links:

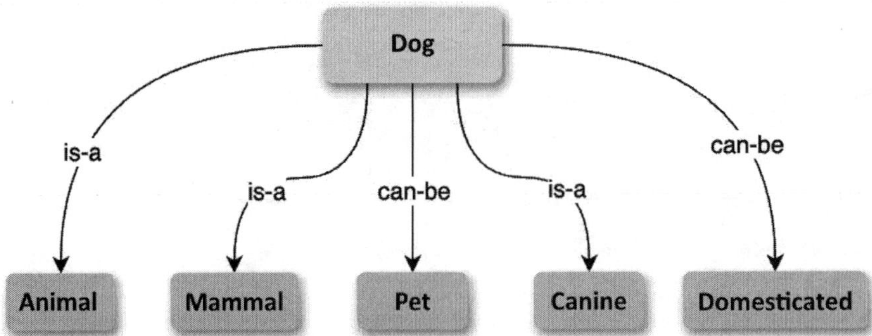

Figure 3.1 – Semantic network representing "Dog" relationships

Unlike strict logic or rigid database schemas, semantic networks provide a flexible knowledge representation where any concept can be associated with any other concept through an appropriate semantic relation. This flexibility enables semantic networks to represent incredibly nuanced domains in an intuitive graphical form. As a real-world example, a medical semantic network could model diseases, symptoms, treatments, and anatomical concepts with relation types such as *"causes,"* *"is-diagnosed-by," "interacts-with,"* and so on:

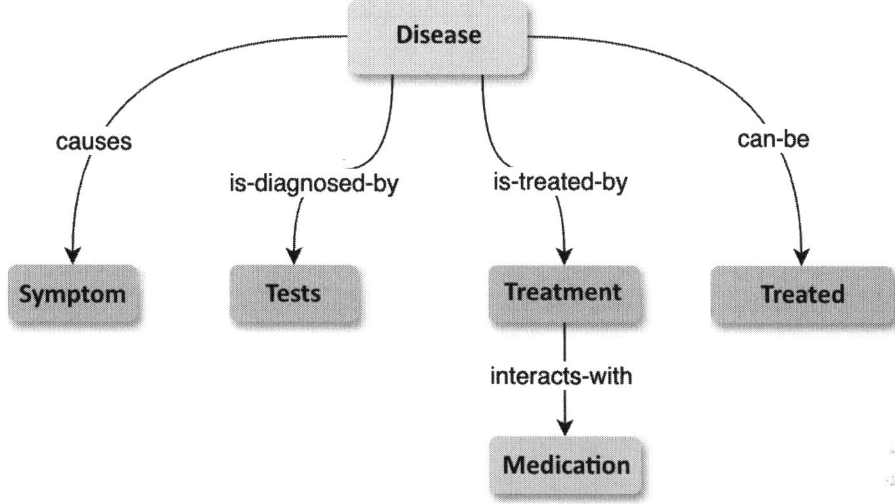

Figure 3.2 – Semantic network representing "Disease" relationships

Semantic networks gain much of their power from their ability to perform generalization through the inheritance of properties along relationship paths. If the network specifies that dogs are a subclass of animals and that animals breathe air, then an agent can semantically infer that dogs also breathe air through inheritance. Algorithms can traverse the graph, chaining sequences of relations together to derive new facts and conclusions from the represented knowledge. For instance, in a semantic network for family relations, one could infer that a person's spouse's parents are also their in-laws.

Additionally, semantic networks integrate naturally with other symbolic reasoning techniques. Their graph-based structure maps well to deductive methods such as **first-order logic**, where nodes become constants or predicates and edges become relations that can participate in logical proofs and inference rules. An intelligent tutoring system could use this combined representational power for logic-based explanations and teach students new concepts based on their semantic knowledge graphs.

Semantic networks provide a robust yet intuitive mechanism for intelligent agents to build rich, expressive models of their environment. Their inherent support for capturing interconnected concepts and deriving new knowledge through relation composition and inheritance makes them an extremely powerful knowledge representation formalism across many real-world domains.

Frames

The frame knowledge representation paradigm provides a structured way for intelligent agents to model concepts and their associated attributes. In this formalism, knowledge about objects, situations, or events is stored in data structures called **frames**.

Each frame consists of a collection of attribute-value pairs that describe the properties and characteristics of the concept being represented. For example, a frame for the concept *"Car"* may contain attributes such as *"make," "model," "year," "color," "fuel type,"* and so on with corresponding values providing specifics for a particular car instance.

Frames are organized hierarchically, allowing for the inheritance of attributes from higher-level, more general frames down to their specialized sub-frames. The *"Car"* frame could inherit properties from a parent *"Vehicle"* frame while adding new attributes unique to cars. This hierarchical taxonomy facilitates efficient knowledge storage by avoiding redundant attribute definitions across related concepts.

A key advantage of frames is their flexibility to represent procedural knowledge alongside factual information. In addition to simple attribute-value slots, frames can contain procedures that supply attribute values dynamically or model operations relevant to the represented concept. For instance, the *"Car"* frame could have methods for calculating fuel efficiency or querying service records. The following figure illustrates the concept of frames with our vehicle example:

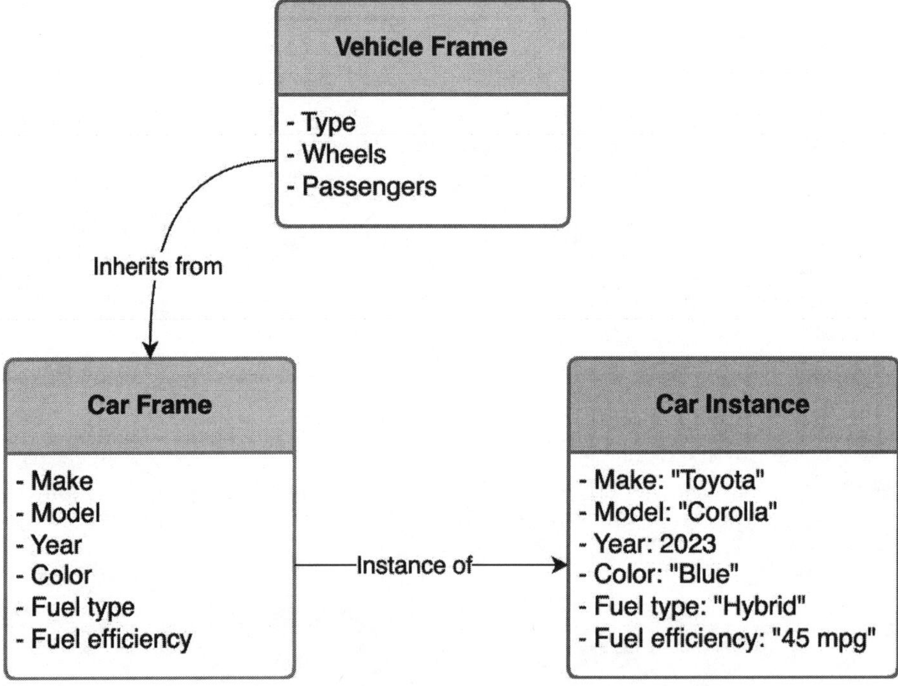

Figure 3.3 – Frames representing "Vehicle" and "Car" relationships

Frames provide an intuitive model for representation that mirrors how humans conceptualize knowledge about the world. Their hierarchical nature aligns with how people form conceptual abstractions and categorize ideas based on shared attributes and relations.

In real-world applications, frame representations are widely used in areas such as the following:

- **Natural language processing**: Linguistic frames model semantic concepts, roles, and relations extracted from text data

- **Expert systems**: Frames capture domain expertise and rules for knowledge-based reasoning engines

- **Object-oriented programming**: Classes in OOP languages are essentially frame-like structures encapsulating attributes and methods

- **Computer vision**: Object detection systems use frame hierarchies to identify and describe visual entities based on attributes such as shape, color, texture, and so on

- **Robotics**: Frames enable robots to represent objects/environments along with associated actions, motion models, and constraints

The frame knowledge representation formalism offers an efficient, structured, and human-compatible way for intelligent agents to capture rich conceptual information suitable for knowledge-based reasoning and decision-making.

Logic-based representations

While semantic networks and frames offer visually intuitive ways to represent knowledge, the logic-based approach takes a more formal, mathematical route. Logic-based knowledge representation employs the machinery of symbolic logic to encode facts, rules, and axioms about a domain.

In this paradigm, statements representing knowledge are translated into well-formed formulae in formal logical languages such as **propositional logic**, **first-order logic**, or **specialized modal/temporal logics**. See this, for example:

- *"All humans are mortal"* can be represented as $\forall x\ (Human(x) \rightarrow Mortal(x))$ in first-order logic

- *"It is raining or it is sunny"* can be expressed as $Rain \lor Sunny$ in propositional logic

- *"Eventually, the system will stabilize"* can be modeled as $\Diamond\ Stable$ in temporal logic

Here:

- $\forall x$: Universal quantifier meaning *"for all x."*

  Example: $\forall x\ (Human(x) \rightarrow Mortal(x))$. Translation: *For all x, if x is a human, then x is mortal.*

- $\lor$: Logical disjunction meaning *"or."*

  Example: $Rain \lor Sunny$. Translation: *It is either raining or sunny.*

- ◇: Diamond operator in temporal logic meaning "*eventually*."

  Example: ◇*Stable*. Translation: *Eventually, the system will stabilize.*

These logical formulae act as the building blocks for constructing a comprehensive knowledge base using strict logical deductive systems with clearly defined axioms, inference rules, and formal semantics. An inference engine can then derive new facts and conclusions from the existing knowledge by applying the rules of logical reasoning.

A key advantage of logic-based representations is their formal rigor and associated strong theoretical properties. Systems built on logical foundations can provide guarantees around soundness (only deriving logically valid conclusions) and completeness (deriving all possible valid conclusions). This mathematical grounding makes logic attractive for knowledge representation in safety-critical domains. Logic-based representations find widespread use in many real-world applications, such as these:

- **Expert systems**: Rule-based expert system engines are essentially theorem provers operating over a logical knowledge base encoding domain expertise

- **Database systems**: Relational databases use relational algebra/calculus – subsets of first-order logic – as the mathematical foundations

- **Automated reasoning**: From software verification to robot planning, logic provides the representational underpinnings for automated reasoning systems

- **Legal/regulatory domains**: Laws, policies, and regulations can be precisely represented as logical rules amenable to formal analysis

- **Semantic web**: Description logics such as OWL (Web Ontology Language) form the knowledge representation backbone of ontologies and the Semantic Web

While logic-based representations aren't as intuitive as semantic networks or frames, their mathematical rigor and ability to support sound, automated reasoning make them invaluable in applications where formal verification, consistency, and completeness guarantees are essential.

Having explored the foundational structures of knowledge representation, which form the basis of an agent's knowledge base, we now turn to examine how intelligent agents harness these representations to perform reasoning tasks, draw inferences, and solve complex problems.

Reasoning in intelligent agents

By employing the language of logic, intelligent agents can build robust knowledge bases, enabling sophisticated querying, deductive inference, and reasoning that are not possible with less expressive representational formalisms. Once an intelligent agent has a robust way to represent its knowledge, reasoning mechanisms allow it to intelligently manipulate and make use of that information. Reasoning capabilities enable agents to derive new insights, draw logical conclusions, explain observations, and ultimately make informed decisions to achieve their goals.

Reasoning in intelligent agents is rarely a singular, monolithic process. Sophisticated agent architectures tend to employ a multi-faceted reasoning approach that combines different reasoning styles and data-driven, analytical, and learned components. For instance, a question-answering system could use semantic parsing to map questions to logical forms, apply deductive reasoning over a logical knowledge base, and then invoke a neural sequence-to-sequence model to render the final answer fluently. There are several fundamental reasoning paradigms, namely, deductive, inductive, and abductive reasoning.

Deductive reasoning

Deductive reasoning is a fundamental form of logical reasoning that follows a top-down approach. In deductive reasoning, an intelligent agent starts with general premises or rules about a domain and applies them to derive specific, logically inescapable conclusions. The classic example illustrating deductive reasoning is the following popular syllogism:

"All men are mortal.

Socrates is a man.

Therefore, Socrates is mortal."

If the initial premises (*"All men are mortal"* and *"Socrates is a man"*) are true, then the conclusion *"Socrates is mortal"* follows inescapably from applying the rules of deductive logic. Deduction provides a way to reach irrefutable conclusions as long as the original premises and rules are correct and factual. The following figure illustrates deductive reasoning with the example:

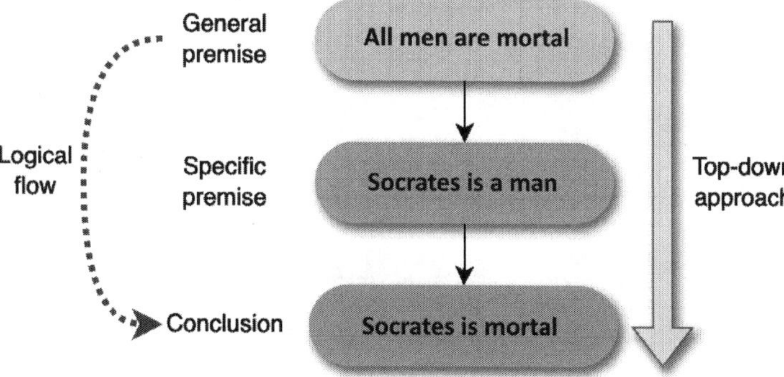

Figure 3.4 – Deductive reasoning – from general premises to specific conclusions

Deductive reasoning finds application across many domains, such as these:

- **Mathematics/geometry**: Formal mathematical proofs are quintessential examples of deductive reasoning, deriving specific theorems from general axioms and previously proven statements

- **Law**: Legal reasoning applies codified laws and precedents to derive judgments about particular cases through deduction

- **Software verification**: Formal verification techniques use deductive reasoning over logical specifications to prove correctness properties of hardware/software systems

- **Network routing**: Routing protocols determine optimal paths by deductively applying rules/constraints about network topology, bandwidth, and so on

Deductive reasoning is particularly powerful when combined with other forms of reasoning such as abduction or induction. For example, a medical diagnosis system could do the following:

- **Abduce** possible disease hypotheses from symptoms (inference to the best explanation)

- **Deduce** expected findings for each hypothesis using rules about disease models

- **Compare** deduced findings to actual patient data to confirm/reject hypotheses

While deduction alone cannot acquire entirely new knowledge, it is indispensable for intelligent agents to logically expand their knowledge, enforcing consistency and enabling rational decision-making. Deductive reasoning provides the rigor to ensure the trustworthiness of an agent's conclusions.

Inductive reasoning

In contrast to the top-down approach of deductive reasoning, inductive reasoning follows a bottom-up methodology. Inductive reasoning involves making generalizations or deriving probable conclusions from a set of specific observations or data points. The following is an example:

"The Sun has risen every day for the past million days.

Therefore, the sun will likely rise again tomorrow."

Based on the repeated instances of the sun rising, an inductive reasoning process allows an intelligent agent to hypothesize or induce that the sun will continue rising in the future. However, unlike deduction, **inductive conclusions** are not logically guaranteed to be true – they merely suggest a likely *possibility* based on the observed evidence. The following figure illustrates the concept with the example:

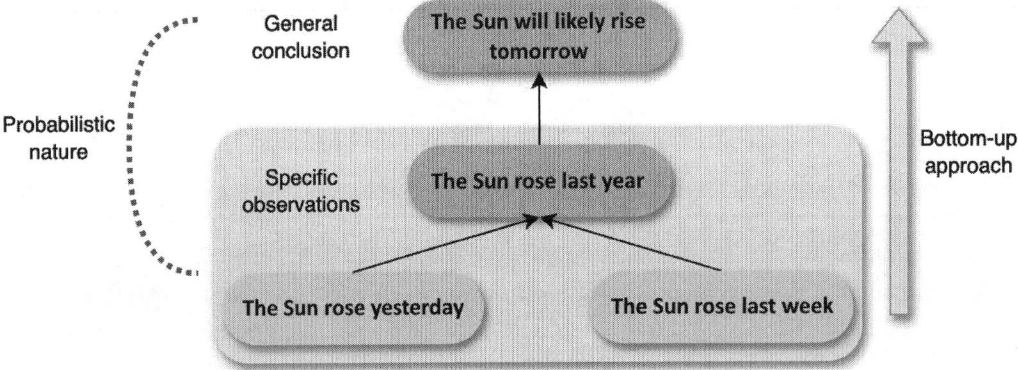

Figure 3.5 – Inductive reasoning – from specific observations to general conclusions

Inductive reasoning has immense applicability in the following real-world domains where data-driven learning and theory formation are crucial:

- **Scientific method**: The process of formulating scientific laws/theories relies heavily on inductively generalizing from experimental observations and data

- **Machine learning**: ML algorithms essentially perform inductive reasoning, inferring general models from training data that can make predictions on new instances

- **Pattern recognition**: Computer vision, signal processing, and other pattern recognition tasks use inductive techniques to classify inputs based on detected statistical regularities

- **Data mining**: Approaches such as association rule mining inductively identify frequently occurring patterns, correlations, or relationships in large datasets

- **Natural language acquisition**: Children learn grammar rules and language models through inductive generalization from the linguistic inputs they receive

While powerful, purely inductive reasoning has limitations since conclusions can be incorrect if the observed instances are an imperfect sample not representative of the entire space. As such, it is often combined with other reasoning approaches such as abduction (inference to the best explanation) and deduction (validating hypotheses) in intelligent agent architectures. Despite not guaranteeing truth, inductive reasoning's ability to extract knowledge, recognize patterns, and formulate theories from specific data makes it indispensable for intelligent agents operating in noisy, uncertain environments where knowledge is not fully available upfront.

Abductive reasoning

Abductive reasoning is a form of reasoning that works backward – attempting to find the most plausible explanations or premises that could account for a given set of observations or data. It is often described as *inference to the best explanation*. Unlike deductive reasoning, which starts with general rules and arrives at guaranteed specific conclusions, abduction begins with observed effects or phenomena and hypothesizes the most likely underlying causes based on current knowledge. An example of abductive reasoning is:

"The lawn is wet.

A plausible explanation: It rained last night."

Here, the observed effect is a wet lawn. Abductive reasoning allows an intelligent agent to rationally deduce or infer that the most likely explanation, based on past experience, is that it rained the previous night, even though that was not directly observed. The following figure illustrates this concept of backward reasoning:

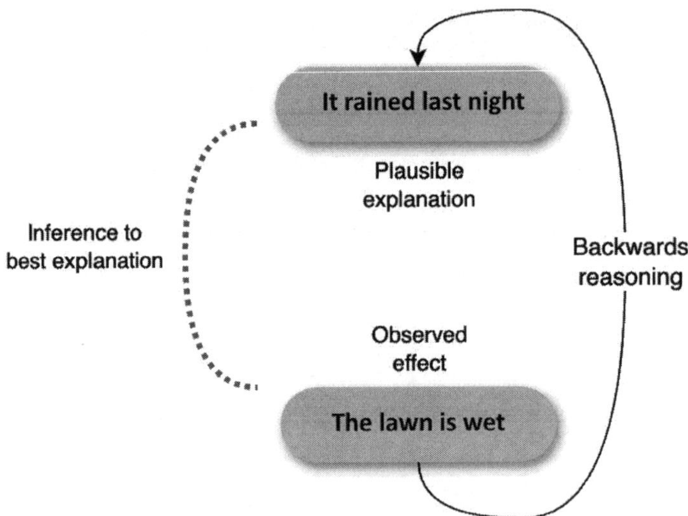

Figure 3.6 – Abductive reasoning – inference to the best explanation

Abductive reasoning is extremely useful in diagnostic domains and applications where root cause analysis is critical, such as these:

- **Medical diagnosis**: Given a set of symptoms, physicians abduce and investigate the most probable diseases or conditions that could explain those symptoms

- **Fault detection**: Monitoring systems in manufacturing use abduction to isolate the most likely faults or failures that led to observed anomalies

- **Forensics/criminal investigation**: From crime scene evidence, detectives abduce possible scenarios and suspect profiles to determine what transpired

- **AI planning**: For agents to achieve desired goals, they must abduce sequences of viable actions by reasoning backward from those goals

- **Scientific discovery**: New scientific theories are often initially inferred by finding explanatory hypotheses for currently unexplained observations or phenomena

A key advantage of abductive reasoning is its ability to generate new plausible premises that deductive or inductive methods cannot produce solely from existing knowledge and data. It facilitates thinking outside the box and exploring novel possible explanations. However, abduction does not guarantee correct explanations – there may be multiple possible hypotheses consistent with the observations. This is why abductive reasoning is commonly used in tandem with deductive reasoning to validate the consistency and plausibility of the explanatory hypotheses formed.

Points to remember here are that implementing abductive reasoning in agentic systems is challenging due to its computational complexity, as generating and evaluating multiple hypotheses can be resource-intensive. It also deals with uncertainty and incomplete data, making it difficult to determine the most plausible explanations. Proper knowledge representation is crucial but difficult to maintain, and evaluating hypotheses often requires subjective criteria. Integrating abductive reasoning with other reasoning modes can lead to conflicts, and scalability becomes an issue as the domain grows. Additionally, handling dynamic environments and ensuring explainability for users may add further complexity to the process. However, by applying abductive reasoning, intelligent agents can exhibit deeper understanding, creativity in postulating tentative explanations, and an increased ability to operate effectively in uncertain environments with partial observability and information. Through robust knowledge representation formalisms and multi-faceted reasoning capabilities, intelligent agents gain the power to build rich models of their environment, draw insights, explain observations, and ultimately make well-informed decisions about how to interact with the world. These capabilities form the bedrock for more advanced agent functionality.

Learning mechanisms for adaptive agents

Learning mechanisms are key to enabling intelligent agents to adapt to changes in their environment or to improve over time. The ability to learn allows agents to continuously refine their knowledge and behavior based on new experiences and data. There are numerous approaches to learning, each with its own strengths and applications:

- **Supervised learning**: This learning paradigm involves training an agent on a dataset where the inputs are paired with corresponding labeled outputs or target values. The aim is for the agent to learn a mapping function that accurately predicts outputs for new unseen inputs. Supervised learning is widely used for classification and regression tasks across domains such as these:

  - Image classification (for example, identifying objects and digits in images)

  - Spam detection (classifying emails as spam or not spam)

  - Machine translation (learning to map text in one language to another)

  - Medical diagnosis (mapping patient symptoms/tests to disease labels

- **Unsupervised learning**: Here, the agent is trained on unlabeled data without any associated target outputs. The goal is to discover inherent patterns, correlations, or groupings within the data itself in an unsupervised manner. Key applications include the following:

  - Customer segmentation (grouping customers based on purchasing behavior)

  - Anomaly detection (identifying unusual data points that differ from the norm)

  - Topic modeling (extracting topics/themes from collections of documents)

  - Dimensionality reduction (finding lower-dimensional representations of high-dimensional data)

- **Reinforcement learning**: This learning approach is inspired by how humans and animals learn – through trial and error using feedback from the environment in the form of rewards or punishments. An RL agent learns optimal behaviors/policies by trying out different actions and updating its strategy based on the observed rewards. RL has seen great success in domains such as the following:

  - Game playing (learning to master games such as chess, Go, and video games)

  - Robotics (learning control policies for robot navigation and manipulation)

  - Supply chain optimization (finding policies to maximize efficiency)

  - Traffic signal control (learning timing policies to improve traffic flow)

- **Transfer learning**: This technique focuses on transferring knowledge learned in one setting to facilitate learning in a different but related setting. By leveraging previously learned patterns and representations, transfer learning can significantly accelerate training speed and sample efficiency for new tasks. Applications span areas such as the following:

  - Natural language processing (transferring language models across domains)

  - Computer vision (using pre-trained models as initialization for new vision tasks)

  - Recommendation systems (transferring user/product embeddings across platforms)

These learning mechanisms, often used in hybrid combinations, equip intelligent agents with the ability to continuously expand their knowledge, refine their behaviors, and grow their problem-solving capabilities – the key hallmarks of intelligence. As learning algorithms advance, agents will only become more adaptable and robust when facing new challenges.

Having explored the learning mechanisms that enable adaptive agents to acquire knowledge and skills, we now turn our attention to how these agents leverage this learning to make decisions and plan their actions in complex environments.

Decision-making and planning in agentic systems

Decision-making and planning are critical capabilities for intelligent agents to achieve their goals effectively in complex environments. Agents need to analyze various possible scenarios, evaluate outcomes, and select the action(s) that will lead to the most desirable outcome based on their preferences and constraints. Although utility functions (tools) and planning will be discussed in detail in later chapters, we will discuss these key components involved in agent decision-making at a high level in the following sections.

Utility function

A utility function quantifies an agent's preferences by mapping outcomes to utility values, enabling the agent to compare and choose actions that maximize expected utility. Utility functions play a central role in decision-making for intelligent agents by providing a quantitative way to represent and reason about preferences over different outcomes or states of the world.

A utility function $u(s)$ maps any given state or outcome to a real-numbered utility value $u(s)$, reflecting the desirability or preference for that state according to the agent's goals, rewards, and penalties. Formally, this is mathematically expressed as:

$$u: S \rightarrow \mathbb{R}$$

$$s \mapsto u(s)$$

This expression may look a little intimidating at first, but the concept is really straightforward. Let us use some example Python code to explain this further:

```python
def travel_utility_function(travel_option):
    price_utility = (1000 - travel_option['price']) * 0.05
    comfort_utility = travel_option['comfort_rating'] * 10
    conv_utility = travel_option['convenience_score'] * 15

    total_utility = price_utility + \
                    comfort_utility + \
                    convenience_utility

    return total_utility
```

To explain this utility function, let us go back to our travel booking example. The given Python utility function evaluates travel options based on price, convenience, and comfort. Lines 2,3, and 4 of the function assign a real numbered utility for price, comfort, and convenience respectively. The numbers 0.05, 10, and 15 are completely arbitrary but are in the order of magnitude of importance of each of the three factors in a person's travel decision-making. For example, in line 2, we assign the price utility to a number; note that we subtract the price from an arbitrary value of `1000`, since the lower the price the better, which means a lower price contributes to more utility. Thus, the price utility number would be higher if the price is lower, that is, an inverse relationship. Similarly, the comfort and convenience utilities are assigned respective utility scores. The comfort and convenience scores are often user provided. For example, travel review websites such as Tripadvisor allow users to post detailed reviews about their travel experience via star ratings.

Applying our utility function to a few travel options will give us a clear picture of how this function works. Let us apply the utility function to two travel options a *Budget Airline* vs *Road Trip*.

A sample input to the utility function is as follows:

```
1  [{
2       'name': 'Budget Airline',
3       'price': 300,
4       'comfort_rating': 3,
5       'convenience_score': 2
6  },
7  {
8       'name': 'Road Trip',
9       'price': 150,
10      'comfort_rating': 4,
11      'convenience_score': 3
12 }]
```

Here's the output of the utility function:

```
1 Budget Airline – Utility: 95.00
2 Road Trip – Utility: 127.50
```

The output clearly shows that the road trip option scores a higher utility score due to higher convenience, comfort, and lower price compared to the budget airline. The full code is available in the `Chapter_03.ipynb` Python notebook in our GitHub repository.

Utility functions encode an agent's preferences by mapping states or outcomes to utility values, allowing any two states to be ranked or compared based on their assigned utilities. Higher utility values correspond to more preferred states or outcomes. This enables rational agents to select actions that maximize their expected utility, which is calculated as the probability-weighted sum of utilities over all possible outcome states resulting from those actions. By quantifying preferences in this way, utility functions provide a systematic mechanism for agents to make rational decisions in pursuit of the most desirable outcomes according to the specified utility measure. Utility functions can take many mathematical forms depending on the domain, such as the following:

- Simple scoring functions that apply weights to quantify preferences between attributes

- Constraint satisfaction functions that are maximized when all hard constraints are met

- Economic utility functions modeling pricing, profits, costs, and so on

- Multiplicative functions modeling preferences between outcomes with independent utility impacts

More sophisticated utility functions can model uncertainty, risk preferences, multi-attribute tradeoffs, changing preferences over time, and dependencies between attributes. In the case of **multi-attribute tradeoffs**, an agent must weigh different attributes (for example, cost, quality, time, or safety) when making decisions. These attributes often conflict, and an agent must find a balance between them, such as choosing between a faster but more expensive option versus a slower, cheaper one. The challenge here lies in quantifying how much an agent values each attribute relative to others, and how changes in one attribute influence the overall utility.

Defining an accurate quantitative utility function that captures all of an agent's preferences is often a major challenge because preferences are often complex and context-dependent. Agents may have different attitudes toward risk (for example, risk-averse or risk-seeking), and preferences may change based on the situation or over time. Additionally, dependencies between attributes – such as how the increase in one attribute (e.g., speed) may negatively affect another (for example, cost) – can complicate the modeling process. Moreover, the uncertainty in predicting outcomes or preferences under changing conditions further complicates the task of creating a utility function that fully reflects the agent's decision-making process. Techniques such as preference elicitation, inverse reinforcement learning, and learning from human feedback are used in such cases.

Planning algorithms

Planning algorithms are algorithms that derive sequences of actions for an agent to take in order to achieve its goals from a given initial state. Some of the most common planning approaches include **graph-based planning**, **heuristic search**, **Monte Carlo tree search (MCTS)**, **hierarchical planning**, and **constraint satisfaction**. Let's discuss each of these planning algorithms in the following sections.

Graph-based planning

Graph-based planning represents a planning problem as a graph, where the nodes correspond to possible states or configurations, and the edges represent actions or transitions that can be taken to move between states. A fundamental concept within graph-based planning algorithms is the **state-space graph**, which is a graph representation where nodes represent all possible states in the problem domain. In such a representation, the edges represent the actions or transitions between the states. This graph representation effectively maps out the entire "space" of possible situations and how they connect with each other via edges.

An **edge cost** is a property of an edge in a weighted graph. Each edge can have an associated cost (or weight) that represents some measure of the "expense" of taking that action or making that transition. Costs could represent factors such as distance, time, energy consumption, financial cost, or any other relevant metric appropriate for the use case.

Using state-space graphs, edges, and edge costs, there are two broad categories of graph-based planning algorithms:

- **Graph search**: In graph search, the planning process involves searching this graph data structure to find a path from the initial state to one of the goal states. The path defines the sequence of actions for the agent to execute to transition between states and reach the goal. Some of the most common algorithms under this category are **depth-first search (DFS)**, **breadth-first search (BFS)**, and Dijkstra's algorithm.

- **Optimal path finding**: This is a specific type of graph search that aims to find not just any path, but the best path according to some criteria (usually minimizing total edge cost). Two of the algorithms in this category are the Bellman-Ford algorithm and the A* search.

The downsides of using graph-based planning algorithms include fixing the state representation (state space) upfront, and the potential for exponential growth in the number of states to represent and store as problems get more complex.

Graph-based planning techniques find numerous real-world applications across domains, where finding optimal sequences of actions to achieve goals is crucial. These applications include navigation and route planning, such as GPS systems using graph representations of road networks to find optimal routes minimizing travel time or distance. Logistics and supply chain applications involve planning optimal sequences of operations for manufacturing products or finding least-cost shipping routes and delivery schedules. AI planning employs graph-based methods for game AI move sequencing in chess, video games, and real-time strategy games, as well as for task planning in AI assistants.

Heuristic search

Heuristic search techniques are widely used when finding optimal solutions through exhaustive search is computationally intractable due to the exponential growth of the search space. By using heuristic functions to guide the search toward promising areas, these methods can find reasonably good approximate solutions much faster.

Heuristic search techniques find widespread use in route planning and navigation applications. When finding truly optimal routes is computationally too expensive, heuristics such as estimating the straight-line distance to the destination can effectively guide the search toward reasonably short driving routes. AI agents in video games also commonly employ heuristic pathfinding algorithms to navigate virtual environments efficiently.

The key benefit of heuristic search is the ability to trade off optimality for computational efficiency, making larger problem instances solvable within limited time/memory constraints by finding approximate solutions. Heuristic design remains a critical challenge tailored to each application domain.

Monte Carlo tree search

The core idea behind MCTS is to iteratively build an asymmetric search tree by running many random simulations (playouts) from the current state. An asymmetric tree means that the tree is not balanced or uniform in its structure. The results of these simulations are used to guide the growth of the most promising branches in the tree at each iteration.

MCTS has seen widespread adoption across various real-world applications involving sequential decision-making under uncertainty. This algorithm has particular benefits in AI agents in situations that are likely to encounter uncertainties, and contain large state spaces, that is, a large number of possible outcomes. MCTS is found to produce reasonable results even with limited computational resources.

The key advantages of MCTS are anytime behavior, the ability to handle large action spaces, and reasoning about long-term outcomes through simulations. However, its efficiency depends on having an effective simulation model and designing good exploration strategies tailored to the domain. Some of the common drawbacks of this algorithm include the computational intensity required for simulations of complex problems and the difficult-to-tune tree policy that helps with outcome selection during simulations.

Hierarchical planning

Hierarchical planning approaches breaking down complex problems into hierarchies of higher-level tasks or goals, and subtasks or subgoals that achieve those higher-level objectives. This hierarchical decomposition allows reasoning about problems more abstractly and reusing solutions to common subproblems.

The core advantages of hierarchical approaches include computational efficiency via reusing subplan solutions, knowledge representation at multiple abstraction levels, and increased scalability to handle highly complex problems through hierarchical reasoning, though not always optimally. This structure also aligns well with how humans conceptualize and tackle complex tasks. The core advantages of hierarchical approaches include the following:

- Computational efficiency by reusing subplan solutions and avoiding reasoning about all details simultaneously

- Knowledge representation at multiple levels of abstraction

- Increased scalability to handle very complex problems

While not always optimal, hierarchical plans can provide good approximations for large problems where optimal solutions may be computationally unmanageable. The structure also maps well to how humans tend to conceptualize and tackle complex tasks.

Constraint satisfaction

Constraint satisfaction problems (CSPs) involve formulating the problem as a set of constraints that must be satisfied, and then using constraint propagation techniques to eliminate inconsistent possibilities from the search space. CSPs represent a powerful framework in AI for solving a wide variety of complex problems. At their core, CSPs involve defining a problem in terms of variables that need to be assigned values, under a set of constraints that restrict the possible combinations of these values. This approach allows for a natural representation of many real-world problems, from scheduling and resource allocation to puzzle-solving and configuration tasks.

The beauty of CSPs lies in their ability to separate the problem representation from the solving method. Once a problem is formulated as a CSP, a variety of general-purpose algorithms can be applied to find a solution. This separation allows researchers and practitioners to focus on accurately modeling the problem without worrying about the intricacies and complexities of the solving algorithm.

Intelligent agents require flexible decision-making capabilities that can weigh constraints, handle uncertainty, learn from experience, and scale to complex real-world problems in pursuit of their goals. Advances in planning, search, reasoning, and learning algorithms continue enhancing these crucial cognitive abilities.

Having examined the foundational aspects of intelligent agents – from knowledge representation and reasoning to learning mechanisms and decision-making processes – we now turn our attention to a cutting-edge development that promises to significantly expand these capabilities: the integration of generative AI into agent systems.

Enhancing agent capabilities with generative AI

Generative AI is transforming the development of intelligent agents by enhancing learning efficiency, improving their understanding of environments, and enabling more complex interactions through generative models. Some of the major developments in ushering generative AI in the space of intelligent agents are as follows:

- **Data augmentation**: Creating synthetic training data with generative models supplements datasets, improving the robustness and efficiency of machine learning agents. For example, self-driving car agents can use generated scene images to learn better object detection and navigation policies.

- **Understanding of context**: Generative AI constructs simulations modeling real-world complexities in fine detail, aiding agents in contextual understanding for informed decisions. For example, virtual assistants such as chatbots can use generative AI to simulate conversations in diverse contexts, helping them better understand user intent and provide more accurate, context-aware responses before interacting with real users.

- **Natural language processing**: Generative language models ease human-agent interaction by improving understanding and generation capabilities. Virtual assistants such as Alexa and chatbots leverage generative NLP for natural conversations.

- **Creative problem solving**: By generating diverse possible solutions, generative AI allows agents to explore creative ideas and evaluate their feasibility. This could allow AI architects to creatively design innovative building layouts while adhering to structural constraints.

The deep integration of generative AI with knowledge representation, learning mechanisms, and decision-making processes yields highly responsive and adaptive intelligent agents capable of operating effectively in dynamic, complex environments. Some examples of how this synergistic combination can enable advanced capabilities are as follows:

- **Learning**: Agents can gather data from various sources such as sensors, human interactions, or simulations to build models based on their operating environment through machine learning techniques such as reinforcement learning

- **Knowledge representation**: The learned environmental data is structured into usable representations such as semantic networks, logical rules, or probabilistic graphical models to capture relationships, constraints, and uncertainties

- **Decision processes**: Based on the represented knowledge, agents use planning and decision-making algorithms (for example, Markov decision processes and MCTS) to derive sequences of actions aiming to achieve their objectives optimally

- **Generative models**: Provide contextual simulations to enhance agents' understanding through generated scenarios accounting for complexities such as noisy sensor data, stochastic dynamics, or extraneous factors absent from training data

- **Feedback loops**: Allow continuous adaptation by feeding real-world interaction outcomes back into the learning mechanisms to refine the agent's knowledge and decision models based on experience

Start building agentic AI

We have learned quite a lot about the characteristics of intelligent agents, how they are built, how they work with different algorithms, and their essential components. It is now time for a gentle introduction to the world of agentic AI and to start building applications using different frameworks.

In subsequent chapters of this book, we will make extensive use of several open source frameworks. The most popular framework for building agentic and multi-agent AI systems is LangChain's LangGraph framework, although some of the other noteworthy frameworks (as of this writing) include AutoGen, CrewAI, and MetaGPT. This is not an exhaustive list of open source frameworks; these are only the most popular frameworks that allow you to build agentic and multi-agent systems with LLMs. Note that although some of these frameworks support different programming languages, we will primarily use Python programming language for our purposes. For consistency, we will use LangGraph and OpenAI GPT models throughout the book; however; there are a number of other LLMs that can be used with agentic AI frameworks.

> **Important note**
>
> Although the code samples are created specifically with OpenAI GPT models, you can use any model of your choice that is supported by LangGraph. LangGraph also works with LLMs offered via several cloud providers such as **Amazon Web Services** (**AWS**), **Microsoft Azure**, and **Google Cloud Platform** (**GCP**). Using AI models or cloud platforms may incur some costs. Refer to the respective AI model documentation for more details.

Now that we have the overview of frameworks and LLMs out of the way, let's start with building our basic travel agent booking. At this stage, we only want the model to respond back with greetings and any follow-up questions. For example, if we ask the agent to *"Book a flight for me"*, then we want the model to respond back with a follow-up question about travel cities, dates, and so on. For the following code, we will directly use OpenAI's Python SDK to build this functionality and use its function calling feature, that is the LLM model's ability to call a function on the user's behalf. Here's the code snippet:

```python
1 import openai from OpenAI
2
3 def book_flight(passenger_name: str,
4                 from_city: str,
5                 to_city: str,
6                 travel_date: str) -> str:
7     return "A flight has been booked"
8
9 tools = [{ "type":"function",
10            "function":{ "name": "book_flight", … }}]
11
12 def travel_agent(user_message: str, messages: list) -> str:
13     messages.append({"role": "user", "content": user_message})
14     try:
15         response = openai.chat.completions.create(
16                 model="gpt-4-turbo",
17                 messages=messages,
18                 tools=tools)
19         if response.choices[0].message.content:
20             return response.choices[0].message.content
21         elif response.choices[0].message.tool_calls:
22             [ … ]
23             confirmation = book_flight(…)
24             [ … ]
25             response = openai.chat.completions.create(
26                     model="gpt-4-turbo",
27                     messages=messages)
28             return response.choices[0].message.content
```

Let us break down what is happening in this code snippet. We first define a book_flight function in line 3 – at the moment, this function just returns a message that says that the flight booking is complete. The travel_agent function in line 12 is where we call the LLM, in this case, OpenAI's gpt-4-turbo model. We call the LLM's API using the OpenAI SDK in line 15, which is where we pass in the user's message, the model's name, and a set of tools. Note that we are using our book_flight function as a *tool* for our intelligent agent and the API takes tools as a parameter.

We will discuss tools in greater detail in the subsequent chapters, but for now, it is sufficient to understand that *tools* are a mechanism by which your intelligent agent can interact with the external world (or external systems) to complete a task. In this case, the task is booking a flight ticket. The LLM is smart enough to indicate to us when to call the `book_flight` tool function when it has all the details from the passenger. In a more complete solution as we will see in future chapters, functions such as `book_flight` will be used to interact with external systems, such as calling APIs to complete the flight booking and so on. Here's how a possible conversation using this code looks:

YOUR AI TRAVEL AGENT

User: Hi i want to book a flight ticket

Travel agent: I can help you with that! Could you please provide me with the following details for your flight booking? 1. Departure City 2. Arrival City 3. Date of Travel 4. Your legal name as it appears on your passport or ID With these details, I'll be able to book the ticket for you.

User: from LA to NY, on Oct 1 2024. Name is Johhny Doe.

Travel agent: Your flight from Los Angeles to New York on October 1, 2024, has been successfully booked for Johnny Doe. If you need any further assistance or additional bookings, feel free to ask. Have a great trip!

Figure 3.7 – A sample conversation with the AI agent

A few things to note here: after the first user message, our agent doesn't directly call the `book_flight` function because it doesn't have all the parameter values to call the function successfully. In a typical heuristics-based approach, you could use string parsing to find out whether the user has provided their name, travel cities, and date of travel. But such logic can be overly complicated and error-prone. This is where the beauty of an intelligent agent comes in. The LLM has better language understanding capabilities and can know when to call the `book_flight` function during the conversation, and if the required values are not provided by the user, it can prompt them to provide these values, that is, their name, travel cities, and date of travel. It can also accurately extract these values from the user's response, which allows us to call the `book_flight` function. For the full code of the intelligent agent, refer to the `Chapter_03.ipynb` Python notebook in the GitHub repository.

Summary

In this chapter, we discussed several aspects and key components of intelligent agents. We started with the understanding and importance of various knowledge representation mechanisms such as semantic networks, frames, and logic-based representations. We also learned about various reasoning techniques such as deductive, inductive, and abductive reasoning to understand how intelligent agents may use these techniques for decision-making to accomplish tasks. We briefly looked at some of the learning mechanisms that intelligent agents may use to adapt themselves to various use cases and explored agent decision-making via utility functions and various planning algorithms. Finally, we wrapped up this chapter with an introduction to intelligent agents with generative AI using an LLM and discussed a simple intelligent agent that is capable of gathering information from user queries for our travel booking agent example.

In the next chapter, we will dive deeper into the advanced intelligent agent concepts such as reflection and introspection. We will learn how reflection and introspection influence an intelligent agent's decision-making capabilities. Before we conclude this chapter, take a moment and try to answer the questions listed in the subsequent sections.

Questions

1. What are the three main types of knowledge representation discussed in the chapter?

2. How does inductive reasoning differ from deductive reasoning?

3. What is the purpose of a utility function in agent decision-making?

4. How does generative AI enhance the capabilities of intelligent agents?

5. What is the role of "tools" in AI frameworks such as the one demonstrated in the travel agent example?

Answers

1. The three main types of knowledge representation discussed are semantic networks, frames, and logic-based representations.

2. Inductive reasoning follows a bottom-up approach, making generalizations from specific observations, while deductive reasoning follows a top-down approach, deriving specific conclusions from general premises.

3. A utility function quantifies an agent's preferences by mapping outcomes to utility values, enabling the agent to compare and choose actions that maximize expected utility.

4. Generative AI enhances agent capabilities through data augmentation, improved context understanding, better natural language processing, and enabling creative problem-solving.

5. Tools in AI frameworks allow agents to interact with external systems or perform specific functions, such as booking a flight in the travel agent example, enhancing the agent's ability to complete complex tasks.

Get This Book's PDF Version and Exclusive Extras

Scan the QR code (or go to `packtpub.com/unlock`). Search for this book by name, confirm the edition, and then follow the steps on the page.

Note: Keep your invoice handly. Purchase made directly from packt don't require one.

Part 2: Designing and Implementing Generative AI-Based Agents

This part equips you with practical techniques and approaches for designing and implementing generative AI-based agentic systems, enabling you to create adaptive, self-aware, and collaborative intelligent agents.

This part contains the following chapters:

- *Chapter 4, Reflection and Introspection in Agents*
- *Chapter 5, Enabling Tool Use and Planning in Agents*
- *Chapter 6, Exploring the Coordinator, Worker, and Delegator Approach*
- *Chapter 7, Effective Agentic System Design Techniques*

4

Reflection and Introspection in Agents

In the previous chapter, we introduced intelligent agents in general, exploring their adaptive, autonomous, and goal-directed behaviors that make them invaluable across diverse applications. We examined the fundamental components that enable these agents to thrive in a complex world – perception, reasoning, and action.

However, the quest for intelligent agents that can not only perform tasks but also continuously improve their performance, emulating aspects of human-like intelligence, has led to the emergence of two developing subfields: reflection and introspection. These disciplines investigate the degree to which agents with reflective capabilities can contribute to their ability to introspect their cognitive processes, gain insights from experience, and adapt their behavior accordingly.

This chapter will dive into the importance of reflection within intelligent agents, exploring various methodologies for embedding reflective functionalities. Through real-world examples, we will explore how these principles find practical applications across business and other domains, enabling agents to transcend mere task execution and evolve toward heightened levels of performance and intelligence.

You will also learn techniques for adding reflective features to agents, such as meta-reasoning, self-explanation, and self-modeling, with practical implementation guidance. Finally, we'll wrap up with real-world examples of reflective agents in different business areas, showing their practical uses and benefits.

This chapter is divided into the following main sections:

- The importance of reflection in agents

- Introspection in intelligent agents

- Implementing reflective capabilities

- Use cases and examples

By the end of this chapter, you'll understand how reflection and introspection help intelligent agents analyze their reasoning, learn from experience, and adapt their behavior, leading to more human-like intelligence.

Technical requirements

You can find the code file for this chapter on GitHub at `https://github.com/PacktPublishing/Building-Agentic-AI-Systems`. In this chapter, we will also use an agentic Python framework known as **CrewAI** to demonstrate the various aspects of AI agents.

The importance of reflection in agents

Reflection in LLM agents refers to their ability to examine their own thought processes, evaluate their actions, and adjust their approach. Like a person who might think, *"that didn't work well, let me try a different way"*, an LLM agent can analyze its own outputs, recognize when its strategies aren't effective, and modify its behavior accordingly. Here are some examples:

- An LLM agent might reflect on a failed attempt to solve a math problem and choose a different solution method

- It could recognize when its response wasn't helpful to a user and adjust its communication style

- It might evaluate whether it has enough information to complete a task and request more details if needed

This self-monitoring and adaptation makes agents more effective than simple input-output systems, since they can learn from their successes and failures. This crucial capability has been recognized as vital for enhanced decision-making, adaptation, ethics, and human-computer interaction, as we will explore in the subsequent sections.

Enhanced decision-making

A reflective agent can replay past deliberations and their outcomes, enabling more informed decision-making in the future. This behavior is akin to *metacognition* in humans, where "thinking about thinking" controls learning and problem-solving. By introspecting on its decision-making process, a reflective agent can identify strengths, weaknesses, and biases, allowing it to refine its approach continuously.

Consider a reflective agent designed to assist users in planning their travel itineraries. By introspecting on its past recommendations and the feedback received from users, the agent can identify patterns and refine its decision-making process over time. Initially, the agent might rely on a set of predefined rules and preferences to suggest travel destinations, accommodations, and activities based on factors such as the user's budget, travel dates, and stated interests. However, through reflection, the agent can learn from the choices made by users and their post-trip feedback.

For instance, the agent might notice that users with similar profiles (for example, age group, family status, or interests) tend to prefer certain types of accommodations or activities over others. It could then adjust the weight it assigns to these preferences in its decision-making process, ensuring that future recommendations better align with the observed patterns. Our reflective travel agent could analyze the reasons behind users' deviations from its initial recommendations. If a significant number of users consistently book more expensive hotels or opt for different activities than suggested, the agent could re-evaluate its assumptions about budget allocations or the importance of certain interests. Additionally, reflective agents can leverage their introspective capabilities to identify knowledge gaps or areas where additional data or expertise is required. They can then proactively seek out relevant information or consult with human experts to enhance their decision-making capabilities.

By engaging in this cycle of reflection, learning, and adaptation, reflective agents can continuously improve their decision-making processes, surpassing the limitations of static, rule-based systems. This ability to learn from experience and adapt to new situations is a crucial step toward developing intelligent agents that can truly emulate human-like reasoning and decision-making capabilities.

Adaptation

Adaptation involves modifying an agent's strategy based on changes in information or context. Reflective agents can introspect on their performance, identify areas for improvement, and adapt their strategies accordingly. This is particularly valuable in dynamic environments where conditions can change rapidly, such as stock trading or network management.

Using the travel agent example, adaptation is crucial as travel conditions, regulations, and user preferences can evolve rapidly. A reflective travel agent can adapt its strategies based on these changing circumstances. Consider a scenario where travel restrictions or advisories are issued due to political unrest, natural disasters in a particular region, or when a situation such as the COVID-19 pandemic occurs. A non-reflective agent might continue recommending destinations and itineraries in that area, oblivious to the potential risks or inconveniences for travelers.

However, a reflective travel agent can introspect on the feedback and experiences of users who have recently traveled to the affected region or can take into account any travel advisory in effect. It might notice an increase in complaints, cancellations, or requests for alternative arrangements. Through this reflection, the agent can identify the need to adapt its strategies and temporarily avoid recommending destinations or activities in that area until the situation stabilizes.

Similarly, the agent could adapt its recommendations based on changing user preferences or travel trends. If it notices a surge in interest in a particular type of travel experience, such as eco-tourism or wellness retreats, the reflective agent can adjust its recommendations to cater to this emerging demand. By continuously monitoring user feedback and preferences, the agent can stay ahead of the curve and provide relevant and appealing suggestions. Additionally, a reflective travel agent can adapt its strategies based on changes in external factors such as airline routes, hotel availability, or pricing fluctuations. By introspecting on the outcomes of its recommendations and analyzing user feedback, the agent can identify instances where its suggestions may have become outdated or suboptimal due to these dynamic conditions. It can then proactively adjust its strategies to ensure that it provides the most current and cost-effective recommendations.

In rapidly evolving environments such as the travel industry, the ability to adapt is crucial for maintaining relevance and providing satisfactory customer service. Through reflection and introspection, a travel agent can continuously monitor its performance, identify areas for improvement, and adapt its strategies accordingly, ensuring that it remains responsive to changing conditions and user needs.

Ethical consideration

Reflection helps agents appraise their actions against ethical norms and human values. In critical applications with significant implications for human life and welfare, reflective agents can reduce the chances of unethical behavior by continuously evaluating their decisions and actions. For example, a reflective agent assisting in autonomous vehicle navigation could prioritize safety and ethical considerations over efficiency.

Using the travel agent example, ethical considerations play a crucial role in ensuring responsible and sustainable tourism practices. A reflective travel agent can introspect on the potential impact of its recommendations and adapt its strategies to align with ethical norms and human values. For instance, the agent might notice a pattern of contributing to overtourism in certain popular destinations, leading to negative consequences such as overcrowding, strain on local resources, and degradation of cultural heritage sites. By reflecting on these observations and feedback from local communities or environmentalists, the agent can recognize the need to adjust its recommendations to promote more sustainable and responsible tourism practices.

The reflective travel agent could then adapt its strategies by suggesting alternative, less-crowded destinations, encouraging travelers to visit during off-peak seasons, or recommending activities that have a lower environmental impact. It could also prioritize eco-friendly accommodations, tour operators, and activities that support local communities and cultures. Additionally, the agent could introspect on the potential ethical implications of recommending certain activities or destinations. For example, it might identify cases where recommended activities could potentially exploit or harm local wildlife or contribute to unethical practices. Through reflection, the agent can reevaluate these recommendations and provide alternatives that align with ethical principles and respect for the environment and local cultures. A reflective travel agent could continuously monitor user feedback and experiences to identify instances where its recommendations may have inadvertently caused harm or disrespected local customs or values. By introspecting on these cases, the agent can learn from its mistakes, adjust its knowledge base, and refine its decision-making process to prevent similar occurrences in the future.

By embedding ethical considerations into its reflective processes, the travel agent can ensure that its recommendations not only provide an enjoyable travel experience but also contribute to the well-being of local communities, preserve cultural heritage, and promote sustainable tourism practices. This commitment to ethical behavior can foster trust and confidence among users, positioning the reflective agent as a responsible and socially conscious travel advisor.

Human-computer interaction

Agents with reflective and introspective capabilities are better equipped to interact with humans. Their ability to deduce and respond to human feelings and intentions enhances cooperation and communication. A reflective virtual assistant, for instance, could adapt its communication style based on the user's emotional state and preferences, fostering a more natural and engaging interaction.

In the context of a reflective travel agent, the ability to engage in effective human-computer interaction is crucial for providing personalized and satisfactory service. By introspecting on its interactions with users, the agent can adapt its communication style and approach to better align with individual preferences and emotional states. Consider a scenario where a user is planning a family vacation and expresses excitement and enthusiasm during the initial interaction with the travel agent. A reflective agent could introspect on the user's positive emotional cues, such as their tone, language choices, and expressions of excitement, and respond accordingly. The agent might adapt its communication style to match the user's upbeat and enthusiastic demeanor, fostering a more engaging and collaborative experience.

Conversely, if the user expresses frustration or dissatisfaction with the travel recommendations provided by the agent, a reflective travel agent can introspect on the user's negative emotional cues and adapt its communication style to be more empathetic and understanding. It could acknowledge the user's concerns, offer alternative solutions or explanations, and adopt a more patient and reassuring tone to help alleviate the user's frustration. The reflective agent may also analyze patterns in user interactions to identify preferred communication styles or preferences. Some users might prefer a more concise and direct approach, while others might appreciate a more conversational and detail-oriented style. By introspecting on these patterns, the agent can tailor its communication to each individual user, fostering a more natural and engaging experience.

Additionally, the reflective travel agent could leverage its introspective capabilities to identify areas where it may lack sufficient information or context to provide satisfactory recommendations or responses. In such cases, it could proactively seek clarification or additional details from the user, engaging in a more collaborative and interactive dialogue. For example, if a user expresses interest in a particular type of activity or destination, but the agent lacks detailed knowledge about it, it could ask follow-up questions to better understand the user's preferences and provide more tailored recommendations.

By continuously adapting its communication style and approach based on user feedback, emotional cues, and preferences, the reflective travel agent can foster a more human-like interaction, enhancing trust, satisfaction, and overall user experience. This ability to effectively communicate and collaborate with users is essential for building long-lasting relationships and establishing the agent as a reliable and personalized travel advisory service. By implementing reflection and introspection, intelligent agents can become more self-aware, adaptable, and aligned with human values, ultimately leading to more intelligent and trustworthy systems.

Having explored why reflective capabilities are essential for agents, let's now dive into the process of implementing them.

Introspection in intelligent agents

Introspection refers to the process by which an intelligent agent examines and analyzes its own cognitive processes, decisions, and behaviors. This capability allows agents to gain deeper insights into their actions, identify patterns, and adjust their strategies based on reflection. Introspection is essential in advancing intelligent agents from simple task performers to systems that can continually evolve and improve over time, similar to the way humans reflect on past experiences to make better future decisions.

In agent-based systems, introspection plays a crucial role in enhancing performance and adaptability. When agents introspect, they evaluate their reasoning and decision-making pathways, allowing them to detect any flaws, biases, or inefficiencies in their processes. This leads to a more refined understanding of the environment and their own functioning, enabling them to make more informed choices and adapt their behavior. For example, introspective capabilities allow agents to learn from both successes and failures. When an agent encounters a situation, it can analyze its actions after the fact to understand why certain decisions led to desired outcomes, while others did not. This feedback loop encourages continuous learning and improvement, which is vital for tasks that require adaptability and long-term performance.

Introspection enhances the agent's ability to deal with ambiguity and uncertainty. By reflecting on past experiences, agents can develop more robust decision-making strategies that accommodate complex, dynamic environments. This makes introspection particularly important for systems that interact with changing data or environments, as it helps agents maintain relevance and effectiveness over time. Introspection allows intelligent agents to evolve from being reactive to becoming proactive learners. By understanding their own thought processes and learning from experience, introspective agents can continually refine their behavior, ultimately enabling them to perform more intelligently and adaptively in a wide range of scenarios. This capability is especially valuable in applications such as autonomous systems, personalized recommendation engines, and adaptive customer support agents, where flexibility and continuous improvement are critical.

By integrating introspection, agents can identify gaps in their knowledge, anticipate future challenges, and adjust their strategies accordingly. This transforms them into systems that not only respond to the present but also prepare for the future, ensuring long-term relevance and efficiency in dynamic and uncertain environments.

Implementing reflective capabilities

There are several techniques for implementing reflective capabilities in intelligent agents, such as travel agents. These techniques enhance the agents' ability to monitor, evaluate, and improve their performance, fostering adaptability and continuous learning. An agent typically combines both *traditional reasoning* and *meta-reasoning* to operate effectively in dynamic environments. We will go through those techniques in the following sections.

Traditional reasoning

Traditional reasoning refers to the logical and systematic process by which an intelligent agent solves specific problems or performs tasks based on predefined rules, algorithms, or learned patterns from data. It operates within a fixed framework to process input and produce output, focusing on immediate goals without considering the reasoning process itself.

In the context of a travel agent, traditional reasoning involves directly handling user queries and performing specific tasks. For example, when a user asks for a flight from Los Angeles to New York, the agent retrieves flight options based on factors such as price, timing, and airline preferences. It applies predefined logic (e.g., sorting by cheapest price or shortest duration) to present the most relevant results to the user. Similarly, if a user requests hotel recommendations near Times Square, the agent uses traditional reasoning to filter hotels based on location, budget, and amenities.

Traditional reasoning is task-oriented and reactive, focusing on solving immediate problems efficiently. However, it does not evaluate or adapt its approach based on the success of its decisions or the changing needs of the user, which is where meta-reasoning comes into play.

Meta-reasoning

Meta-reasoning refers to the processes that monitor and control reasoning activities, allowing agents to reflect upon their own reasoning processes and make adjustments where appropriate. In the context of a reflective travel agent, meta-reasoning plays a crucial role in enabling the agent to continuously evaluate and refine its decision-making processes.

For example, consider a scenario where the travel agent recommends a particular destination or itinerary to a user based on their stated preferences and constraints. However, upon receiving feedback from the user after their trip, the agent learns that certain aspects of the recommendation did not align well with the user's actual experiences or desires. Through meta-reasoning, the travel agent can analyze this feedback and introspect on the reasoning process that led to the initial recommendation. It might identify patterns or flaws in how it interpreted the user's preferences, weighted certain factors over others, or made assumptions about the destination or activities. Armed with this insight, the agent can then make adjustments to its reasoning process. It might recalibrate the importance it assigns to different user preferences, introduce new decision-making heuristics, or refine its data sources to ensure more accurate and relevant information.

Meta-reasoning can also help the travel agent optimize its resource allocation. For complex or high-stakes trip planning scenarios, such as organizing a multi-destination family vacation or a large group tour, the agent could allocate more computational resources to perform deeper reasoning and analysis. This might involve considering a wider range of options, simulating various scenarios, or leveraging more sophisticated algorithms to generate optimal recommendations. Conversely, for routine or straightforward requests, such as booking a simple weekend getaway, the agent could rely on more streamlined reasoning processes or pre-defined rules, conserving computational resources for more complex tasks.

Meta-reasoning can enable the travel agent to adapt its reasoning strategies based on the user's level of expertise or familiarity with travel planning. For novice users, the agent might adopt a more guided approach, providing detailed explanations and recommendations tailored to their needs. Conversely, for experienced travelers, the agent could employ more concise reasoning processes, focusing on presenting a curated selection of options that align with the user's preferences and travel history.

By continuously monitoring and adjusting its reasoning processes through meta-reasoning, the reflective travel agent can provide increasingly personalized and satisfactory recommendations, adapt to evolving user needs and preferences, and optimize its resource utilization for efficient and effective trip planning.

Refer to the following code snippet, (the full code can be found in the sample notebook Chapter_04.ipynb) where the concept of meta-reasoning is demonstrated through the agent's ability to reflect and adjust its decision-making process based on user feedback. This section of the meta-reasoning method evaluates the feedback from the user (feedback == 1 for positive and feedback == -1 for negative) and adjusts the internal reasoning (preferences_weights) accordingly. If the feedback is negative, the agent reduces the associated weight (for example, reducing the emphasis on *luxury* for *Paris*). If the feedback is positive, it increases the associated weight, improving the agent's recommendations for future interactions. This allows the agent to continuously refine its decision-making process based on past feedback:

```python
1   if feedback == -1:  # Negative feedback indicates dissatisfaction
2       if destination == "Paris":
3           preferences_weights["luxury"] *= 0.9
4       elif destination == "Bangkok":
5           preferences_weights["budget"] *= 0.9
6       elif destination == "New York":
7           preferences_weights["budget"] *= 0.9
8
9   elif feedback == 1:  # Positive feedback indicates satisfaction
10      if destination == "Paris":
11          preferences_weights["luxury"] *= 1.1
12      elif destination == "Bangkok":
13          preferences_weights["budget"] *= 1.1
```

```
14      elif destination == "New York":
15          preferences_weights["budget"] *= 1.1
```

While this example is based on heuristics (simple `if-else` based), we can implement an AI agent that is capable of meta-reasoning. In the case of an LLM, we may have the model generate an `adjustment_factor` value, which is used to adjust the base weights of the system based on user feedback, instead of hardcoding 0.9 and 1.1 as we did in this example. The Python notebook shows an example of implementing an AI agent-based system using the CrewAI framework, which does just that. Rather than simply making a recommendation, the agent evaluates the outcome of its suggestions and adapts its internal reasoning by adjusting preference weights, allowing it to improve future recommendations.

Let us get a few definitions out of our way before we look into CrewAI-based agent sample code. In CrewAI's context, an *agent* is an independent unit powered by an LLM that can perform specific tasks, make decisions based on its role and goal, use tools to accomplish said tasks, communicate with other agents, and so on. You can use any supported LLM with a CrewAI agent. As such, in our case, we use OpenAI's **gpt-4o-mini** model. A *task* is essentially a specific assignment to be completed by an agent. You may provide the agent with *tools* to accomplish and complete the task. Here's a sample code snippet where we define agents for our example with CrewAI:

```
1  from crewai import Agent
2
3  preference_agent = Agent(
4      name="Preference Agent",
5      role="Travel destination recommender",
6      goal="Provide the best travel destination based on user
              preferences and weights.",
7      backstory="An AI travel expert adept at understanding user
              preferences.",
8      verbose=True,
9      llm='gpt-4o-mini',
10     tools=[recommend_destination])
11
12 meta_agent = Agent(
13     name="Meta-Reasoning Agent",
14     role="Preference weight adjuster",
15     goal="Reflect on feedback and adjust the preference weights to
              improve future recommendations.",
16     backstory="An AI optimizer that learns from user experiences to
              fine-tune recommendation preferences.",
17     verbose=True,
18     llm='gpt-4o-mini',
19     tools=[update_weights_on_feedback])
```

Next, we define tasks to be completed by the agents:

```python
1 from crewai import Task
2
3 generate_recommendation = Task(
4     name="Generate Recommendation",
5     agent=preference_agent,
6     description=(
7       f"Use the recommend_destination tool with these preferences:
          {state['preferences']}\n"
8       "Return only the destination name as a simple string (Paris,
          Bangkok, or New York)."
9     ),
10    expected_output="A destination name as a string")
11
12 adjust_weights = Task(
13     name="Adjust Weights Based on Feedback",
14     agent=meta_agent,
15     description=(
16        "Use the update_weights_on_feedback tool with:\n"
17        "1. destination: Get from first task's output
           (context[0])\n"
18        "2. feedback: Get from second task's output (context[1])\n"
19        "3. adjustment_factor: a number between 0 and 1 that will be
           used to adjust internal weights based on feedback\n\n"
20        "Ensure all inputs are in their correct types (string for
           destination, integer for feedback)."
21     ),
22     expected_output="Updated weights as a dictionary",
23     context=[generate_recommendation, user_feedback])
```

In this code snippet, we first define two agents: `preference_agent` and `meta_agent`. The `preference_agent` agent is responsible for recommending a travel destination to the user based on some pre-defined internal weights (in our case, equal weights are given to `budget`, `luxury`, and `adventure`) with some initial user preference weights. The `preference_agent` agent uses the tool named `recommend_destination`, which does the weights calculation and returns a desired destination for the user. The `meta_agent` agent is responsible for the meta-reasoning part, where it evaluates the user's feedback based on the recommended destination and sets an `adjustment_factor`, which is then used by the `update_weights_on_feedback` tool to update the system's internal weights based on the user's feedback. This enables the model to improve its recommendation capabilities in subsequent user interactions.

We will then set up a crew with the defined agents and tasks and kick off the process:

```
1 from crewai import Agent, Task, Crew
2 crew = Crew(
3     agents=[preference_agent, meta_agent],
4     tasks=[generate_recommendation, adjust_weights],
5     verbose=True)
6
7 crew.kickoff()
```

The output would look something like this:

```
# Agent: Travel destination recommender
## Task: Use the recommend_destination tool with these preferences:
{'budget': 0.04, 'luxury': 0.02, 'adventure': 0.94}
Return only the destination name as a simple string (Paris, Bangkok,
or New York).


# Agent: Travel destination recommender
## Thought: I need to analyze the user's preferences which heavily
favor adventure and very little for budget and luxury.
## Using tool: Recommend travel destination based on preferences.
## Tool Input:
"{\"user_preferences\": {\"budget\": 0.04, \"luxury\": 0.02,
\"adventure\": 0.94}}"
## Tool Output:
New York


# Agent: Travel destination recommender
## Final Answer:
New York


# Agent: Preference weight adjuster
## Task: Use the update_weights_on_feedback tool with:
1. destination: Get from first task's output (context[0])
2. feedback: Get from user input
3. adjustment_factor: a number between 0 and 1 that will be used to
adjust internal weights based on feedback
Ensure all inputs are in their correct types (string for destination,
integer for feedback).


# Agent: Preference weight adjuster
## Thought: I need to adjust the preference weights based on the
provided feedback for the destination 'New York', which received
a dissatisfied feedback of -1. I will choose an adjustment factor
between 0 and 1; for this case, I will use 0.1 for a slight
```

```
adjustment.
## Using tool: Reasoning tool to adjust preference weights based on
user feedback.
## Tool Input:
"{\"destination\": \"New York\", \"feedback\": 1, \"adjustment_
factor\": 0.1}"
## Tool Output:
{'budget': 0.33, 'luxury': 0.32, 'adventure': 0.34}
# Agent: Preference weight adjuster
## Final Answer:
{'budget': 0.33, 'luxury': 0.32, 'adventure': 0.34}
```

Figure 4.1 shows a visual understanding of this flow:

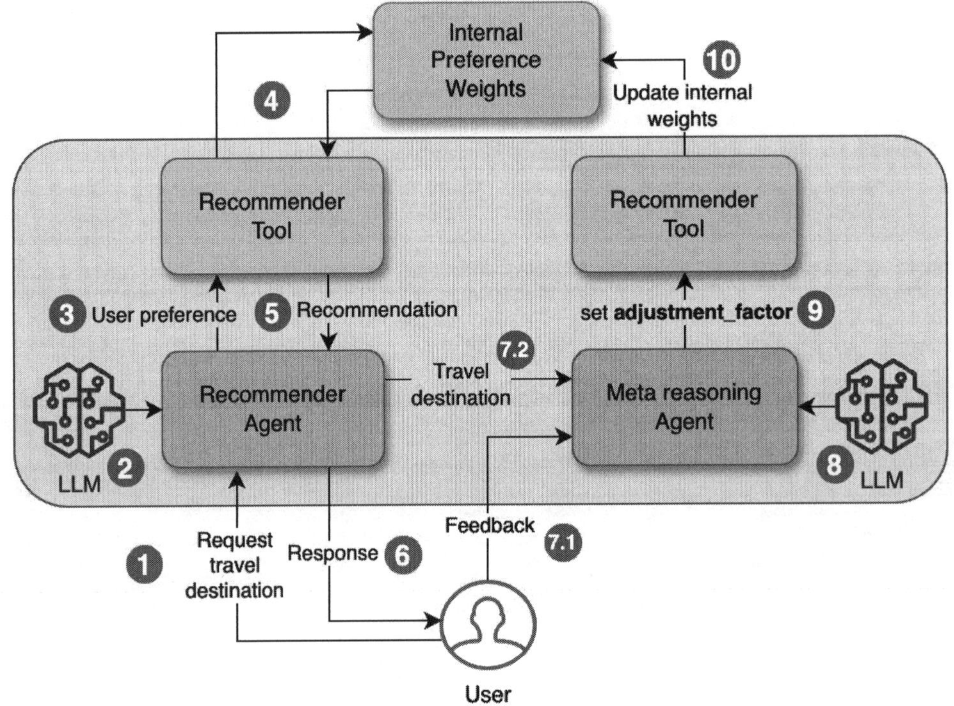

Figure 4.1 – Meta-reasoning with AI agents and CrewAI framework

The system initially begins with a pre-defined internal set of weights that puts equal emphasis on budget, luxury, and adventure. This set of system weights is then combined with an initial presumptive user preference weight to arrive at a final travel destination recommendation. Subsequently, the user may like or dislike the recommendation that is marked by feedback = 1 (for satisfied) or feedback = -1 (for dissatisfied). The meta-reasoning agent then looks at the recommendation it made in the previous step, the user's feedback (1 or -1), decides on an `adjustment_factor` value between 0 and 1, and passes it on to a tool that uses this information to update the system's internal weights. So, in this example, the system started with a recommendation with more emphasis on adventure and the user liked this recommendation (New York, hence, feedback = 1). The meta_agent then increases the internal system weight for adventure to 0.34. This means, the system now has a better understanding that the user prefers adventurous destinations for subsequent interactions.

This process exemplifies continuous learning, where each piece of feedback helps the agent better understand the user's preferences and refine its decision-making, ensuring an ongoing cycle of evaluation and improvement. Though resource optimization isn't explicitly shown in the simplified example, the concept can be extended to more complex scenarios, where the agent allocates greater computational resources for intricate decisions while streamlining simpler ones. Potential enhancements may include persistent learning, where feedback and weights are stored for future sessions, enabling the agent to maintain its knowledge and evolve over time. More complex feedback, such as detailed ratings or specific user comments, could allow for even finer adjustments, while advanced algorithms might provide more intelligent analysis of the feedback and adjustments to the preference weights. Additionally, expanding the number of destinations and incorporating a broader range of attributes – such as climate or cultural experiences – would enrich the recommendation process.

Meta-reasoning allows agents to reflect upon their own reasoning processes and make adjustments where appropriate. This encompasses performance monitoring and resource allocation, which are further detailed in the following sections.

Performance monitoring

A reflective travel agent can monitor its success rates and spot patterns in its decision-making processes. For instance, it could track the satisfaction levels of users with the recommended itineraries, accommodations, or activities. By identifying patterns, such as certain types of recommendations consistently receiving lower ratings, the agent can adjust its reasoning strategy to improve future performance. Continuous performance monitoring is a crucial aspect of a reflective travel agent's ability to learn and adapt. By systematically tracking and analyzing user feedback and satisfaction metrics, the agent can gain valuable insights into the effectiveness of its recommendations and decision-making processes. Setting clear baselines and thresholds for performance metrics is equally important, as it helps determine when an adjustment to reasoning strategies or decision-making processes is necessary.

A reflective travel agent can continuously monitor its performance by tracking various metrics to evaluate the effectiveness of its recommendations and decision-making processes. These metrics can include user satisfaction levels, ratings, and reviews for recommended itineraries, accommodations, activities, and transportation. Performance monitoring enables the agent to spot patterns, identify areas for improvement, and make data-driven adjustments to enhance its reasoning strategies and outcomes.

For example, the travel agent could solicit post-trip feedback from users, asking them to rate aspects such as hotel quality, activity suitability, transportation convenience, and overall experience. By aggregating and analyzing this feedback, the agent can uncover trends and areas where its recommendations may fall short.

Specific metrics to track

Here are some specific metrics to track to evaluate the effectiveness of its recommendations and decision-making processes:

- **User ratings and reviews**: Ratings for accommodations, activities, and overall trip experience help gauge user satisfaction and pinpoint areas of improvement

- **Recommendation acceptance rates**: Metrics such as the percentage of users selecting the recommended flights, hotels, or activities indicate how well the agent aligns with user preferences

- **Complaint and return rates**: Tracking issues reported by users, such as dissatisfaction with services or canceled trips, reveals gaps in the agent's decision-making

- **User engagement metrics**: Data on how frequently users interact with recommendations or ask for revisions provides insights into the agent's relevance and accuracy

- **Demographic-specific insights**: Understanding how different user segments (e.g., families, solo travelers, couples) respond to recommendations helps the agent tailor its strategies

How metrics adjust behavior

If the agent notices consistently lower ratings for accommodations in a particular destination, it might reevaluate its prioritization of factors such as price, location, or amenities. For instance, the agent might realize it overemphasizes cost savings while neglecting other crucial factors such as proximity to attractions or user reviews.

Similarly, if feedback reveals that adventure sports consistently receive low ratings across various destinations, the agent might conclude that it lacks a comprehensive understanding of user preferences for these activities. By adjusting its reasoning strategies – such as incorporating additional user preference data or using more diverse activity sources – the agent can improve the accuracy and personalization of its recommendations.

The agent might also analyze feedback based on demographics. For example, if family-friendly recommendations receive high ratings but solo traveler suggestions do not, it could refine its reasoning to better cater to individual needs, such as offering more budget-conscious or culturally immersive options for solo users.

By systematically tracking and analyzing these metrics, the travel agent can iteratively refine its reasoning strategies. This approach not only enhances the quality and personalization of recommendations but also builds trust and loyalty among users by delivering consistently reliable and satisfying travel experiences. Through continuous performance monitoring, the agent evolves into a more intelligent, adaptive, and user-focused advisor.

Resource allocation

Through meta-reasoning, the travel agent can optimize its resource allocation. For complex or high-stakes trip planning, the agent might allocate more computational resources for deeper reasoning and analysis. Conversely, for routine or straightforward requests, it could fall back on simpler heuristics or pre-defined rules, conserving resources. Efficient resource allocation is crucial for a reflective travel agent to operate effectively and provide timely responses to users. By employing meta-reasoning, the agent can dynamically adjust the allocation of its computational resources based on the complexity and significance of each trip planning request.

Consider a scenario where the travel agent receives a request to plan an elaborate multi-destination vacation spanning multiple countries or regions. Such a request typically involves intricate logistics, coordination of various travel components (flights, accommodations, activities, and so on), and the need to balance numerous constraints and preferences. In this case, the agent could allocate more computational resources to perform deeper reasoning and analysis. This might involve running complex algorithms to generate optimal itineraries, considering a vast number of potential combinations and permutations of travel options, and evaluating each option against a multitude of factors such as cost, travel time, user preferences, and potential risks or disruptions. However, allocating excessive computational resources to optimize complex itineraries might lead to diminishing returns or inefficiencies. For instance, the agent could become overly focused on achieving perfection in the itinerary, potentially delaying the response time or consuming unnecessary resources. Moreover, the agent might overlook simpler, yet equally satisfactory, solutions that could meet the user's needs without requiring exhaustive simulations or analysis. Balancing computational effort with practical outcomes is essential to avoid over-engineering and ensure timely, efficient responses.

Additionally, the agent could allocate resources to simulate various scenarios and contingency plans, ensuring a robust and adaptable travel plan.

On the other hand, if the request is for a routine or straightforward trip, such as a weekend getaway to a nearby destination, the reflective travel agent could conserve computational resources by relying on simpler heuristics or pre-defined rules. These might include prioritizing popular or highly-rated destinations and accommodations based on user preferences, applying standard algorithms for route planning or activity recommendations, and leveraging pre-compiled data and travel packages.

By using meta-reasoning to dynamically adjust its resource allocation, the travel agent can strike the right balance between computational efficiency and the depth of analysis required for each trip planning task. This not only ensures timely responses to users but also optimizes the agent's overall resource utilization, preventing unnecessary computational overhead for routine tasks while dedicating sufficient resources to complex or high-stakes scenarios.

The reflective travel agent could employ meta-reasoning to continuously monitor and adjust its resource allocation strategies based on evolving user demands, system performance metrics, or the availability of new computational resources. For example, if the agent consistently struggles to provide timely responses during peak travel seasons, it could proactively allocate additional resources or implement load-balancing techniques to maintain optimal performance. Through intelligent resource allocation driven by meta-reasoning, the reflective travel agent can provide a seamless and efficient trip planning experience, tailoring its computational efforts to the specific needs and complexity of each user request while ensuring optimal resource utilization and system performance.

A reflective travel agent can leverage a variety of algorithms and strategies for dynamic resource allocation, ensuring optimal performance and personalized user experiences. **Reinforcement Learning (RL)** is one such approach, enabling the agent to learn allocation strategies through trial and error, dynamically adjusting computational resources based on the complexity of tasks, such as multi-destination itinerary planning. **Multi-Armed Bandit (MAB)** offers another example by balancing exploration and exploitation, helping the agent allocate resources effectively to tasks such as price comparisons or hotel recommendations to maximize user satisfaction. Bayesian optimization uses statistical methods to identify the most promising resource configurations, while dynamic programming simplifies complex allocation problems into manageable sub-problems, ensuring optimal decisions throughout the trip planning process.

Heuristic-based methods, such as allocating more resources to international travel due to its inherent complexity, provide practical rule-of-thumb solutions, whereas game-theoretic approaches model resource allocation as a strategic game, balancing competing tasks such as itinerary optimization and preference analysis. Task prioritization algorithms, such as weighted round robin, allocate resources based on the urgency or importance of tasks, while resource-aware scheduling techniques such as Min-Min focus on completing simpler tasks quickly, freeing up resources for more complex computations. By integrating these strategies with meta-reasoning, the agent can assess task complexity in real time and select the most effective approach, delivering adaptive and efficient solutions that enhance the overall trip planning experience.

Self-explanation

Self-explanation is a process through which agents verbalize their reasoning processes, generating explanations for decisions reached. This technique serves several crucial purposes for reflective agents, particularly in the context of our travel agent example, as discussed in the following sections.

Self-explanation serves two distinct purposes: enhancing transparency and facilitating learning. When used for **transparency**, self-explanation focuses on making the agent's decisions understandable to humans. For example, a reflective travel agent might explain why it recommended a specific itinerary by highlighting factors such as cost, user preferences, or destination popularity. This type of self-explanation builds trust by providing users with clear insights into the reasoning behind the agent's suggestions, ensuring they feel confident in its decisions.

On the other hand, self-explanation for **learning** is centered on the agent's ability to improve its decision-making processes. Here, the agent generates explanations for its own decisions, not just to communicate with users but to reflect on its reasoning and identify potential areas for improvement. For instance, if a travel agent consistently receives negative feedback for certain hotel recommendations, it can analyze its explanations to detect flaws in how it evaluates hotels, such as overemphasizing price over user reviews. This process allows the agent to refine its strategies, learning from its past explanations to deliver better recommendations in the future.

Thus, while self-explanation for transparency is outward-facing and user-focused, self-explanation for learning is inward-facing, enabling the agent to continuously adapt and improve.

Transparency

By generating self-explanations for its recommendations and decisions, the reflective travel agent can provide users with insights into its thought processes and decision-making rationale. This transparency fosters trust and confidence in the agent's capabilities, as users can better understand the reasoning behind the suggested itineraries, accommodations, or activities.

For example, the travel agent could explain that it recommended a particular hotel based on its proximity to popular tourist attractions, high ratings from previous travelers with similar preferences, and competitive pricing within the user's specified budget range. By articulating these factors and the underlying reasoning process, the agent demonstrates a level of transparency that can reassure users and increase their willingness to follow the recommendations.

Looking back at our sample code, we first implement a transparency self-explanation agent by prompting the model to explain why it gave a response the way it recommended a particular hotel or destination. With the CrewAI framework, the code looks something like this:

```
1 travel_agent = Agent(
2     role="Travel Advisor",
3     goal="Provide hotel recommendations with transparent reasoning.",
4     backstory="An AI travel advisor specializing in personalized
                travel planning.
5                You always explain the steps you take to arrive at a
                conclusion.",
6     tools=[recommend_hotel]
7   )
8
9 recommendation_task = Task(
10     name="Recommend hotel",
11     description="""
12     Recommend a hotels based on the user's query {query}.
13     """,
14     agent=travel_agent,
15     expected_output="The name of the hotel with explanations"
16   )
```

In this code sample, we define an agent and specify that it always must explain the steps it takes to arrive at a conclusion – this is specified in the `backstory` parameter of the agent. We then assign it the task of finding a hotel using the `recommend_hotel` tool, which is responsible for looking up hotels. When the agent is invoked with the query *"I am looking for a hotel in Paris under $300 a night"*, it recommends a hotel and the rationale behind its decision to recommend said hotel. The output may look something like this:

```
Hotel: Hotel du Petit Moulin

Reason:
I found several hotels in Paris, but most of them exceeded the budget
of $300. The only suitable option is Hotel du Petit Moulin, which is
priced at $300 per night. Located in the 3rd arrondissement, it offers
moderate transportation convenience with the nearest metro station,
Saint-Sébastien Froissart, being approximately 1.9 kilometers away.
This hotel is a great choice for budget-conscious travelers who still
want to enjoy the charm of Paris.
```

A conceptual flow of how an agentic system with self-explanation and transparency would look is shown in *Figure 4.2*:

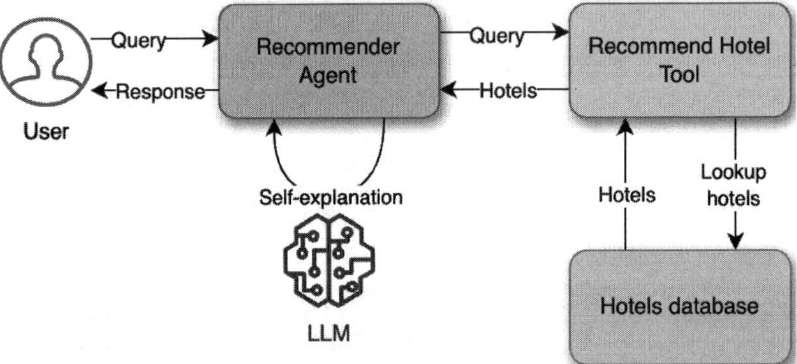

Figure 4.2 – Self-explanations transparency with AI agents

Here, each response from the model would go through an explanation cycle where the agent generates a proper explanation and rationale behind its responses. These explanations may then be surfaced up to the user, or may simply be logged for explainability purposes.

Learning and refinement

The act of verbalizing its reasoning processes can also serve as a learning mechanism for the reflective travel agent. As the agent generates self-explanations, it may uncover flaws, inconsistencies, or oversights in its decision-making process. By introspecting on these self-explanations, the agent can identify areas for improvement and refine its reasoning strategies accordingly.

For instance, if a user provides feedback indicating dissatisfaction with a recommended activity, the travel agent could revisit its self-explanation for that recommendation. In doing so, it might recognize that it failed to consider certain user preferences or overlooked crucial factors that should have influenced its decision. This realization can then inform the agent's learning process, leading to adjustments in its reasoning algorithms or knowledge base to prevent similar oversights in the future. In our previous example, the AI suggested a hotel that has moderate convenience from public transport accessibility, however, the user may not be satisfied with this result and may be ready to pay a little extra to be near public transport.

To implement learning and refinement, we will simply extend our previous transparency flow and augment it with an agent/task pair that can consume the recommendation and the user feedback and use these bits of information to perform refinement of the strategy. Refer to the Python notebook for code samples. *Figure 4.3* shows the high-level flow:

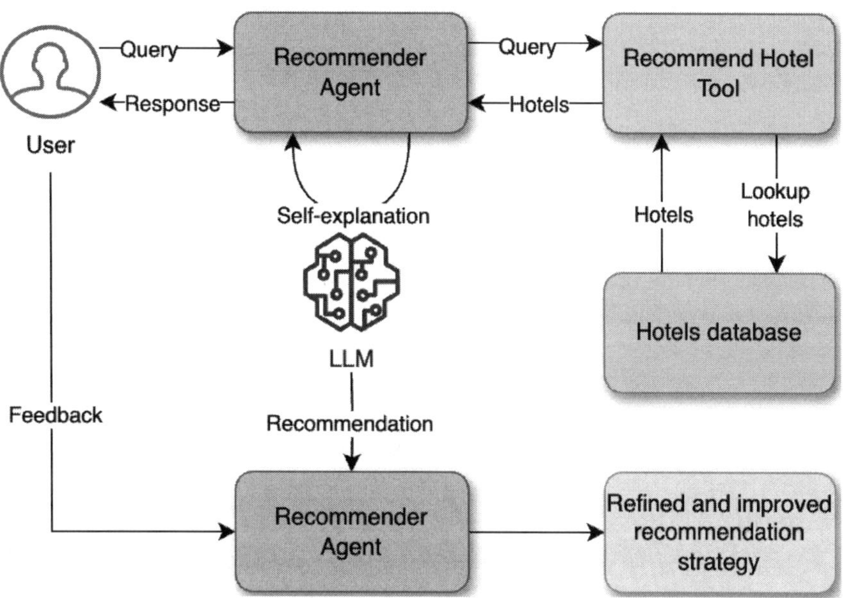

Figure 4.3 – Learning and refinement with AI agents

User engagement and collaboration

Self-explanations can also facilitate more engaging and collaborative interactions between the travel agent and users. By providing explanations for its recommendations, the agent invites users to provide feedback, ask follow-up questions, or offer additional context or preferences. This two-way dialogue can lead to a more personalized and iterative trip planning process, where the agent continuously refines its recommendations based on the user's input and clarifications.

For example, if a user expresses concerns or uncertainties about a particular recommendation, the travel agent could provide a detailed self-explanation, outlining the factors it considered and inviting the user to share their perspective or additional requirements. This collaborative approach can help the agent better understand the user's needs and preferences, leading to more tailored and satisfactory recommendations. By now, we have seen several examples of how agents are capable of consuming human input and recommending and re-strategizing their task execution. While a similar sample of user engagement collaboration is present in the Python notebook, it is important to recognize that human collaboration is often implemented via conversational interfaces such as chatbots.

By incorporating self-explanation capabilities, the reflective travel agent can foster transparency, trust, continuous learning, and collaborative user interactions. This multi-faceted approach not only enhances the overall trip planning experience but also contributes to the agent's ability to provide increasingly personalized and accurate recommendations over time. Next, let's explore self-modeling with AI agents.

Self-modeling

Self-modeling is a crucial aspect of reflective agents, allowing them to maintain an internal representation of their goals, beliefs, and knowledge. This self-model serves as a foundation for decision-making and reflection, enabling the agent to adapt and evolve in response to changing circumstances or newly acquired information. To clarify a bit further, the term *modeling* in this context means the agent's initial environment and state. The agent (or group of agents) starts with some initial state with a specific environment, and as the agent learns more via human-machine interactions or via its task executions, it continues to update that internal state, thus changing its own environment within which it operates. In the context of a reflective travel agent, self-modeling plays a vital role in ensuring that the agent's recommendations and decision-making processes remain aligned with the user's evolving needs and preferences, as well as incorporating new knowledge and experiences. *Figure 4.4* gives a high-level overview of agent self-modeling as we further discuss the two components of internal state. Agents may have individual internal states that they independently self-model within an agentic system, or they may have shared internal state that they collaboratively self-model.

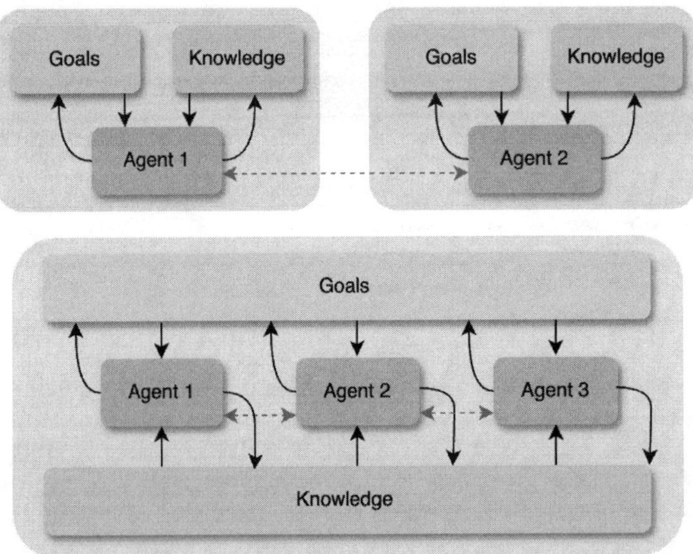

Figure 4.4 – Individual and shared internal states for self-modeling

This internal state may comprise several components, but most crucially, at a high-level, they can be categorized into two categories: *goal management* and *knowledge update*, as we will explore next.

Goal management

A reflective travel agent maintains an internal model of its goals, which can range from providing personalized and satisfactory trip recommendations to optimizing travel experiences based on user preferences and constraints. However, these goals are not static; the agent must be able to rethink and adjust its goals as circumstances change or new information becomes available.

For example, if a user's travel dates or budget constraints change during the trip planning process, the reflective travel agent can leverage its self-model to reevaluate and update its goals accordingly. It might shift its focus from maximizing luxury accommodations to prioritizing cost-effectiveness or adjust its itinerary recommendations to align with the new travel dates.

Additionally, if the agent learns new information about a user's evolving interests or travel preferences through feedback or interactions, it can update its goals to better cater to these changing needs. For instance, if a user expresses a newfound interest in eco-friendly or sustainable travel practices, the agent can adjust its goals to prioritize recommending environmentally conscious accommodations, activities, and transportation options.

Knowledge update

A key aspect of self-modeling is the ability to automatically update the agent's knowledge base based on new experiences and insights. As the reflective travel agent interacts with users, receives feedback, and learns from its own recommendations and decisions, it can continuously refine and expand its knowledge about destinations, accommodations, activities, user preferences, and travel trends.

For instance, if a user reports a negative experience with a recommended hotel or activity, the agent can update its knowledge base to reflect this feedback, potentially adjusting its rating or removing the option from future recommendations. Conversely, if a user provides glowing reviews and feedback about a particular destination or experience, the agent can reinforce its knowledge about the positive aspects of that recommendation, increasing the likelihood of suggesting it to users with similar preferences in the future.

By maintaining a self-model and automatically updating its knowledge base, the reflective travel agent lays the groundwork for improved decision-making and recommendation accuracy over time. As its knowledge base grows and evolves, the agent can leverage these insights to provide increasingly personalized and satisfactory trip planning experiences for its users.

In our example, our self-modeling travel agent would not only provide recommendations based on user preferences but would also continuously adapt and refine its recommendations. By maintaining an internal self-model and updating its knowledge base based on user feedback, the agent(s) can improve its recommendations over time, ensuring they are more personalized and relevant to the user's evolving needs and preferences. Self-modeling can enable the agent to identify knowledge gaps or areas where its information is lacking or outdated. In such cases, the agent can proactively seek out new sources of information or leverage external data sources to enhance its knowledge base, ensuring that its recommendations are based on the most up-to-date and comprehensive information available.

By combining goal management and knowledge updating capabilities through self-modeling, the reflective travel agent can continuously adapt and improve its performance, ensuring that it remains a reliable and valuable resource for users seeking personalized and tailored travel experiences.

While we have been discussing our travel agent example to understand the concepts in this chapter, there are numerous real-world use cases and examples that we will discuss in the next section. Do keep in mind that these examples are in no way exhaustive, so a good exercise at the end of this chapter would be to think of ways agent reflection and introspection techniques can be utilized in other real-world scenarios.

Use cases and examples

Reflective intelligent agents have been equipped to support a number of emerging business applications. A reflective agent can efficiently apply self-assessment and introspection to improve its performance against changing environments for the purpose of making more effective business decisions, thus continuing to improve in a transparent and explainable manner. Some examples of reflective agents applied in real business applications are as follows.

Customer service chatbots

Reflective customer service chatbots employ self-assessment methodologies to continuously improve their ability to provide effective and satisfactory responses to users. By introspecting on past conversations, these chatbots can identify patterns, strengths, weaknesses, and areas for improvement, enabling them to refine their knowledge base, response strategies, and overall interaction capabilities.

One key aspect of self-assessment is the ability to analyze the outcomes of past conversations. Chatbots can review user feedback, sentiment analysis, and conversation metrics to gauge the success or failure of their responses. For instance, a chatbot might identify conversations where users expressed frustration or dissatisfaction through negative sentiment or low satisfaction ratings. By reflecting on these instances, the chatbot can pinpoint potential issues, such as misunderstandings, inadequate information, or inappropriate tone or language. Conversely, the chatbot can also analyze conversations that went well, where users expressed satisfaction or gratitude for the provided solutions. By studying the characteristics of these successful interactions, the chatbot can reinforce effective response strategies, identify best practices, and replicate them in future conversations.

Reflective chatbots can introspect on the specific content and flow of conversations to identify patterns and areas for improvement. They might recognize recurring questions or topics that frequently lead to user confusion or dissatisfaction, indicating a need to enhance their knowledge base or refine their response templates. Alternatively, they could identify frequent requests for specific information or functionalities, prompting the development of new conversational flows or integrations to better serve user needs. In addition to content analysis, reflective chatbots can also assess the effectiveness of their communication styles and language usage. By analyzing user feedback and reactions, they can determine which tones, wordings, or levels of formality resonate better with different user groups or contexts. This insight can then inform the chatbot's ability to adapt its communication style dynamically, fostering more natural and personalized interactions.

Moreover, self-assessment can help chatbots identify knowledge gaps or areas where their understanding is limited. By recognizing instances where they struggle to provide satisfactory responses, chatbots can proactively seek out additional information or consult with human experts to expand their knowledge base and improve their ability to handle a wider range of queries effectively.

Software companies such as **Zendesk** and **Drift** use AI-powered chatbots that learn from conversations. These chatbots monitor ratings and comments made by users regarding their satisfaction levels. By reflecting on this feedback, the chatbots can better develop responses and improve their ability to provide satisfactory solutions in the future. For instance, if a chatbot notices that users frequently express frustration or dissatisfaction with its responses on a particular topic, it can analyze those conversations, identify patterns or gaps in its knowledge, and refine its response strategies accordingly. Additionally, the chatbot could learn to adapt its tone, language, and communication style based on user preferences and feedback, fostering a more natural and personalized interaction experience.

Personal marketing agents

Personalized marketing also makes use of reflective agents. Reflective agents analyze consumer behavior and feedback for successful marketing strategies. They mull over the successes and failures of past campaigns to make adjustments based on key performance metrics for upcoming ones.

For example, Amazon uses reflective AI agents that implement studying customer buying trends and reviews to suggest identical products. These continue to learn with the users, thereby perfecting the suggestions and the parameters for marketing to ensure better sales and customer interaction.

Personalized marketing has become increasingly crucial in today's competitive business landscape, and reflective agents play a pivotal role in delivering tailored and effective marketing strategies. These agents leverage self-assessment and introspection to analyze consumer behavior, feedback, and the success or failure of past campaigns, enabling them to continuously refine and optimize their marketing approaches. At the core of reflective personal marketing agents is their ability to collect and analyze vast amounts of data on consumer behavior, preferences, and interactions. By studying patterns in purchasing decisions, browsing histories, reviews, and engagement metrics, these agents can gain insights into what resonates with different consumer segments and what factors drive purchasing decisions.

The key aspect of reflection in personal marketing agents is their ability to evaluate the success or failure of past marketing campaigns. These agents can analyze **key performance indicators (KPIs)** such as click-through rates, conversion rates, and customer acquisition costs, and correlate them with the specific strategies, messaging, and targeting employed in each campaign. By introspecting on these metrics, the agents can identify which approaches were most effective and which ones fell short, enabling them to make data-driven adjustments for future campaigns.

For example, a reflective personal marketing agent employed by an e-commerce company might analyze the performance of a targeted email campaign promoting a specific product line. If the campaign yielded lower-than-expected engagement or conversion rates, the agent could introspect on factors such as the messaging, subject lines, timing, and audience segmentation. Based on this analysis, the agent could refine its strategies for future campaigns, adjusting the messaging to better resonate with the target audience, optimizing the timing and frequency of communications, or refining the segmentation criteria to reach more relevant consumers.

The example of Amazon's reflective AI agents highlights the practical application of these principles. By continuously studying customer trends, purchasing behaviors, and product reviews, Amazon's agents can refine their product recommendations and personalized marketing strategies. As customers interact with the platform and provide feedback, the agents learn and adapt, perfecting their suggestions and optimizing the parameters used for targeted marketing campaigns. This continuous learning and adaptation cycle ensures that Amazon's marketing efforts remain relevant, personalized, and effective, fostering better sales and customer interactions.

Financial trading systems

The use of reflective agents will continue to rise within financial markets, since the former enhances the latter within the core of developing trading strategies. They may analyze market data and past trades for better algorithms and decision-making processes. For example, trading hedge funds, such as Renaissance Technologies, are utilizing reflective trading agents that learn from marketplace circumstances and from previous trading results. As a consequence, at any moment in time, it is capable of exercising different trading methods to reach profitable trades that may reduce risks.

Financial trading systems are complex and dynamic environments where the ability to adapt and optimize decision-making processes is paramount. In this context, reflective agents play a crucial role in enhancing trading strategies by analyzing market data, past trades, and the performance of existing algorithms, enabling continuous improvement and risk mitigation.

One of the key advantages of reflective agents in financial trading systems is their ability to introspect on the success or failure of past trades. By analyzing the outcomes of previous trading decisions, these agents can identify patterns, trends, and correlations between various market factors and trading results. This introspection enables the agents to refine their decision-making algorithms, adjusting the weight assigned to different variables, incorporating new data sources, or modifying risk management strategies.

For instance, a reflective trading agent might notice that certain trading strategies consistently underperform in specific market conditions or during particular economic events. By introspecting on these patterns, the agent can adapt its algorithms to avoid or minimize exposure to such scenarios, reducing potential losses and optimizing risk management.

Furthermore, reflective agents can leverage market data and historical trends to forecast future market movements or identify potential opportunities. By analyzing vast amounts of data, including financial news, economic indicators, and social media sentiment, these agents can uncover subtle patterns or correlations that may not be immediately apparent to human traders. This predictive capability allows the agents to proactively adjust their trading strategies, positioning themselves for potential market shifts or capitalizing on emerging opportunities.

The example of Renaissance Technologies' utilization of reflective trading agents highlights the practical application of these principles. These agents continuously learn from market circumstances and the outcomes of previous trades, enabling them to adapt their decision-making processes and trading strategies in real time. By introspecting on past performance and market conditions, the agents can identify profitable trading opportunities while mitigating risks, providing a competitive edge in the ever-evolving financial markets.

Forecast agents

Such reflective agents take advantage of sales forecasting too. They reflectively analyze past sales information including market trends. Using such information, the agents can analyze what corrections to make based on previous forecasts, hence adjusting their models.

For example, Salesforce's Einstein Analytics uses reflective AI to deliver insights to sales teams based on historical data. In the process, it learns about historical sales trends, corrects errors and inaccuracies, and then updates future forecasts so that the business can move on to its next level of decisions related to resource distribution and strategy.

Accurate sales forecasting is crucial for businesses to make informed decisions regarding resource allocation, inventory management, and strategic planning. Reflective agents play a vital role in enhancing the accuracy and reliability of sales forecasts by continuously analyzing past data, identifying patterns and trends, and adapting forecasting models based on previous performance.

One of the key advantages of reflective agents in sales forecasting is their ability to introspect on past forecasts and compare them with actual sales figures. By analyzing the discrepancies between forecasted and actual sales data, these agents can identify potential sources of error or inaccuracy in their forecasting models. This introspection allows the agents to make necessary adjustments, such as recalibrating the weighting of various factors, incorporating new data sources, or refining the algorithms used for forecasting.

Furthermore, reflective agents can leverage historical sales data and market trends to uncover valuable insights that can inform and enhance their forecasting capabilities. By analyzing past sales patterns, seasonal fluctuations, and external factors such as economic conditions or consumer behavior shifts, these agents can identify correlations and predictive variables that may have been overlooked in previous forecasting models. This continuous learning and adaptation process enables the agents to refine their forecasting accuracy over time, providing more reliable and actionable insights for business decision-making.

The example of Salesforce's Einstein Analytics illustrates the practical application of reflective AI in sales forecasting. Einstein Analytics leverages historical data to learn about and understand past sales trends, identify errors or inaccuracies in previous forecasts, and subsequently update future forecasts accordingly. By continuously refining its forecasting models based on introspection and data analysis, Einstein Analytics empowers sales teams with accurate and reliable insights, enabling businesses to make informed decisions regarding resource distribution, inventory management, and strategic planning.

Moreover, reflective agents in sales forecasting can incorporate machine learning techniques to further enhance their predictive capabilities. By ingesting and analyzing vast amounts of data from various sources, such as market research reports, social media sentiment, and competitor intelligence, these agents can uncover complex patterns and relationships that may not be immediately apparent. This ability to learn and adapt dynamically enables agents to stay ahead of market trends and continuously refine their forecasting models, providing businesses with a competitive edge in anticipating and responding to market shifts.

In the dynamic business landscape, accurate sales forecasting is essential for effective resource allocation, strategic planning, and maintaining a competitive advantage. Reflective agents offer a powerful solution for enhancing the accuracy and reliability of sales forecasts by leveraging introspection, data analysis, and continuous learning. By continuously refining their forecasting models based on past performance and emerging trends, these agents empower businesses with actionable insights, enabling them to make informed decisions and stay ahead of the curve in their respective markets.

Price strategies in e-commerce

Another area of application of these reflective agents is in optimizing pricing strategies within e-commerce. These agents collect data about competitors' pricing, customer behavior, and sales data, and give recommendations on the best pricing strategy that needs to be deployed.

For example, AI-powered pricing agents take into account the situation in the market and the reactions of consumers to fluctuate prices dynamically. Companies such as Walmart and Target utilize such agents. It helps the companies to reach maximum sales by not increasing prices excessively, and in turn, increasing profit margins.

In the highly competitive and dynamic e-commerce landscape, effective pricing strategies are crucial for attracting customers, maximizing sales, and maintaining profitability. Reflective agents play a vital role in optimizing pricing strategies by continuously analyzing market conditions, competitor pricing, customer behavior, and sales data, enabling businesses to make informed and adaptive decisions.

One of the key advantages of reflective agents in e-commerce pricing is their ability to monitor and respond to changes in the market and customer behavior in real time. These agents can collect and analyze vast amounts of data from various sources, including competitor websites, social media sentiment, and customer reviews. By introspecting on this data, the agents can identify patterns, trends, and consumer preferences that influence pricing decisions.

For instance, a reflective pricing agent might notice that a competitor has launched a promotional campaign, offering discounts on certain products. By analyzing customer reactions and sales data, the agent can determine whether a price adjustment is necessary to remain competitive and maintain market share. If the agent determines that a pricing adjustment is warranted, it can recommend an appropriate pricing strategy, taking into account factors such as profit margins, inventory levels, and customer demand.

Furthermore, reflective agents can leverage historical sales data and customer behavior patterns to optimize pricing strategies over time. By analyzing the effectiveness of previous pricing decisions and their impact on sales and profitability, these agents can refine their pricing models and algorithms, ensuring that future recommendations align with the business's objectives and customer expectations.

Reflective agents in e-commerce pricing can incorporate machine learning techniques to enhance their decision-making capabilities further. By ingesting and analyzing vast amounts of data from various sources, such as market research reports, social media sentiment, and customer purchase histories, these agents can uncover complex patterns and relationships that may not be immediately apparent. This ability to learn and adapt dynamically enables agents to stay ahead of market trends and continuously refine their pricing strategies, providing businesses with a competitive edge in the ever-evolving e-commerce landscape.

In the competitive world of e-commerce, effective pricing strategies are essential for attracting and retaining customers, maximizing sales, and maintaining profitability. Reflective agents offer a powerful solution for optimizing pricing strategies by leveraging introspection, data analysis, and continuous learning. By continuously monitoring market conditions, analyzing customer behavior, and refining their pricing models based on past performance, these agents empower businesses with data-driven insights and adaptive pricing strategies, enabling them to stay ahead of the competition and achieve their sales and profitability goals.

Summary

The ability of LLM agents to reflect and introspect emerges as a crucial differentiator, enabling agents to transcend static rule-based systems and exhibit human-like intelligence. This chapter looked into the significance of reflection and self-assessment, exploring practical techniques for embedding these capabilities and showcasing their real-world applications across various business domains.

Through the implementation of meta-reasoning, self-explanation, and self-modeling, intelligent agents gain the ability to monitor and control their reasoning processes, verbalize their decision-making rationale, and manage their goals and knowledge based on changing circumstances and new experiences. These capabilities not only foster transparency and trust but also pave the way for continuous learning, adaptation, and optimization of agent performance. These abilities enable agents to learn from their experiences, adapt to changing environments, and refine their decision-making processes, ultimately leading to improved performance, personalized user experiences, and competitive advantages for businesses.

The case studies and examples presented in this chapter underscore a wide range of utilities of reflective agents, ranging from customer service chatbots that provide personalized and natural interactions to supply chain optimization agents that dynamically adjust logistics and inventory management strategies. From financial trading systems that mitigate risks and capitalize on emerging opportunities to project management tools that enhance resource allocation and team dynamics, reflective agents have proven their value across diverse business domains.

While we touched on the topic of tool use in this chapter, in the next chapter we will dive deeper into agent tool use and look at various ways tools can supercharge your agentic workflows. We will also explore more about how agents can plan their course of action to complete a given task via agent planning.

Questions

1. How do meta-reasoning capabilities contribute to an intelligent agent's performance optimization?

2. What is the relationship between self-explanation and user interaction in AI systems?

3. How does self-modeling contribute to an agent's adaptive capabilities?

4. What are the key business benefits of implementing reflective capabilities in AI systems?

5. Why are reflection and introspection considered essential components for developing human-like AI capabilities?

Answers

1. Meta-reasoning enables intelligent agents to monitor and control their reasoning activities while dynamically adjusting strategies and optimizing resource allocation. This allows agents to evaluate their own thought processes, make real-time adjustments to their problem-solving approaches, and efficiently distribute computational resources where they're most needed.

2. Self-explanation promotes transparent decision-making processes and enables natural interactions with users by allowing the AI system to articulate its reasoning process. This transparency helps users understand how the system reaches conclusions, builds trust, and facilitates continuous learning through clear communication of the system's decision-making rationale.

3. Self-modeling empowers agents to adapt by enabling them to manage goals based on changing circumstances, update their knowledge from new experiences, and improve decision-making over time. This creates a dynamic learning system that can evolve and adjust its behavior based on new information and changing environmental conditions.

4. Implementing reflective capabilities in AI systems leads to several business advantages, including improved decision-making processes, the ability to deliver more personalized user experiences, and competitive advantages through enhanced adaptability and learning capabilities. These benefits stem from the system's ability to continuously learn, adapt, and optimize its performance.

5. Reflection and introspection are essential because they enable AI systems to analyze their reasoning processes, learn from experiences, and adapt behavior dynamically – qualities that are fundamental to human intelligence. Through techniques such as meta-reasoning, self-explanation, and self-modeling, agents can develop more sophisticated understanding and decision-making capabilities that mirror human cognitive processes.

Subscribe to AI_Distilled, the go-to newsletter for AI professionals

To keep up with the latest developments in the fields of Generative AI and LLMs, subscribe to our weekly newsletter, AI_Distilled, at `https://packt.link/8Oz6Y`.

5

Enabling Tool Use and Planning in Agents

In the previous chapter, we looked into the intricate concepts of reflection and introspection in intelligent agents. These capabilities empower agents to reason about their own cognitive processes, learn from experiences, and dynamically modify their behaviors.

A significant step forward in AI agents comes from combining how agents plan and use tools. This chapter looks at how tools work, different planning algorithms, how they fit together, and real examples showing how useful they are in practice. We will explore the concept of tool use by intelligent agents that extend their capabilities beyond decision-making and problem-solving. We will look at different types of tools that agents can utilize, such as APIs, databases, and software functions. We will then delve into planning algorithms essential for agents, including state-space search, reinforcement learning, and hierarchical task network planning. We will discuss integrating tool use and planning by reasoning about available tools, assessing their suitability based on goals, selecting appropriate tools, and generating efficient action sequences that leverage those tools.

This chapter is divided into the following main sections:

- Understanding the concept of tool use in agents
- Planning algorithms for agents
- Integrating tool use and planning
- Exploring practical implementations

By the end of this chapter, you will know what tools are, how they can be used to power your agentic systems, and how they work in conjunction with planning algorithms.

Technical requirements

You can find the code file for this chapter on GitHub at `https://github.com/PacktPublishing/Building-Agentic-AI-Systems`. In this chapter, we will also use agentic Python frameworks such as CrewAI, AutoGen, and LangChain to demonstrate the various aspects of AI agents.

Understanding the concept of tool use in agents

At its core, tool usage by an intelligent agent refers to the LLM agent's capability of leveraging external resources or instrumentation to augment the agent's inherent functionality and decision-making processes. This concept extends beyond the traditional notion of an agent as a self-contained (isolated) entity, relying solely on its internal knowledge (training data) and algorithms. Instead, it acknowledges the potential for agents to transcend their intrinsic limitations by strategically harnessing the power of external tools and systems.

For example, when you send a query ("*What's the weather?*") to an agent in isolation, the model is free to either respond with any made-up answer or it may respond that it doesn't know how to find the weather. In this case, the agent will rely on the LLM's training data, which will not have up-to-date information about real-time weather data. On the other hand, if the LLM agent has access to a real-time weather lookup tool, it may be able to answer the question accurately. Tool usage enables agents to access real-time data, execute specialized tasks, and manage complex workflows that go beyond their built-in knowledge and algorithms. *Figure 5.1* shows this isolated versus tool-powered behavior:

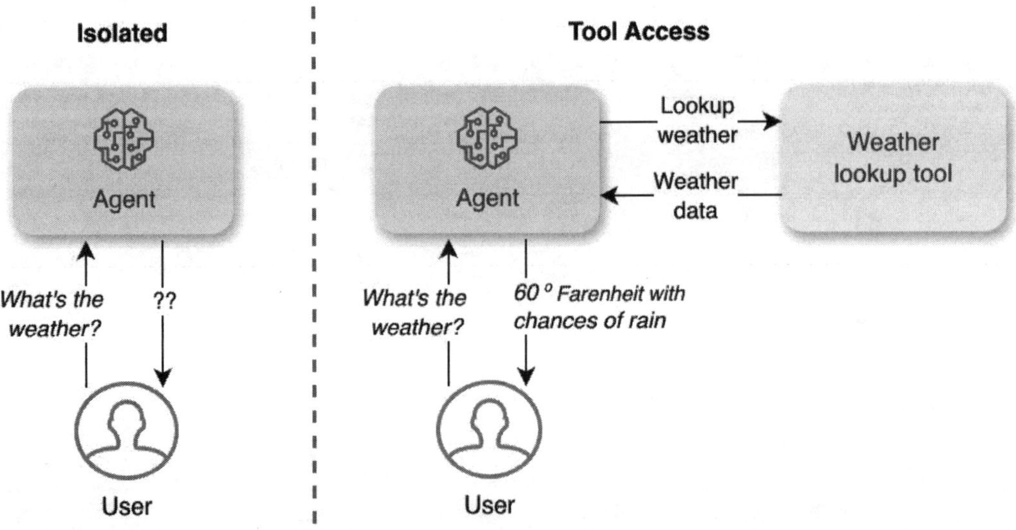

Figure 5.1 – Agent behavior in isolation versus with access to a tool

The significance of tool use lies in its ability to broaden the scope of an agent's (and, in turn, the LLM that powers the agent's) competencies, enabling it to tackle complex, real-world challenges that may be beyond the reach of its native problem-solving capabilities. By integrating and orchestrating the use of various tools, an agent can effectively offload specific tasks or access supplementary data and functionalities, thereby enhancing its overall performance and expanding its scope of achievable objectives. Before we go into the details of tools, let's first understand how LLM tool calling works.

Tool and function calling

While *tool calling* and *function calling* are often used interchangeably in the context of LLMs, they have distinct technical differences. **Function calling** refers to an LLM generating structured calls to predefined functions within the same runtime, typically executing internal tasks such as database lookups or calculations. **Tool calling**, on the other hand, enables LLMs to interact with external APIs, services, or systems, allowing them to access real-time data and perform specialized tasks beyond their intrinsic capabilities. For example, an LLM using function calling might retrieve a user's profile from a local database, while tool calling would involve querying a weather API for live updates. Understanding this distinction is crucial for designing AI agents that seamlessly integrate internal logic with external systems to enhance functionality.

When an LLM invokes a tool or function, it doesn't actually execute any code. Instead, it generates a structured response indicating the following:

- Which tool/function it wants to use

- What parameters should be passed to that tool/function

- How those parameters should be formatted

Think of it like writing a detailed instruction rather than performing the action itself. The LLM acts as a sophisticated dispatcher, determining what needs to be done and how, but the actual execution of the tool or function must be handled by an external runtime environment or an *Agent Controller*. For example, when asked about the weather in Boston, an LLM might recognize the need for the weather lookup function and respond with a structured call such as the following:

```
{
    "function": "weather_lookup",
    "parameters": {
        "location": "Boston",
        "date": "10/01/2024"
    }
}
```

This structured response is then interpreted and executed by the Agent Controller that actually has the capability to run the specified function with the provided parameters. The `weather_lookup` tool (or function) may look something like this:

```
 1 import requests
 2
 3 def weather_lookup(location: str, date: str) -> dict:
 4     """A function to lookup weather data that takes location and date
       as input"""
 5     API_KEY = "api_key"
 6     base_url = "<api URL>"
 7
 8     params = {
 9         "q": location,
10         "appid": API_KEY,
11         "units": "imperial"  # For Fahrenheit
12     }
13     response = requests.get(base_url, params=params)
14     if response.status_code == 200:
15         data = response.json()
16         return data
```

At the minimum, the LLM agent requires the tool's description of what the tool does and what input it expects. You can also specify which parameters (in this case, `location` and `date`) are mandatory and which ones are optional. *Figure 5.2* demonstrates the flow between an LLM agent, tool, and the Agent Controller:

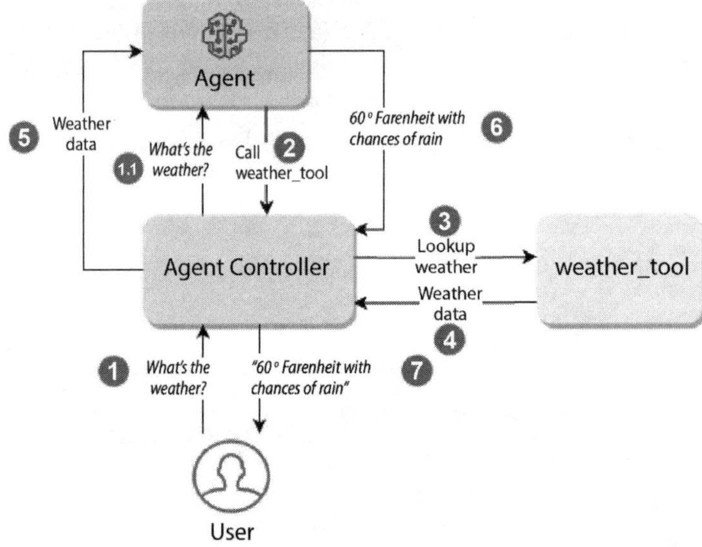

Figure 5.2 – LLM agent tool calling and tool execution by the Agent Controller

It is worth noting that not all LLMs are capable or efficient (or rather accurate) in tool/function calling. While larger models are more capable of tool calling, some larger models (such as OpenAI's GPT-4 and -4o, Anthropic's Claude Sonnet, Haiku, Opus, and Meta's Llama 3 models) are explicitly trained for tool calling behavior. While other models are not explicitly trained on tool calling, they may still be able to achieve similar functionality with aggressive prompt engineering, but with varying degrees of success.

Defining tools for agents

Tools are defined with clear descriptions, typically using docstrings or a JSON schema, to communicate their purpose, required inputs, and expected outputs to the agent. There are two main approaches to defining tools, depending on whether you're using a framework or working directly with LLM APIs.

Framework approach – using docstrings

In frameworks such as CrewAI or LangGraph, tools are defined using docstrings – descriptive text that appears at the beginning of a function. Here's an example of a weather lookup tool:

```
1 def weather_lookup(location: str, date: str = None):
2     """
3     A tool that can lookup real-time weather data.
4     Arguments:
5         location (str): The location to lookup weather for
6         date (str) Optional: The date in MM/DD/YYYY format
7     """
8   # function code and logic
```

The docstring, enclosed within triple quotes (`"""`), provides crucial information about the following:

- The tool's purpose

- Required and optional arguments

- Expected return values

This approach makes tool creation intuitive for developers, as it uses standard programming practices. While Python uses triple quotes for docstrings, other programming languages may have different conventions for defining such documentation.

Direct LLM integration

When working directly with LLM APIs (such as Anthropic's Claude or OpenAI's GPT) without a framework, tools must be defined using a specific JSON schema format:

```
{
  "name": "weather_lookup",
  "description": "A tool that can lookup real-time weather data",
  "input_schema": {
     "type": "object",
     "properties": {
        "location": {
           "type": "string",
           "description": "The city and state, e.g. San Francisco, CA"
        }
     },
     "required": ["location"]
  }
}
```

Multiple tools can be used as a list (or array) of JSON schema objects with the tool definition when invoking the model, such as the following:

```
tools = [
  { "name": "weather_lookup",
    "description": "A tool that can check weather data",
    ... },
  {
   "name": "flight_booking",
   "description": "A tool that can book flights",
    ... },
  ...
]
```

Note that this is model-dependent, so you must refer to the model's documentation to learn more about how its APIs require you to specify tools. If your project uses multiple models that have different ways of defining tools, then it can quickly become cumbersome to define, manage, and maintain tool definitions. This is one of the reasons why there is an increase in affinity toward using libraries or frameworks such as CrewAI, LangGraph, and AutoGen, which provide a simplified way of defining tools regardless of the LLM being used for the agents.

Types of tools

LLM agents can leverage various types of toolkits to enhance their capabilities and perform complex tasks. Here are the main categories:

- **Application programming interfaces (APIs)**: APIs serve as the primary gateway for agents to access external services and data in real time. They provide standardized methods for interacting with third-party systems, enabling agents to seamlessly integrate with various services. For instance, in a travel planning context, APIs allow agents to access weather services, payment processing systems, navigation and mapping services, and flight and hotel booking systems. This real-time connectivity ensures agents can provide up-to-date information and services to users.

- **Database tools**: Database tools enable agents to store, retrieve, and manage structured (or semi-structured) data efficiently. These tools support both reading and writing operations, allowing agents to maintain persistent information across sessions. Agents commonly use databases to store customer profiles and preferences, maintain historical transaction records, manage product catalogs, and access domain-specific knowledge bases. This persistent storage capability enables agents to learn from past interactions and provide personalized services.

- **Utility functions**: Utility functions are custom software components designed for specialized tasks that run locally within the agent's environment. These functions handle essential operations such as data processing and analysis, format conversion, mathematical calculations, and natural language processing tasks. They serve as the building blocks for more complex operations and help agents process information efficiently. Utility functions are particularly valuable for tasks that require consistent, repeatable operations.

- **Integration tools**: Integration tools specialize in connecting different systems and services, enabling seamless workflow automation. These tools handle crucial tasks such as calendar synchronization, document processing, file management, and communication systems integration. They act as bridges between different platforms and services, allowing agents to orchestrate complex workflows that span multiple systems and data sources.

- **Hardware interface tools**: Hardware interface tools enable agents to interact with physical devices and systems, bridging the gap between digital and physical worlds. These tools are essential for controlling IoT devices, integrating with robotics systems, processing sensor data, and managing physical automation systems. Through hardware interface tools, agents can extend their influence beyond digital interactions to affect real-world changes and monitor physical environments.

Each tool type serves specific purposes and can be combined to create powerful agent capabilities. The choice of tools depends on the agent's role, requirements, and the complexity of tasks it needs to perform.

Understanding how agents work with these tools involves the following several key considerations that affect their effectiveness and reliability. These aspects are crucial for developing robust agent systems that can handle complex real-world tasks while maintaining security, handling errors gracefully, and adapting to changing requirements:

- **Tool composition and chaining**: Agents often need to combine multiple tools to accomplish complex tasks. Tool composition allows agents to create sophisticated workflows by chaining tools together. For example, a travel planning agent might first use an API to check flight availability, then a database tool to retrieve user preferences, and, finally, a utility function to calculate optimal itineraries. This chaining capability significantly extends what agents can accomplish beyond using tools in isolation.

- **Tool selection and decision-making**: One of the most critical aspects of tool usage is the agent's ability to select the appropriate tool for a given task. Agents must evaluate the context, understand the requirements, and choose the most suitable tool or combination of tools. This involves considering factors such as tool capabilities, reliability, performance, and cost. The agent must also handle cases where multiple tools could solve the same problem, selecting the most efficient option.

- **Error handling and fallbacks**: When working with tools, agents must be prepared for potential failures and have strategies to handle them. This includes detecting failed API calls, managing database connection issues, or handling incorrect function outputs. Robust error handling often involves implementing fallback mechanisms, where agents can switch to alternative tools or approaches if the primary method fails.

- **Tool state management**: Many tools maintain state or require specific initialization and cleanup procedures. Agents need to manage these tool states effectively, ensuring proper resource allocation and release. This includes managing database connections, maintaining API authentication tokens, and handling session states for various services.

- **Tool updates and versioning**: Tools evolve over time with new versions and capabilities. Agents need strategies to handle tool updates, version compatibility, and deprecated features. This might involve maintaining compatibility with multiple versions of a tool, gracefully handling deprecated features, and adapting to new tool interfaces.

- **Tool security and access control**: Security considerations are crucial when agents interact with tools, especially those accessing sensitive data or critical systems. This includes managing authentication credentials, implementing proper authorization checks, and ensuring secure communication channels. Agents must also respect rate limits and usage quotas imposed by various tools.

Consider a practical example of interaction between a user and our AI travel agent using tools effectively.

User: "I need flight and hotel options for Rome for 2 adults, June 15–22, 2024, with a total budget of $3,000."

Using the CrewAI framework in the following code snippet, we will demonstrate how agents use tools in this focused travel planning scenario:

```
1 class TravelTools:
2   def search_flights(self, ...) 6 -> dict:
      """Basic flight search simulation"""
3    return {
4      "flights": [ {"airline": "Alitalian airlines",
                     "price": 800, "duration": "9h"}]
5
6      }
7
8  def check_hotels(self, ...) -> dict:
9       """Basic hotel search simulation"""
10      return {
11          "hotels": [ {"name": "Roma Inn",
12                       "price": 150, "rating": 4.0}]
13       }
14
15 travel_agent = Agent(
16    role='Travel Agent',
17    goal='Find suitable flight and hotel options within
            budget',
18  tools=[TravelTools().search_flights,
19          TravelTools().check_hotels]
20  )
21
22 search_task = Task(
23    description="Find flights and hotels for 2 adults to
                  Rome, June 15-22, budget $3000",
24    agent=travel_agent )
25
26 crew = Crew(agents=[travel_agent], tasks=[search_task])
27 result = crew.kickoff()
```

In this example, we can see several key concepts in action:

- **Tool definition**: The `TravelTools` class implements focused tools for specific travel-related tasks

- **Agent configuration**: The travel agent is configured with appropriate tools and a clear goal

- **Task specification**: The task is defined with precise parameters for the agent to work with

- **Tool integration**: The agent seamlessly integrates multiple tools (flight and hotel search) to accomplish its task

- **Execution flow**: The CrewAI framework manages the overall execution and coordination of the agent and its tools

This streamlined implementation demonstrates how agents can effectively use tools while maintaining clarity and purpose in their operations. In our example, the `TravelTools` class uses simplified JSON responses for clarity. However, in a real-world implementation, these tools would interact with actual external services and handle much more complex data.

Note that this is a rather simple implementation, and the actual implementation would involve integrating with various APIs, databases, and software tools specific to the travel domain. Additionally, advanced AI planning algorithms could be employed to optimize the itinerary construction and activity planning steps. This comprehensive tool usage allows the AI travel agent to provide a seamless, end-to-end, trip-planning experience far beyond just searching flights and hotels. You can find the full code in the Python notebook (`Chapter_05.ipynb`) in the GitHub repository.

The significance of tools in agentic systems

The paradigm shift toward tool use is driven by the recognition that many complex problems demand a diverse array of specialized tools and resources, each contributing a unique set of capabilities. Rather than attempting to encapsulate all requisite knowledge and functionalities within the agent itself, a more efficient and scalable approach involves intelligently leveraging the appropriate tools as needed.

For instance, an agent tasked with providing personalized healthcare recommendations could exploit tools such as medical databases, clinical decision support systems, and advanced diagnostic algorithms. By judiciously combining these external resources with its own reasoning capabilities, the agent can deliver more accurate and comprehensive guidance, tailored to individual patient profiles and conditions.

The concept of tool use in intelligent agents is not limited to software-based tools alone. In certain domains, such as robotics and automation, agents may interact with physical tools, machinery, or specialized equipment to extend their capabilities into the physical realm. For example, a robotic agent in a manufacturing plant could leverage various tools and machinery to perform intricate assembly tasks, quality inspections, or material handling operations.

Ultimately, the ability to effectively utilize external tools and resources is a hallmark of truly intelligent agents, capable of adapting and thriving in dynamic, complex environments. By going beyond the limitations of their native capabilities, these agents can continually evolve, leveraging the collective power of diverse tools and systems to achieve ambitious objectives.

Another good example is that of a virtual travel agent that has the capability to access multiple APIs, databases, and software tools to plan and book complete travel itineraries for users. Such a travel agent could leverage APIs from airlines, hotels, rental car companies, and travel review sites to gather real-time data on flight schedules, availability, pricing, and customer ratings. It could also tap into databases of travel advisories, travel document requirements, and destination information. By integrating and reasoning over all this data from various tools, the agent can provide personalized recommendations, make intelligent trade-offs, and seamlessly book and coordinate all aspects of a trip tailored to the user's preferences and constraints. Naturally, the set of tools used in such a case is diverse and they all operate in their unique ways.

We've looked at what tools are and how they work. Next, we will explore another critical aspect of agentic systems – planning – and some of the planning algorithms.

Planning algorithms for agents

Planning is a fundamental capability of intelligent agents, enabling them to reason about their actions and devise strategies to achieve their objectives effectively. Planning algorithms form the backbone of how LLM agents determine and sequence their actions. An algorithm is a step-by-step set of instructions or rules designed to solve a specific problem or complete a task. It is a sequence of unambiguous and finite steps that takes inputs and produces an expected output in a finite amount of time.

There are several planning algorithms in AI, each with its own strengths and approaches. However, when working with LLM agents, we need to consider their practicality in handling natural language, uncertainty, and large state spaces (all possible situations or configurations that an agent might encounter during its task). For example, in a simple robot navigation task, state spaces might include all possible positions and orientations, but in LLM agents, state spaces become vastly more complex as they include all possible conversation states, knowledge contexts, and potential responses.

Among the known planning algorithms – **Stanford Research Institute Problem Solver (STRIPS)**, **hierarchical task network (HTN)**, **A* planning**, **Monte Carlo Tree Search (MCTS)**, **GraphPlan**, **Fast Forward (FF)**, and **LLM-based planning** – they can be categorized by their practicality for LLM agents.

STRIPS, A* planning, GraphPlan, and MCTS, while powerful in traditional AI, are less practical for LLM agents due to their rigid structure and difficulty handling natural language. FF shows moderate potential but requires significant adaptation. The most practical approaches are LLM-based planning and HTN, as they naturally align with how language models process and decompose tasks. Let's discuss them in detail.

Less practical planning algorithms

As mentioned earlier, less practical planning algorithms include STRIPS, A* planning, GraphPlan, and MCTS. Here's a detailed overview.

STRIPS

STRIPS works with states and actions defined by logical predicates, making it effective for clear, binary conditions. However, it's unsuitable for LLM agents because natural language interactions can't be effectively reduced to simple `true`/`false` conditions. For example, while STRIPS can easily model `true`/`false` states, it struggles with nuanced language states such as *partially understanding a concept* or *somewhat satisfied with a response*, making it too rigid for language-based planning.

A* planning

A* planning, while powerful for pathfinding problems, faces fundamental challenges with LLM agents. The algorithm requires a clear way to calculate both the cost of actions taken and a heuristic estimate of the remaining cost to reach a goal. In language-based interactions, defining these costs becomes highly problematic – how do you quantify the "distance" between different conversation states or estimate the "cost" of reaching a particular understanding? These mathematical requirements make A* impractical for natural language planning.

GraphPlan

GraphPlan builds a layered graph structure representing possible actions and their effects at each time step. When applied to LLM agents, this approach breaks down because language interactions don't fit neatly into discrete layers with clear cause-and-effect relationships. The combinatorial explosion of possible language states and the difficulty in determining mutual exclusion relationships between different conversational actions make GraphPlan computationally intractable for language-based planning.

MCTS

For LLM agents, **MCTS** becomes impractical for two main reasons. First, each "simulation" would require actual LLM calls, making it prohibitively expensive in terms of computation and cost; second, the vast space of possible language interactions makes random sampling inefficient for finding meaningful patterns or strategies. The algorithm's strength in game-like scenarios becomes a weakness in open-ended language interactions.

Moderately practical planning algorithm – FF

FF planning is considered to be a moderately practical planning algorithm that can be used in LLM agents. It uses a heuristic search with a simplified version of the planning problem to guide its search. Its focus on goal-oriented planning could be adapted for LLM agents, though it would require modifications to handle natural language effectively. FF planning uses heuristic search with a simplified version of the planning problem to guide its search.

For LLM agents, FF planning offers several compelling advantages that make it worth considering. Its goal-oriented approach naturally aligns with how LLMs handle task completion, while its relaxed planning mechanism provides useful approximations for complex language tasks. The heuristic guidance helps manage the vast search space inherent in language-based planning, and its flexibility allows modification to work with partial state descriptions, which is particularly valuable in natural language contexts.

However, FF planning also faces significant challenges when applied to LLM agents. The original numeric heuristics that make FF effective in traditional planning don't translate smoothly to language states, and relaxed plans risk oversimplifying the rich context present in language interactions. There's also considerable difficulty in defining clear delete effects – what aspects of a conversation state are removed or changed by an action – in language-based planning. Perhaps most challengingly, the fundamental state representation requires substantial adaptation to work effectively with natural language. In practice, FF could be adapted for LLM agents as follows:

```python
1  class LLMFastForward:
2      def create_relaxed_plan(self,
3                              current_state: str,
4                              goal: str) -> list:
5          """Create a simplified plan ignoring complexities"""
6          # Use LLM to generate a high-level plan
7          prompt = f"Given current state: {current_state}\nAnd
                 goal: {goal}\n"
8          prompt += "Generate a simplified step-by-stepplan"
9              return self.llm.generate_plan(prompt)
10
11     def select_next_action(self, relaxed_plan: list):
12         """Choose next action based on the relaxed plan"""
13         # Implement action selection logic
14         return relaxed_plan[0]  # Simplified selection
```

This code demonstrates a simplified adaptation of FF planning for LLM agents. Let me explain its key components. The `LLMFastForward` class has two main methods:

- `create_relaxed_plan`: This method takes the current state and goal as text strings and uses an LLM to generate a simplified plan. Think of it as asking the LLM, *"Given where we are now, and where we want to go, what are the main steps we should take?"*. It ignores many complexities, similar to how traditional FF planning ignores delete effects.

- `select_next_action`: This method chooses the next action from the relaxed plan. In this simplified version, it just takes the first action from the plan (`relaxed_plan[0]`). In a more sophisticated implementation, it would use additional logic to select the most appropriate next action.

In essence, this code shows how FF planning's core concept of using simplified plans to guide decision-making can be adapted to work with language models, even though it's a significant simplification of both FF planning and LLM capabilities. While this adaptation shows potential, implementing FF for LLM agents requires careful consideration of how to represent states, actions, and relaxed problems in a language-model context. This makes it moderately practical – possible but requiring significant modifications from its original form.

Most practical planning algorithms

When it comes to planning algorithms for LLM agents, two approaches stand out as particularly effective: LLM-based planning and HTN planning. These algorithms have proven especially suitable for language models because they naturally align with how LLMs process information and handle complex tasks. While traditional planning algorithms often struggle with the ambiguity and complexity of natural language, these approaches embrace the fluid, contextual nature of language-based planning. Let's explore each of these algorithms and understand why they've become the preferred choices for modern AI agent frameworks.

LLM-based planning

Modern approaches leverage LLMs to generate plans in a more flexible and natural way. This approach can handle complex, real-world scenarios and understand context better than traditional planning algorithms. LLM-based planning operates on the principle that language models can understand complex goals, generate appropriate steps to achieve them, and adapt these steps based on changing contexts. Unlike traditional planners that require explicit state representations, LLM planners work with natural language descriptions of states and actions, making them inherently more flexible and expressive. Let's visualize the planning process using *Figure 5.3*:

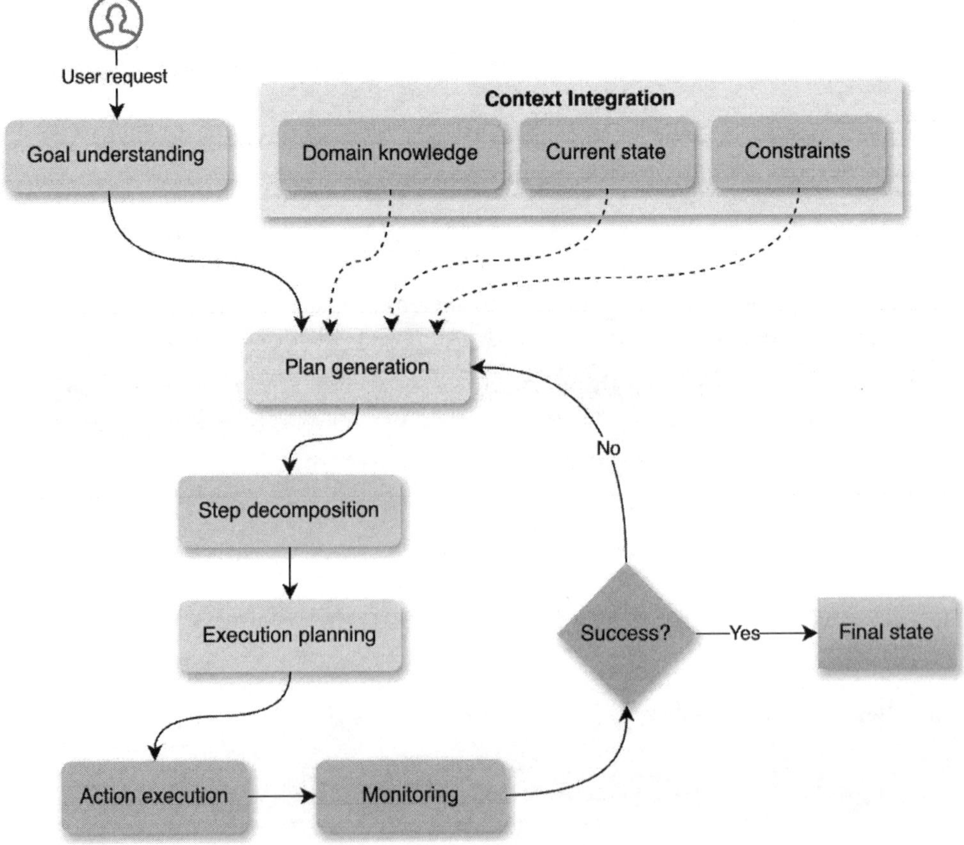

Figure 5.3 – LLM-based planning algorithm flow

Let's examine a practical implementation using CrewAI that demonstrates this planning approach. In this example, we'll create a travel planning system with two specialized agents: a *Travel Planning Strategist* who breaks down travel requests into manageable steps, and a *Travel Researcher* who validates and finds specific options. The system processes natural language travel requests and generates comprehensive travel plans through collaborative agent interaction. Here's the implementation:

```python
1 class TravelPlanner:
2     def __init__(self):
3         self.planner = Agent(
4             role='Travel Planning Strategist',
5             goal='Create comprehensive, personalized travel plans',
6             ... # Other parameters
7         )
8         self.researcher = Agent(
9             role='Travel Researcher',
10            goal='Find and validate travel options and
opportunities',
11            ... # Other parameters
12        )
13
14    def create_travel_plan(self, request: str) -> Dict:
15        planning_task = Task(
16            description=f"""
17            Analyze the following travel request and
18            create a detailed plan:
19            {request}
20            Break this down into actionable steps by:
21            1. Understanding client requirements
22            3. Specific booking requirements
23            4. Required validations
24            """, agent=self.planner )
25
26        research_task = Task(
27            description="""
28            Based on the initial plan, research and
29            validate: Flight availability, hotel options,
30            and local transportation
31            """, agent=self.researcher)
32
33        crew = Crew(
34            agents=[self.planner, self.researcher],
35            tasks=[planning_task, research_task],
36            process=Process.sequential )
37        return crew.kickoff(inputs={"request": request})
```

This implementation demonstrates several key advantages of LLM-based planning. The planner can understand complex natural language requests, dynamically generate appropriate steps, and adapt to different types of travel planning scenarios. The agents can work together, sharing context and building upon each other's outputs. The system's sophistication comes from its ability to handle nuanced requirements. For instance, when a user requests *"a relaxing beach vacation with some cultural activities,"* the planner understands these abstract concepts and can translate them into concrete recommendations.

However, developers should be mindful of certain caveats. LLM-based planning systems can sometimes generate overly optimistic or impractical plans if not properly constrained. They may also struggle with highly specific numerical constraints or strict timing requirements unless these are explicitly handled in the implementation. A significant advantage of LLM-based planning over traditional algorithms lies in the system's adaptability. While STRIPS or A* planning would require explicit state representations for every possible travel scenario, LLM-based planning can handle novel situations by leveraging its understanding of language and context. This makes it particularly suitable for domains where requirements are often ambiguous or evolving. This planning approach also excels at handling uncertainty and partial information, something traditional planners struggle with. When information is missing or ambiguous, the system can generate reasonable assumptions and include contingency steps in its plans.

HTN

HTN planning breaks down complex tasks into simpler subtasks, creating a hierarchy of actions. Unlike STRIPS, which works with primitive actions, HTN can work with abstract tasks and decompose them into more concrete steps. This makes it particularly well-suited for real-world planning problems where tasks naturally decompose into subtasks. HTN planning works by breaking down high-level tasks into progressively smaller subtasks. Consider the following example code:

```
1 def buy_groceries_task():
2     return [
3         ('go_to_store', []),
4         ('select_items', []),
5         ('checkout', []),
6         ('return_home', [])
7     ]
8
9 def select_items_task():
10     return [
11         ('check_list', []),
12         ('find_item', []),
13         ('add_to_cart', [])
14     ]
```

HTN planning operates on the principle of task decomposition, where high-level tasks (compound tasks) are broken down into smaller, more manageable subtasks until reaching primitive tasks that can be directly executed. This hierarchical structure allows for intuitive problem representation and efficient solution finding. In our example, `buy_groceries_task` is a high-level task broken down into four subtasks. One of these subtasks, `select_items`, is further decomposed into three more specific actions, and so on. In the context of our travel agent example, we can use a similar hierarchical breakdown of complex tasks decomposed into smaller tasks. Visually, *Figure 5.4* shows how this may look:

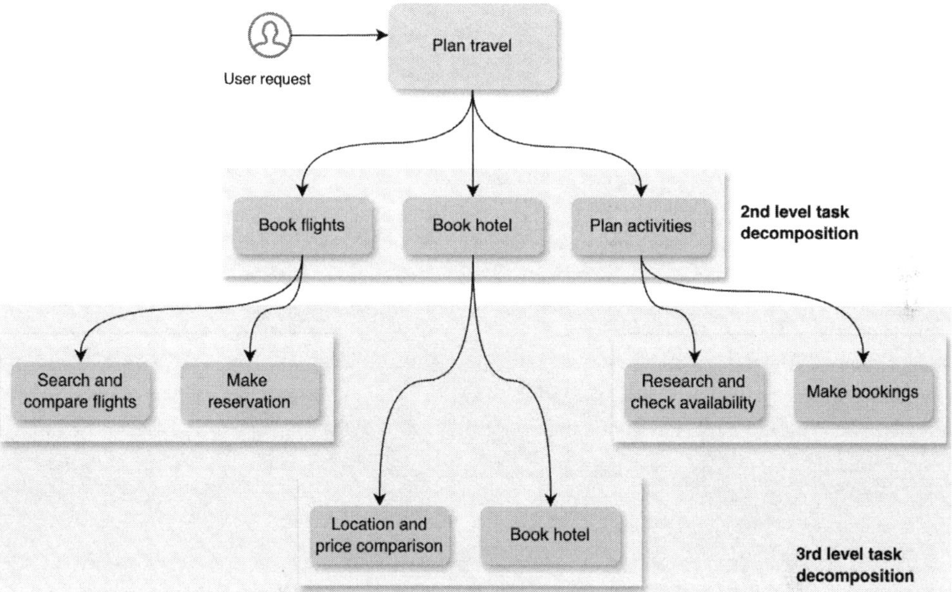

Figure 5.4 – HTN decomposition

To implement this with CrewAI, we can use CrewAI's *hierarchical* processing, where tasks are broken down into a hierarchical manner as explained using the HTN planning algorithm. With the CrewAI framework, the hierarchical method requires a **manager** unit, which would be responsible for breaking down the tasks and *delegating* individual tasks to the agents. The Manager can either be an agent or it can be the LLM itself. If the Manager is an agent, then you can control how the manager breaks down the tasks to *n*-level tasks as per the workflow's needs. If the Manager is an LLM, then it will use the arbitrary plan generated by the LLM itself based on the user's query. With a Manager LLM, you may be able to control how the task breakdown works and how the delegation works using some prompt engineering; however, it is generally less flexible and is meant for simpler workflows. Here's a sample code for an HTN-like workflow for the travel planner:

```
1 flight_specialist = Agent(
2     role='Flight Planning Specialist',
3     goal='Handle all aspects of flight arrangements',
```

```python
 4        backstory='Expert in airline bookings and flight
                     logistics.')
 5
 6 accommodation_specialist = Agent(
 7     role='Accommodation Specialist',
 8     goal='Manage all accommodation-related planning',
 9     backstory='Expert in hotel and accommodation booking')
10
11 activity_specialist = Agent(
12     role='Vacation Activity Specialist',
13     goal='Manage all activity-related planning',
14     backstory="Expert in recreational activity
                     arrangements.",)
15
16 manager_llm = ChatOpenAI(model="gpt-4o-mini")
17 travel_planning_task = Task(
18     description=f"""
19        Plan a comprehensive flight itinerary based on the
20        following request:
21        {request}
22        The plan should include: Flight arrangements,
23        Accommodation bookings, other relevant travel
24          components
25        """,
26        expected_output="A detailed flight itinerary
             covering all requested aspects.",
27        agent=None) #No agent; the manager will delegate
                      subtasks
28
29 crew = Crew(
30             agents=[self.flight_specialist,
31                     self.accommodation_specialist,
32                     self.activity_specialist],
33             tasks=[travel_planning_task],
34             process=Process.hierarchical,
35             manager_llm=self.manager_llm,)
36     return crew.kickoff()
```

The output of this execution may look as shown (output has been trimmed for brevity):

```
Final Travel Plan:
Here's the complete travel itinerary for a 5-day trip to Paris from
New York for two adults:
---
```

```
Travel Itinerary for Paris Trip
From New York (JFK) to Paris (CDG)
Travelers: 2 Adults , Duration: 5 Days
---
1. Flights:
- Departure Flight: ...
- Total Flight Cost: $2,960
---
2. Hotel Accommodations:
- Hotel: ...
- Estimated Total = €800.
---
3. Airport Transfers:
- Option 1: ...
- Option 2: ...
---
4. Day Trip to Versailles:
- Transportation: Round-trip via RER C train from …
    - Cost: Approximately …
    - Departure Time: 9:00 AM from …
    - Return Time: 5:00 PM from Versailles.
    ...
    - Overall Total for Day Trip: Approximately €364.20.
---
Grand Total Estimated Cost:
- Flights: $2,960
- Accommodation: €800 (with Le Fabe Hotel)
- Airport Transfers: €100 (may vary)
- Day Trip to Versailles: Approximately €364.20
- Convert Total Costs as Necessary to USD.
...
```

Note that, in this case, the agentic system has no access to external tools or lookup, so whatever response it generates is going to be completely fictional and non-factual. This underscores the importance of tools, which we will look at in the next section. For now, the previous example shows how you can use the framework for task breakdown and have a Manager manage several agents to perform decomposed simplified tasks from a user's request. You can see the full code in the Python notebook (`Chapter_05.ipynb`) in the GitHub repository.

HTN planning offers several significant advantages that make it particularly effective for complex planning scenarios. Its natural problem representation mirrors human thinking patterns, making it intuitive to understand and maintain. The hierarchical approach enables better scalability by breaking down complex problems into manageable subtasks, effectively reducing the search space. HTN's structure excels at encoding expert knowledge through its task hierarchies, allowing for reusable patterns across similar problems. Additionally, its flexibility in handling both abstract and primitive tasks makes it adaptable to various planning situations, enabling planners to work at different levels of abstraction as needed.

So far, we've learned about tools and several planning algorithms, but together they can enable LLM agents to perform more complex, multi-step tasks by combining strategic planning with effective tool use. Let's further explore how we can effectively integrate tool use with planning within agentic systems.

Integrating tool use and planning

Most of the earlier work in AI planning and tool usage was done in isolation, focusing on either planning algorithms or tool capabilities separately. However, to achieve truly intelligent agents, there is a need to integrate tool use with planning effectively. As we already saw in the previous section, our travel planner gave us a detailed travel plan but none of the details were factual – that is, it contained information that the LLM simply made up. In order to infuse our system with actual flight, hotel, and activity data so that the travel plan is grounded in facts, we will need to utilize tools along with the planning algorithm. This section will discuss how to combine these two aspects to generate relevant responses and complete tasks accurately.

Reasoning about tools

Agents need the ability to reason about the available tools at their disposal, understanding the functionality, capabilities, and limitations of each tool, as well as the contexts and conditions under which they can be applied effectively. The reasoning process involves assessing the available tools based on the current goals and objectives, and then choosing the most appropriate ones that can be utilized in the given situation or problem domain.

For example, in the case of our travel planner, the agent will have access to various tools such as flight booking APIs, hotel reservation systems, and activity planning software. The agent needs to reason about the capabilities of each tool, such as which tools can be used for booking flights or book hotels, and which ones can provide information about local attractions.

When working with LLM agents, reasoning about tools is largely handled by the language model's inherent capabilities. Modern LLMs are trained to understand tool descriptions, purposes, and appropriate usage contexts. This means we don't need to explicitly program complex reasoning mechanisms – instead, we provide clear tool descriptions and let the LLM determine when and how to use them. For example, let's look at our travel planner agent scenario:

```
1 from crewai import Agent
2
3 travel_agent = Agent(
4    role='Travel Planner',
5    goal='Plan comprehensive travel itineraries',
6    tools=[
```

```
7          flight_search_tool,      # Tool for finding and booking flights
8          hotel_booking_tool,      # Tool for hotel reservations
9          activity_planner_tool    # Tool for local activities and
                                       attractions
10    ])
```

The LLM agent can naturally understand the following:

- Which tool to use for each task (for example, `flight_search_tool` for air travel)

- When to use tools in combination (for example, coordinating flight and hotel dates)

- How to adapt tool usage based on user requirements (for example, budget constraints)

This built-in reasoning capability means we can focus on providing well-defined tools with clear descriptions, rather than implementing complex reasoning mechanisms. The LLM will handle the decision-making process of tool selection and application based on the context and requirements of each situation. However, not all language models are equally capable of effective tool reasoning. This capability typically requires models that have been specifically trained or fine-tuned for tool use and function calling. Smaller models or those without tool-use training may have the following issues:

- Failing to understand when a tool is needed

- Making incorrect assumptions about tool capabilities

- Using tools in the wrong sequences

- Missing opportunities to use available tools

- Ignoring tool constraints or requirements

Even capable models can face limitations such as the following:

- Difficulty with complex tool combinations requiring many steps

- Inconsistency in tool selection across similar scenarios

- Challenges with tools that have subtle differences in functionality

- Struggles with error recovery when tools fail

This is why frameworks such as CrewAI, LangGraph, and AutoGen often work best with more advanced models that have demonstrated strong tool reasoning capabilities, and why it's important to test your agent's tool usage patterns before deployment.

Planning for tool use

The planning process in modern AI agents is fundamentally driven by LLM capabilities, building upon the principles we discussed in LLM-based planning and HTN approaches. Rather than following rigid planning algorithms, agents leverage their language model's understanding to create flexible, context-aware plans for tool usage. *Figure 5.5* depicts this process:

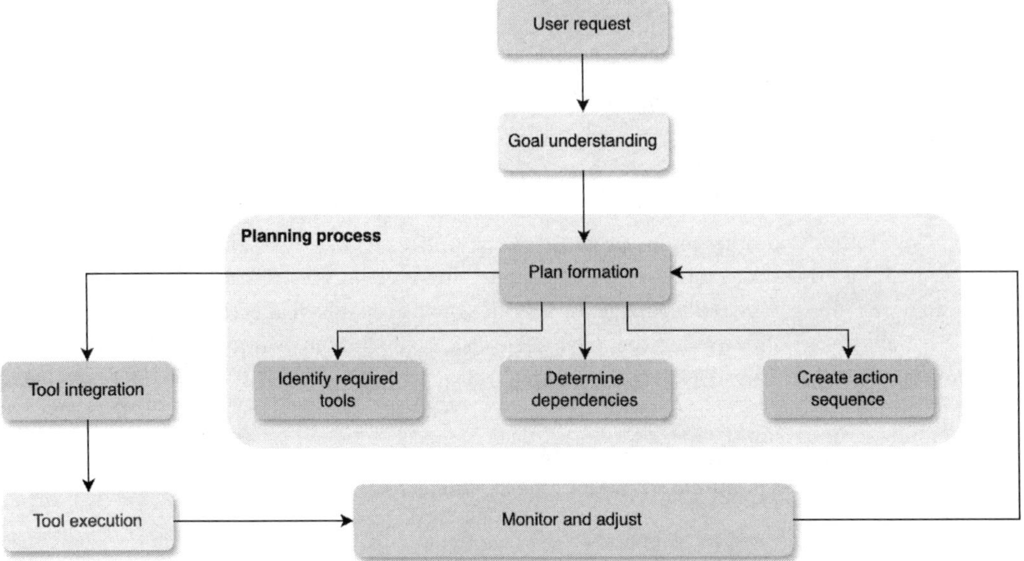

Figure 5.5 – Tool planning flow

When an agent receives a request, it first understands the goals through natural language processing. For a travel agent, this might mean comprehending that a family vacation request requires not just flight bookings but also family-friendly accommodation and activities. This goal-understanding phase draws directly from the LLM's trained comprehension abilities.

The planning process then shifts to identifying which tools are needed and in what sequence they should be used. This mirrors the hierarchical decomposition we saw in HTN planning but with the flexibility of LLM-based decision-making. The agent doesn't just follow predefined decomposition rules; it adapts its planning based on the specific context and requirements of each request.

Tool integration into the plan happens naturally as part of this process. The agent understands tool capabilities through their descriptions and can sequence them appropriately. For instance, when planning a vacation, the agent knows that flight dates need to be confirmed before booking hotels, and that activity planning should consider the location and timing of both.

This planning approach combines the structured nature of traditional planning algorithms with the adaptability of language models. The agent can adjust its plans based on new information or changing circumstances, much like a human travel agent would modify their approach based on client feedback or availability changes.

The success of this planning process relies heavily on the LLM's ability to understand context and generate appropriate sequences of actions. This is why frameworks such as CrewAI often implement this type of planning, allowing agents to leverage their language understanding capabilities while maintaining the systematic approach needed for complex task completion.

Exploring practical implementations

To demonstrate how various AI/ML frameworks can be used to create intelligent agents capable of executing complex tasks through tool use and planning, let's explore examples using CrewAI, AutoGen, and LangGraph (the agentic framework of LangChain). You can find the full code for each of the framework examples in the `Chapter_05.ipynb` Python notebook in the GitHub repository.

CrewAI example

Let's examine how CrewAI implements tool-based reasoning through a practical travel planning example. The framework's Python library provides a `@tool` decorator that allows us to define tools with clear descriptions and documentation. Here's how we can create a set of travel-related tools:

```python
1 @tool("Search for available flights between cities")
2 def search_flights(...) -> dict:
3     """Search for available flights between cities."""
4     # Call flight API and other tool logic
5
6 @tool("Find available hotels in a location")
7 def find_hotels(...) -> dict:
8     """Search for available hotels in a location."""
9    # Call hotels API and other tool logic
10
11 @tool("Find available activities in a location")
12 def find_activities(...) -> dict:
13     """Find available activities in a location."""
14  # Call activities API and other tool logic
```

The tools are then assigned to an agent that understands how to use them in context. The agent is created with a specific role, goal, and backstory that helps guide its decision-making:

```python
1 Agent(
2     role='An expert travel concierge',
3     goal='Handle all aspects of travel planning',
4     backstory="Expert in airline bookings and flight
            logistics, hotel bookings, and booking vacation
```

```
                activities.",
5        tools=[search_flights, find_hotels, find_activities],
6        verbose=False
7 )
```

When given a task, the agent uses these tools based on the context and requirements:

```
1 travel_planning_task = Task(
2     description=f"""
3     Plan a comprehensive travel and leisure itinerary
4     based on the following request:
5     {request}
6     The plan should include:
7     - Flight arrangements
8     - Accommodation bookings
9     - Any other relevant travel components
10    """,
11    expected_output="A detailed travel itinerary covering
          all requested aspects.",
12    agent=self.travel_specialist )
```

When `crew.kickoff()` is called, CrewAI orchestrates the tool usage in the following ways:

- Understanding the task requirements through the task description

- Identifying which tools are needed based on the agent's role and the task goals

- Using the tools in a logical sequence to build the travel plan

- Processing tool outputs and incorporating them into the final response

This implementation demonstrates how CrewAI combines tool definitions, agent capabilities, and task specifications to create a coherent planning system. The framework handles the complexity of tool reasoning while allowing developers to focus on defining clear tool interfaces and agent behaviors.

AutoGen example

AutoGen provides a platform for developing AI agents that can engage in conversations and, through these interactions, arrive at solutions for given tasks. AutoGen approaches multi-agent collaboration through a RoundRobinGroupChat system where specialized agents interact to create a comprehensive travel plan. The implementation defines four key agents: a flight planner, a hotel planner, an activities planner, and a summary agent, each with specific responsibilities and tools.

Each agent is initialized with the following:

- A name and description

- A model client (in this case, OpenAI's GPT-4o-mini)

- Specific tools they can access

- A system message defining their role and responsibilities

The key differentiators from CrewAI lie in the execution model:

- **Agent communication**: While CrewAI uses a hierarchical task-based approach, AutoGen implements a round-robin group chat where agents take turns contributing to the solution. The `RoundRobinGroupChat` class orchestrates this conversation flow, allowing agents to build upon each other's suggestions.

- **Termination handling**: AutoGen uses an explicit termination condition through the `TextMentionTermination` class. The travel summary agent can end the conversation by mentioning `"TERMINATE"` when a complete plan is ready. This differs from CrewAI's task-completion-based termination. Here are the parameters of `TextMentionTermination`:

  - `mention_text (str)`: The keyword or phrase that triggers termination (e.g., `"TERMINATE"`)

  - `case_sensitive (bool, optional)`: Whether the keyword matching should be case-sensitive

  - `strip_whitespace (bool, optional)`: Whether to ignore leading/trailing spaces in the detected text

  - `regex_match (bool, optional)`: Allows for using regular expressions for more flexible termination triggers

- **Tool integration**: Instead of CrewAI's decorator-based tool definition, AutoGen associates tools directly with agents during initialization. Each agent has access to specific tools relevant to their role.

- **Coordination pattern**: While CrewAI often uses a manager-worker pattern, AutoGen's round-robin approach creates a more collaborative environment where agents contribute equally to the solution, with the summary agent responsible for creating the final integrated plan.

This implementation showcases AutoGen's strength in handling complex multi-agent conversations while maintaining clear role separation and specialized tool usage for each agent. The following is how you define agents with AutoGen:

```
1 flight_agent = AssistantAgent(
2     name="flight_planner",
3     model_client=model_client,
4     tools=[travel_tools.search_flights],
```

```
5      description="A helpful assistant that can plan flights
                itinerary for vacation trips.",
6      system_message="You are a helpful assistant that can
            plan flight itinerary for a travel plan for a
            user based on their request." )
7
8 hotel_agent = AssistantAgent(
9     name="hotel_planner",
10    model_client=model_client,
11    tools=[travel_tools.search_flights],
12    description="...", system_message="..." )
```

Once agents are defined, a `RoundRobinGroupChat` class can be defined using the agents and a conversation with the multi-agent system can be invoked:

```
2 group_chat = RoundRobinGroupChat(
3     [flight_agent, hotel_agent],
4     termination_condition=termination)
6  await Console(group_chat.run_stream(task="I need to plan
                a trip to Paris from New York for 5 days."))
```

LangGraph example

LangChain provides a framework for developing applications that can leverage LLMs alongside other tools and data sources. In the context of agentic systems, LangChain provides a sub-framework known as LangGraph that is used to build powerful LLM agent-based workflows. LangGraph approaches agent-based travel planning through a workflow graph system, offering a different paradigm from both CrewAI and AutoGen. Let's examine how this implementation works and its distinguishing characteristics.

LangGraph uses a state machine approach where the workflow is defined as a graph with nodes and edges. The implementation centers around two main nodes:

- An agent node that processes messages and makes decisions

- A tool node that executes the requested tools (flight search, hotel booking, and activity planning)

The workflow follows a cycle where the agent node evaluates the current state and either makes tool calls or provides a final response. This is controlled through a function that interprets the model's next move (that is, call a tool or end the response), which determines whether to route to the tools node or end the conversation. Just like CrewAI, LangGraph also uses the @tool decorator (for Python) with which the tool functions can be defined:

```
1 @tool
2 def search_flights(...) -> dict:
3     """Search for available flights between cities."""
```

```
4    # Emulate JSON data from an API
5    return data
```

Once nodes are defined with or without tools, they can be connected to each other to build a full graph structure of the workflow. For example, in our case, the following code defines a state graph-based workflow using LangGraph, where a task cycles between two nodes: agent and tools. The graph starts at the agent node (defined as the entry point), which calls a function (`call_model`) to process input. After the agent runs, a conditional function (`should_continue`) determines the next node – either looping back to the tools node or ending the workflow. The tools node (`tool_node`) processes intermediate tasks and always transitions back to the `agent` node, creating a repetitive cycle until the conditional function decides to stop. A `MemorySaver` checkpoint is used to persist the state across runs, and the graph is compiled into a LangChain-compatible runnable. Finally, the workflow is invoked with an initial input message about planning a trip, and the final message content is printed after the graph execution concludes:

```
1 workflow = StateGraph(MessagesState)
2 workflow.add_node("agent", call_model)
3 workflow.add_node("tools", tool_node)
4 workflow.add_edge(START, "agent")
5 workflow.add_conditional_edges("agent",should_continue)
6 workflow.add_edge("tools", 'agent')
7 checkpointer = MemorySaver()
8 app = workflow.compile(checkpointer=checkpointer)
9 final_state = app.invoke(
10    {"messages": [HumanMessage(content="I need to plan a
             trip to Paris from New York for 5 days")]},
11     config={"configurable": {"thread_id": 42}})
```

LangGraph's approach offers several notable advantages. For example, its graph structure provides explicit flow control, making workflows easy to visualize and understand, while built-in state management with checkpointing capabilities ensures robust handling of the application state. However, these benefits come with certain trade-offs. The framework requires a solid understanding of graph-based programming concepts, and its initial setup involves more overhead compared to CrewAI's more straightforward agent definition. The full code implementation can be found in the `Chapter_05.ipynb` Python notebook in the GitHub repository.

Table 5.1 illustrates some key differences between LangGraph, CrewAI, and AutoGen:

	LangGraph	**CrewAI**	**AutoGen**
State management	Uses explicit state management	Manages state through agent instances and their task context	Handles state through group chat message history
Tool integration	Tools are managed through a dedicated tool node	Uses a decorator-based tool definition with direct agent association	Associates tools directly with specific agents
Flow control	Uses a graph-based workflow	Uses hierarchical task decomposition or sequential flow	Implements round-robin turn-taking between agents

Table 5.1 – Comparison of LangGraph, CrewAI, and AutoGen implementation approaches

The preceding table shows the differences between LangGraph, CrewAI, and AutoGen based on our implementation.

Summary

In this chapter, we learned about the crucial role of tools and planning in AI agent systems. We discussed what tool/function calling is and how LLM agents exhibit this property. We also learned about various tool types and saw examples of how to use tools with frameworks or natively with an LLM. Subsequently, we explored various planning algorithms, from traditional approaches such as STRIPS and HTN to modern LLM-based planning methods, understanding their relative practicality in the context of language models. Through a practical travel planning example, we saw how tools can be defined, integrated, and utilized within each framework to create sophisticated planning systems.

We learned how integrating tool calling with planning can supercharge agentic systems by making them more capable of handling complex tasks. We also reviewed the implementation patterns across three frameworks (CrewAI, AutoGen, and LangGraph), which revealed distinct approaches to agent coordination and tool usage.

In the next chapter, we will dive into the concepts of the coordinator, worker, and delegator approach in agentic systems, and learn how they can help with completing complex real-world tasks.

Questions

1. What is the purpose of tools in AI agents, and how do docstrings help in tool definition?

2. Explain the difference between traditional planning algorithms (such as STRIPS) and modern LLM-based planning. Why are traditional algorithms less practical for LLM agents?

3. How does HTN planning work, and why is it considered one of the more practical approaches for LLM agents?

4. What role does reasoning play in tool selection for LLM agents, and what are its limitations?

5. When comparing frameworks (CrewAI, AutoGen, and LangGraph), what are the key factors to consider for an AI agent implementation?

Answers

1. Tools in AI agents are functions that enable agents to perform specific tasks or access external services. Docstrings provide crucial information about the tool's purpose, expected parameters, and return values, helping the LLM understand when and how to use each tool effectively. This documentation serves as the context that guides the model's decision-making process.

2. Traditional planning algorithms such as STRIPS rely on explicit state representations and predefined action sets, working with binary conditions and clear state transitions. LLM-based planning, however, operates with natural language understanding and can handle ambiguous states and actions. Traditional algorithms struggle with LLMs because they can't effectively represent the nuanced, contextual nature of language-based tasks.

3. HTN planning works by breaking down complex tasks into progressively simpler subtasks in a hierarchical structure. It's practical for LLM agents because this hierarchical decomposition mirrors how language models naturally process and understand tasks. The approach allows for both structured planning and the flexibility needed for language-based interactions.

4. Reasoning in LLM agents is largely handled by the model's built-in capabilities to understand context and make decisions. While this makes tool selection more natural, not all models are equally capable. Limitations include potential inconsistencies in tool selection, difficulties with complex tool combinations, and challenges in error recovery when tools fail.

5. Key factors for framework selection include the complexity of the workflow (structured versus conversational), the need for state management, multi-agent collaboration requirements, and development complexity. CrewAI offers straightforward implementation, AutoGen excels at multi-agent interaction, and LangGraph provides robust workflow control but requires more setup.

Get This Book's PDF Version and Exclusive Extras

Scan the QR code (or go to `packtpub.com/unlock`). Search for this book by name, confirm the edition, and then follow the steps on the page.

Note: Keep your invoice handly. Purchase made directly from packt don't require one.

6

Exploring the Coordinator, Worker, and Delegator Approach

In the previous chapter, we looked into the concepts of tool use and planning, which lay an essential foundation for intelligent agents to enhance their problem-solving capabilities. We explored various planning algorithms, including state space search techniques and **hierarchical task networks (HTNs)**, and examined how these algorithms can be seamlessly integrated with external tools and resources to enable agents to perform optimally.

Building upon this foundation, in this chapter, we will ground our understanding by exploring a powerful organizational framework for intelligent agents: the **coordinator-worker-delegator (CWD)** approach. This chapter is divided into the following main sections:

- Understanding the CWD model
- Designing agents with role assignments
- Communication and collaboration between agents
- Implementing the CWD approach in generative AI systems

By the end of this chapter, you will have a comprehensive understanding of how to design and implement multi-agent systems using the CWD approach. You'll know how to effectively assign roles to different agents, establish robust communication protocols between them, and orchestrate their interactions to tackle complex problems.

Technical requirements

You can find the code file for this chapter on GitHub at `https://github.com/PacktPublishing/Building-Agentic-AI-Systems`. In this chapter, we will also use the Python frameworks that we have already used in previous chapters to demonstrate the various aspects of the CWD approach and agent roles.

Understanding the CWD model

The CWD model is a comprehensive framework designed to facilitate the development of multi-agent systems, emphasizing collaboration, specialization, and effective distribution of tasks and resource management. Just as human organizations benefit from clear role delegation and hierarchical structures, intelligent agents can achieve greater effectiveness through thoughtful division of labor. The CWD framework, as shown in *Figure 6.1*, draws inspiration from organizational psychology and management theory, adapting proven principles of human coordination to the field of intelligent agents. This approach is particularly valuable as agent systems grow in complexity and need to handle increasingly intricate tasks that require multiple specialized capabilities working in concert. This model is particularly well suited for environments where autonomous agents must collaborate to achieve complex objectives that may be beyond the capabilities of a single agent.

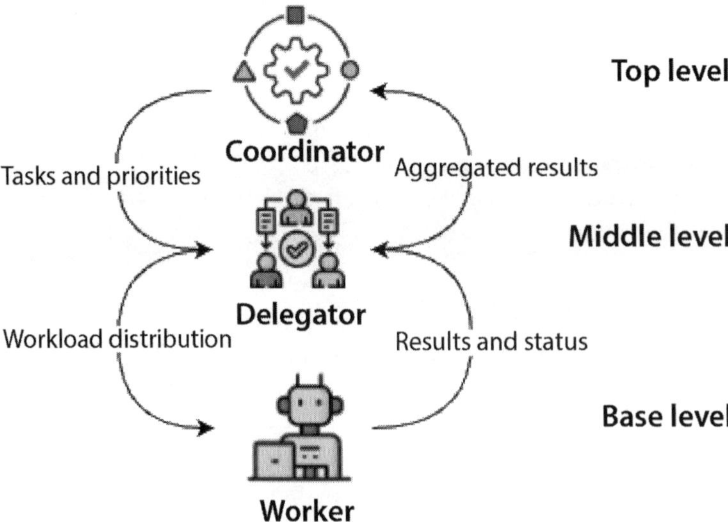

Figure 6.1 – The CWD model

The CWD model establishes three distinct roles that work together to accomplish complex tasks:

- **Coordinators**: Coordinators are agents responsible for managing tasks, resources, and the overall workflow of the system. Their primary responsibilities encompass facilitating progress monitoring, assigning tasks to appropriate agents, and enabling effective collaboration among workers. coordinators play a crucial role in ensuring smooth operations and keeping the system aligned with its objectives. They act as orchestrators, overseeing the entire process and coordinating the various components to work in harmony. Coordinators prioritize workloads by dynamically allocating tasks based on urgency, resource availability, and dependencies. They monitor progress, adjust assignments as needed, and ensure seamless collaboration among agents. By optimizing task distribution and workflow execution, they maintain system efficiency and alignment with overall objectives.

- **Workers**: Workers are specialized agents dedicated to carrying out specific tasks or functions within the system. These agents possess diverse capabilities and expertise, reflecting a broad range of skills that can be applied to various tasks. When assigned a task by the delegators, workers leverage their specialized knowledge and proficiency to efficiently realize the task's objectives. The diversity of worker agents allows for a division of labor and the allocation of tasks to the most suitable agents, optimizing the system's overall performance.

- **Delegators**: Delegators serve as intermediaries between coordinators and workers, responsible for implementing workload assignments to workers based on resource availability and system needs. They act as interfaces, facilitating the communication and coordination between the coordinators and workers. delegators play a crucial role in dispatching and balancing the workload across multiple workers, ensuring that tasks are assigned to the appropriate agents in a timely and efficient manner. The most critical function of delegators is optimizing overall performance by assigning tasks to the right workers at the right time, considering their capabilities and the system's constraints. Delegators optimize performance by balancing **throughput, latency**, and **resource utilization**. They ensure tasks are assigned efficiently to minimize delays (low latency), maximize completed tasks per unit time (high throughput), and prevent resource bottlenecks (optimal resource utilization). By dynamically adjusting assignments based on worker capacity and system constraints, they enhance overall efficiency and responsiveness.

The CWD model defines distinct roles—coordinators, workers, and delegators—that work together to enhance system efficiency and collaboration. By structuring task allocation, communication, and execution, it ensures operational harmony, driven by key principles that underpin its effectiveness.

Key principles of the CWD model

The CWD model is founded on several key principles that guide its design and implementation:

- **Separation of concerns**: The fundamental philosophy behind CWD is the clear separation of responsibilities between strategic planning (coordinator), resource management (delegator), and task execution (worker). This separation allows each component to focus on its core competencies while maintaining system flexibility and scalability.

- **Hierarchical organization**: The model implements a hierarchical structure that mirrors successful organizational patterns found in human institutions:

  - **Top level**: Strategic oversight and planning

  - **Middle level**: Resource management and coordination

  - **Base level**: Specialized task execution

- **Information flow and feedback loops**: The CWD model emphasizes bidirectional communication flows:

  - **Downward flow**: Task assignments, priorities, and constraints

  - **Upward flow**: Progress updates, results, and resource utilization

- **Adaptability and resilience**: The model is designed to be inherently adaptable through the following:

  - **Dynamic resource allocation**: Agents continuously assess workload demands and redistribute computational or operational resources in real time to optimize efficiency and prevent bottlenecks

  - **Fault tolerance through redundancy**: The system employs multiple agents with overlapping capabilities, allowing seamless handoff and recovery in case of failures, and ensuring uninterrupted operations

  - **Load balancing across agents**: Tasks are intelligently distributed among agents based on their availability, expertise, and current workload, preventing performance degradation and improving responsiveness

  - **Runtime role reassignment**: Agents can adapt their roles based on evolving system needs, stepping into different responsibilities as required to maintain workflow continuity and operational effectiveness

These mechanisms collectively enhance the system's ability to adapt, recover, and function efficiently, even in unpredictable conditions, ensuring sustained performance and reliability.

The CWD model's key principles ensure clarity, organization, and adaptability by defining roles, fostering hierarchy, and enabling robust communication. This structured approach enhances efficiency and resilience, making it versatile for various applications, including the development of an intelligent travel agent system.

The CWD model for the intelligent travel agent

As an example, let's discuss how the CWD model may be implemented for the intelligent travel agent system. The overall structure and flow may be as follows:

- **Coordinator agent**: This agent will act as the travel planning coordinator. This agent will be responsible for the following:

  - Managing the overall travel planning process based on a user request

  - Facilitating progress monitoring and effective collaboration among worker agents

  - Assigning tasks and coordinating the workflow based on the customer's travel requirements

- **Worker agents**: There can be a number of different agents, each specializing in its own domain and expertise within travel and hospitality management:

  - **Flight booking worker**: Specialized in searching for and booking flight options based on travel dates, destinations, and preferences

  - **Hotel booking worker**: Focused on finding and reserving suitable accommodations based on location, amenities, and customer preferences

  - **Activity planning worker**: Responsible for researching and planning activities, tours, and experiences at the travel destination, tailored to the customer's interests

  - **Transportation worker**: Specialized in arranging ground transportation, such as rental cars, airport transfers, or local transportation options

- **Delegator agent**: This agent will act as the travel task delegator agent. This agent performs the following:

  - Acts as an interface between the travel planning coordinator and the specialized worker agents

  - Receives travel planning tasks from the coordinator

  - Assesses the capabilities and availability of worker agents

  - Assigns appropriate tasks to the suitable worker agents based on their expertise and workload

  - Coordinates and balances the workload among the worker agents

Figure 6.2 depicts an extension and adaptation of our previous high-level CWD model diagram to this travel planning scenario:

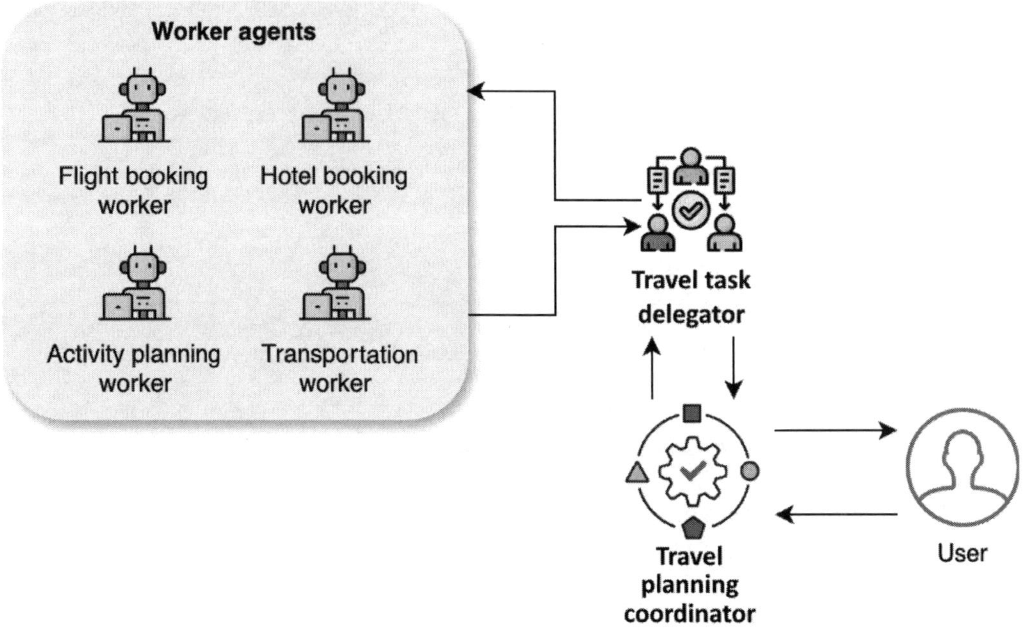

Figure 6.2 – The CWD model for the travel planner

Let's walk through an example of the user requirement and workflow:

1. A user approaches the intelligent travel agent system with their travel requirements, such as destination, travel dates, budget, and preferences (for example, family-friendly, cultural experiences, and beach vacation).

2. The travel planning coordinator analyzes the customer's requirements and breaks down the overall travel planning task into subtasks. This is where the task decomposition happens, as we learned about in the previous chapter.

3. The coordinator communicates these subtasks to the travel task delegator.

4. The delegator assesses the available worker agents and assigns tasks accordingly.

5. The worker agents collaborate and coordinate with each other as needed, sharing relevant information and ensuring a cohesive travel plan.

6. The delegator monitors the progress of the tasks and ensures workload balance among the worker agents.

7. Once all the tasks are completed, the worker agents submit their respective outputs (for example, flight bookings, hotel reservations, activity itineraries, and transportation arrangements) to the delegator.

8. The delegator compiles and integrates the outputs from the worker agents into a comprehensive travel plan.

9. The travel planning coordinator reviews the final travel plan, makes any necessary adjustments, and presents it to the customer for approval.

In this example, we've seen how the CWD model can be effectively applied to create a sophisticated travel planning system. The model demonstrates how complex tasks can be broken down and managed efficiently through specialized agents, each handling specific aspects of the travel planning process. This approach not only ensures thorough coverage of all travel requirements but also maintains clear communication channels and responsibility allocation throughout the planning process. By structuring the system this way, we can handle multiple travel requests simultaneously while maintaining quality and attention to detail for each customer's unique needs.

For those interested in implementing this system, the complete code implementation, including detailed examples and documentation, can be found in the `Chapter_06.ipynb` Python notebook in the GitHub repository. This code sample uses many of the concepts of tool and planning to implement the CWD travel planner. It also utilizes popular frameworks such as CrewAI and AutoGen.

In this section, we've explored the CWD model, a framework that mirrors effective human organizational practices to build scalable, efficient, and collaborative multi-agent systems. This model's emphasis on role delineation, adaptability, and structured communication ensures that it can manage complex, multi-faceted tasks such as travel planning seamlessly. Understanding this model is essential, as it provides a foundation for designing intelligent agent systems capable of handling specialized roles while working in concert to achieve overarching goals.

In the next section, we will dive deeper into the principles of agent design, focusing on how assigning roles and responsibilities can optimize system performance and align agent behavior with specific objectives. This builds directly on the CWD framework, equipping you with practical tools to create intelligent systems tailored to diverse real-world applications.

Designing agents with role assignments

In the context of the CWD model, designing agents with appropriate role assignments is crucial for ensuring the effective functioning of a multi-agent system. Careful consideration must be given to the specific roles and contributions of each agent toward achieving the overall system objectives. This is perhaps very easily explained using CrewAI agents, which can be initialized with a role, a goal, and a backstory.

When designing these agents, the role definition serves as the foundation for their behavior and responsibilities within the system. The role explicitly defines what the agent is supposed to do and how it fits into the larger system architecture. For instance, a coordinator agent might be assigned the role of *Strategic Planning Manager*, which immediately establishes their authority in overseeing and directing the overall workflow.

Equally important is the backstory, which provides depth and context to how the agent approaches its responsibilities. The backstory isn't just a biography – it's a carefully crafted narrative that shapes the agent's decision-making process and interaction style. Consider a coordinator agent with a backstory of *"A veteran project manager who has successfully led diverse teams in Silicon Valley start-ups, known for balancing innovation with practical execution."* This backstory naturally influences how the agent makes decisions, communicates with other agents, and approaches problem-solving. It's important to note that this backstory is a CrewAI-specific implementation and CrewAI merges this backstory along with the role in the LLM's system prompt, which helps set the context for the model. Here's an example with CrewAI:

```
coordinator = Agent(
    role="Strategic Planning Manager",
    backstory="A veteran project manager who has successfully led
               diverse teams in Silicon Valley startups, known for
               balancing innovation with practical execution. Expertise
               in bridging communication gaps between technical and
               non-technical teams while maintaining focus on key
               deliverables.",
    verbose=True
)
```

The combination of role and backstory creates a more nuanced and effective agent that can operate within the complex dynamics of a multi-agent system while maintaining a clear purpose and direction. Within CWD-based systems, several typical agent roles can be identified, as follows:

- **Manager**: The Manager agent is responsible for monitoring the system's operations, managing resources, and ensuring timely task completion. Manager agents are synonymous with **coordinators** in the CWD model. Managers play a critical role in overseeing the entire system and ensuring its overall effectiveness. In the context of an intelligent travel agent system, the Manager agent could be responsible for tasks such as the following:

  - Monitoring the progress of travel planning processes

  - Allocating resources (for example, computational resources and access to external APIs) to other agents

  - Ensuring that travel plans are generated within specified time constraints

- **Analyst**: The Analyst agent possesses expertise in analyzing data and providing insights and recommendations based on its findings. These agents can inform and guide decision-making processes within the system. In the travel agent scenario, an Analyst agent could be employed for the following:

  - Analyzing customer preferences and travel trends

  - Providing recommendations for popular destinations or activities based on data analysis

- Identifying potential cost-saving opportunities or optimal travel routes

- Summarizing outcomes and recommendations for the user

- **Reflector**: The Reflector agent observes the system's performance and identifies areas for improvement. By continuously monitoring the system's operations, the Reflector can suggest changes or adjustments that would enhance efficiency and effectiveness. In the travel agent context, a Reflector agent could do the following:

  - Analyze customer feedback and satisfaction levels

  - Identify bottlenecks or inefficiencies in the travel planning process

  - Propose improvements to the system's algorithms or workflows

- **Searcher**: The Searcher agent explores the problem space, constantly seeking new solutions and sharing relevant information with other agents. This role often involves innovation, as the Searcher adapts the system to cope with novel situations. In the travel agent domain, a Searcher agent could do the following:

  - Discover new travel destinations or activities

  - Explore alternative transportation options or travel routes

  - Share information about emerging travel trends or regulations with other agents

  Note that the Analyst, Reflector, and Searcher roles fit squarely under **workers** in the CWD model.

- **Task Interpreter**: The Task Interpreter agent serves as a bridge between the coordinators and workers, mapping high-level tasks into lower-level, concrete, and performable actions for the worker agents. This role ensures that tasks are well defined and understood by the workers. Task interpreters are synonymous with **delegators** in the CWD model. In the travel agent system, a task interpreter agent could do the following:

  - Break down a customer's travel request into specific subtasks (for example, flight booking, hotel reservation, or activity planning)

  - Translate the customer's preferences into actionable tasks for the worker agents

  - Ensure that the tasks assigned to the worker agents are clear and unambiguous

The concept of multi-agent systems isn't new, and neither is role assignment – in fact, a study was done more than a decade ago by Kazík (2010) (`https://physics.mff.cuni.cz/wds/proc/pdf10/WDS10_103_i1_Kazik.pdf`), which comprehensively explored role-based approaches in multi-agent system development. The study highlighted how roles serve as abstract representations of stereotypical behavior common to different agent classes, providing interfaces through which agents obtain knowledge of and affect their environment. The study highlighted how roles serve as abstract representations of stereotypical behavior common to different agent classes, providing interfaces through which agents obtain knowledge of and affect their environment. While these foundational concepts were initially developed for traditional multi-agent systems, they provide valuable insights for designing modern LLM-based agent systems.

The key principles of role-based modeling – including separation of interaction logic from inner algorithmic logic, dynamic role assignment, and modular system organization – are particularly relevant as we design collaborative LLM agents that need to coordinate effectively while maintaining clear responsibilities and interaction patterns. By assigning specific roles to agents based on their capabilities and the system's requirements, designers can achieve a role-based abstraction that supports the separation of concerns and allows for modular and reusable design in multi-agent systems. For example, in the intelligent travel agent system, agents could be assigned roles such as coordinator, worker, delegator, and so on.

Roles and responsibilities of each agent

Here is an overview of the roles and responsibilities of each agent within our intelligent travel planning multi-agent system, and how they collectively work toward achieving the system's objectives.

- **Travel planning agent (coordinator)**: This agent functions as the strategic overseer of the entire travel planning operation. With expertise in project management and travel coordination, they break down customer requests into manageable components, establish timelines, and ensure all aspects of travel planning align with customer expectations. They maintain a holistic view of each travel plan, ensuring all elements work together cohesively while managing contingencies and adjusting plans as needed.

    To better understand how the CWD model applies to real-world scenarios, consider the example of a travel planning agent functioning as the coordinator, as shown in the following snippet. This agent oversees the travel planning process, ensuring all components of the plan align with customer expectations while managing resources and contingencies effectively. To illustrate the functionality of core travel worker agents in the CWD model, the following example snippet showcases their specialized roles and expertise. Each agent contributes to the seamless execution of specific travel planning tasks:

```
coordinator = Agent(
    role="Travel Planning Executive",
    backstory="A seasoned travel industry veteran with 15 years
of experience in luxury travel planning and project management.
Known for orchestrating seamless multi-destination trips for
high-profile clients and managing complex itineraries across
different time zones and cultures. Expert in crisis management
and adaptive planning.",
    goals=["Ensure cohesive travel plans", "Maintain high
customer satisfaction", "Optimize resource allocation"]
)
```

- **Core travel worker agents**: These agents comprise the following roles:

  - **Flight booking worker**: This agent specializes in navigating the complex world of airline reservations, understanding fare classes, routing rules, and alliance partnerships. It stays updated on airline schedules, pricing trends, and booking policies while maintaining relationships with airline representatives for special requests or problem resolution, as shown in the following snippet:

```python
flight_specialist = Agent(
    role="Aviation Booking Specialist",
    backstory="Former airline revenue management expert with
deep knowledge of global aviation networks. Skilled in finding
optimal flight combinations and hidden fare opportunities. Has
handled over 10,000 flight bookings across all major airlines
and alliances.",
    goals=["Secure optimal flight arrangements", "Maximize value
for money", "Ensure booking accuracy"]
)
```

  - **Hotel booking worker**: An expert in global hospitality, this agent understands hotel categories, room types, and amenity offerings across different markets. It maintains extensive knowledge of hotel loyalty programs, seasonal pricing patterns, and special promotional offers, as displayed in the following snippet:

```python
hotel_specialist = Agent(
    role="Hospitality Accommodation Expert",
    backstory="Previous luxury hotel chain executive with
extensive connections in the hospitality industry. Expert in
boutique hotels and major chains alike, with deep knowledge of
room categories, seasonal trends, and upgrade opportunities
across global markets.",
    goals=["Find perfect accommodation matches", "Secure best
available rates", "Ensure special requests are met"]
)
```

  - **Activity planning worker**: This agent combines deep cultural knowledge with practical experience in tour operations. It excels at matching activities to traveler interests and abilities while considering factors such as seasonal availability, local customs, and logistical constraints, as highlighted in the following snippet:

```python
activity_planner = Agent(
    role="Destination Experience Curator",
    backstory="Professional tour guide turned experience
designer with expertise in creating memorable travel moments.
Has lived in 5 continents and personally vetted thousands of
local experiences. Specialist in combining cultural authenticity
with traveler comfort.",
```

```
        goals=["Create engaging itineraries", "Balance activities
and free time", "Ensure cultural authenticity"]
)
```

- **Transportation worker**: This agent focuses on ground logistics and local transportation solutions. It understands various transportation options across different destinations, from private car services to public transportation systems, as shown in the following snippet:

```
transport_coordinator = Agent(
    role="Ground Transportation Logistics Specialist",
    backstory="Former urban mobility consultant with extensive
experience in transportation systems worldwide. Expert in
coordinating seamless transfers and creating reliable ground
transportation plans across diverse global locations.",
    goals=["Ensure reliable transfers", "Optimize local
transportation", "Maintain backup options"]
)
```

- **Analysis and intelligence worker agents**: In these agents, we have the following roles:

- **Travel data analyst worker**: This agent focuses on transforming raw travel data into actionable insights. It analyzes booking patterns, customer preferences, and market trends to inform decision-making and enhance travel recommendations, as shown here:

```
analyst = Agent(
    role="Travel Intelligence Specialist",
    backstory="Data scientist with deep expertise in travel
industry analytics. Previously led data science initiatives at
major online travel platforms. Developed predictive models for
travel trends and customer behavior that increased customer
satisfaction scores by 25%. Expert in combining quantitative
analysis with qualitative travel insights.",
    goals=["Generate actionable insights", "Identify travel
trends", "Optimize customer matching"]
)
```

- **Travel experience worker (Reflector)**: This agent acts as the system's quality assurance and continuous improvement specialist. It analyzes feedback, monitors performance, and suggests systemic improvements to enhance the travel planning experience, as shown here:

```
reflector = Agent(
    role="Travel Experience Optimization Expert",
    backstory="Customer experience strategist with background in
both luxury hospitality and digital transformation. Pioneered
feedback analysis systems that revolutionized service delivery
in major hotel chains. Passionate about creating memorable
travel experiences through systematic improvements.",
```

```
        goals=["Analyze customer feedback", "Identify improvement
areas", "Enhance service quality"]
    )
```

- **Travel opportunity worker (Searcher)**: This agent functions as the system's explorer and innovator, constantly seeking new destinations, unique experiences, and emerging travel opportunities that could enhance the service offering, as shown here:

```
searcher = Agent(
    role="Travel Discovery Specialist",
    backstory="Former travel journalist and destination
researcher with a network spanning 100+ countries. Has uncovered
numerous hidden gems and emerging destinations that became major
travel trends. Combines deep cultural understanding with a
keen eye for unique travel opportunities. Expert in identifying
experiences that match evolving traveler preferences.",
    goals=["Discover unique opportunities", "Identify emerging
destinations", "Expand service offerings"]
    )
```

- **Delegator agent**: The critical link between strategy and execution, this agent excels at task prioritization and resource allocation. They understand each worker agent's capabilities and current workload, ensuring optimal task distribution and workflow management, as shown here:

```
delegator = Agent(
    role="Travel Operations Orchestrator",
    backstory="Experienced project manager with a background
in both travel operations and workflow optimization. Known for
exceptional ability to match tasks with the right expertise and
maintain balanced workloads across teams. Previously managed
large-scale travel operations for Fortune 500 companies.",
    goals=["Optimize task distribution", "Maintain workflow
efficiency", "Ensure quality standards"]
    )
```

So far, this structured role-based agent approach creates a well-defined hierarchy with clear responsibilities while maintaining flexibility for handling complex travel planning scenarios. Each agent's role and backstory provide depth and context to their function within the larger system, enabling more natural and effective interactions. Let's define the Manager, Analyst, Reflector, and Searcher agents. *Figure 6.3* is a further adaptation of our CWD model with role-based agents for the travel planning system:

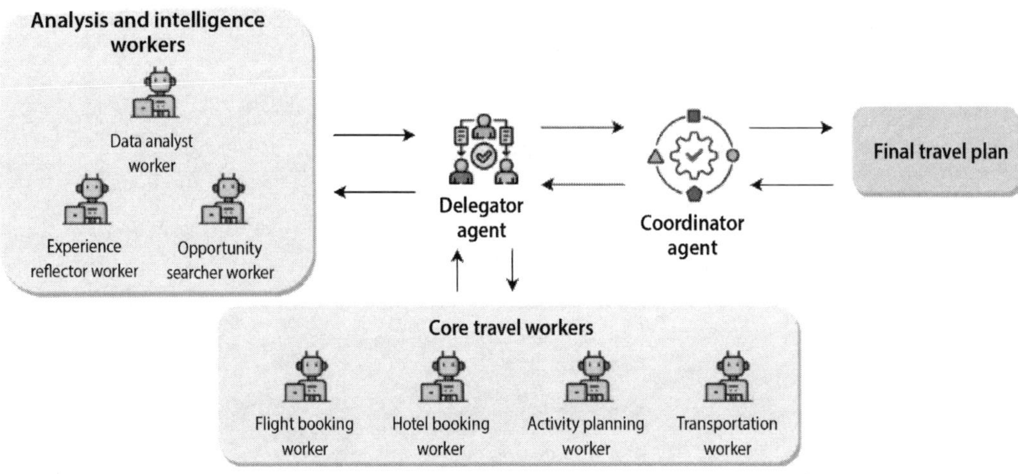

Figure 6.3 – Role-based agents within the CWD model for travel planner

Let's examine how our travel planning multi-agent system orchestrates a seamless journey from initial customer request to final travel plan. The system leverages a hierarchical structure where the coordinator agent provides strategic oversight, the delegator agent manages task distribution, and specialized worker agents execute both core travel tasks and analytical functions in parallel. This coordinated workflow demonstrates the practical application of the CWD model, enabling efficient and intelligent travel planning through clear role definition and effective collaboration. Here's the breakdown of the steps:

1. **Initial request and planning**:

    I.   The customer submits their travel requirements to the system.

    II.   The coordinator agent analyzes these requirements and develops a strategic plan.

2. **Task distribution**:

    I.   The coordinator agent passes the strategic plan to the delegator agent.

    II.   The delegator agent breaks down the plan into specific tasks for both core and analysis workers.

3. **Parallel processing (core travel tasks)**: The delegator agent assigns specialized tasks to core travel workers, as follows:

    *   The **flight booking worker** searches for and reserves optimal flights

    *   The **hotel booking worker** identifies and books suitable accommodations

    *   The **activity planning worker** creates an itinerary of experiences

    *   The **transportation worker** arranges ground transport solutions

4. **Parallel processing (analysis and intelligence)**: Simultaneously, the delegator agent engages analysis workers, as follows:

    - The **data analyst worker** processes customer data and travel patterns

    - The **experience reflector worker** reviews similar past itineraries

    - The **opportunity searcher worker** identifies unique options/alternatives

5. **Integration and refinement**:

    I.   All workers submit their outputs back to the delegator agent.

    II.   The delegator agent consolidates the information.

    III. The coordinator agent receives the consolidated plan.

6. **Final review and delivery**:

    I.   The coordinator agent reviews and optimizes the complete travel plan.

    II.   The final travel plan is presented to the customer.

This flow showcases the collaboration between the various agent roles, leveraging their specialized expertise and contributions to generate a personalized and optimized travel plan for the customer. Each agent plays a specific role, and their outputs are consolidated and integrated by the Manager agent (travel operations manager) and the coordinator agent (travel planning coordinator) to deliver the final travel plan.

By carefully designing agents with well-defined roles, the CWD-based multi-agent system can effectively collaborate, leverage specialized expertise, and distribute tasks efficiently, ultimately delivering personalized and optimized travel plans tailored to customer requirements. However, the success of such a sophisticated multi-agent system heavily depends on how these agents communicate and interact with each other. Let's explore how effective communication and collaboration are achieved between these agents in the next section.

Communication and collaboration between agents

In multi-agent systems based on the CWD model, effective communication and collaboration among agents are crucial for achieving successful outcomes. Agents need to be capable of sharing information, coordinating their actions, and behaving cooperatively to work toward common goals. Communication and collaboration in CWD-based systems involve the key aspects as discussed in the following subsections.

Communication

Agents should follow well-defined protocols for their interactions, including the format of messages and interaction patterns. These protocols ensure that agents can understand each other clearly and act appropriately. For example, in a travel agent system, the agents may employ a standardized message format and communication protocol to exchange information about flight options, hotel availability, or customer preferences. By adhering to these protocols, agents can effectively communicate and interpret messages from other agents, enabling seamless collaboration.

The agents in the example travel agent system can follow a standardized communication protocol, such as the FIPA **Agent Communication Language** (**ACL**), to exchange messages and information. For instance, when the hotel booking worker agent needs to communicate with the flight booking worker agent to coordinate travel dates, it can send a message in the FIPA ACL format, specifying the content (for example, requested travel dates), the sender (hotel booking worker), and the recipient (flight booking worker).

Coordination mechanism

Coordinators play a vital role in establishing mechanisms for coordination that align the activities of worker agents with the overall objectives of the system. These coordination mechanisms allow for the control of dependencies and ensure that tasks are completed within the required timeframes. In the context of a travel agent system, the travel planning coordinator agent could implement a coordination mechanism that involves task prioritization, resource allocation, and progress monitoring to ensure that the travel planning process proceeds smoothly and efficiently.

The travel planning coordinator agent can implement a coordination mechanism to align the activities of the worker agents with the overall travel planning objectives. For example, it could employ a task prioritization mechanism based on customer preferences or travel dates. If a customer prioritizes finding suitable accommodations first, the coordinator agent can instruct the delegator agent to assign the hotel booking worker agent a higher priority than the other worker agents. Additionally, the coordinator agent can monitor the progress of each worker agent and reallocate resources or adjust priorities as needed to ensure timely task completion.

Negotiation and conflict resolution

In complex multi-agent systems, there may be cases where the goals or actions of different agents conflict with one another. To address such situations, agents should be equipped with negotiation strategies or mechanisms for conflict resolution. These strategies help maintain harmony in the working environment by facilitating compromise or reaching mutually acceptable solutions. For instance, if multiple worker agents in a travel agent system propose conflicting activity plans or transportation options, a negotiation mechanism could be employed to resolve the conflict based on predefined criteria or by involving the coordinator agent for mediation.

Suppose the activity planning worker agent and the transportation worker agent propose conflicting plans for a particular day of the trip. The activity planning worker agent might have scheduled a full-day tour, while the transportation worker agent has arranged for a rental car to be available for the entire day. In such a scenario, a negotiation mechanism can be employed to resolve the conflict. The delegator agent could act as a mediator, gathering the conflicting plans from both worker agents and proposing alternative solutions, such as rescheduling the tour or modifying the rental car reservation. If a resolution cannot be reached, the coordinator agent can intervene and make a final decision based on predefined criteria or customer preferences.

Knowledge sharing

Agents should have the capability to share knowledge, insights, and findings from their research or experiences with other agents in the system. This knowledge-sharing facilitates continuous learning and adaptation, enabling the system to improve its overall performance over time. In the travel agent context, the travel data analyst agent could share insights derived from customer preference analysis with other agents, enabling them to make more informed decisions. Similarly, the travel opportunity searcher agent could share information about new travel destinations or emerging trends, allowing the system to stay up-to-date and adapt its offerings accordingly.

The travel data analyst agent can analyze customer preferences, travel trends, and feedback from past trips to generate insights and recommendations. These insights can be shared with other agents in the system to improve their decision-making processes. For example, the travel data analyst agent might identify a growing trend for eco-friendly travel options and share this information with the activity planning worker agent and the transportation worker agent. These agents can then adjust their offerings to include more sustainable activities and transportation options, reflecting the changing customer preferences. The travel opportunity searcher agent may continuously explore new travel destinations, unique experiences, or emerging travel trends. This agent can share its findings with other agents, enabling them to incorporate these new opportunities into their respective planning processes. For instance, if the travel opportunity searcher agent discovers a newly opened eco-resort in a popular destination, it can share this information with the hotel booking worker agent and the activity planning worker agent, allowing them to consider this new option when generating hotel recommendations and activity plans.

The CWD model's role-based approach establishes clear boundaries for communication channels and agent responsibilities. By implementing well-defined protocols for communication, coordination, and knowledge sharing, the system harnesses its agents' collective intelligence to deliver adaptable and efficient travel planning services. This structured collaboration enables the system to tackle complex challenges while continuously improving its performance over time.

While this section has outlined the theoretical framework for communication and collaboration in our CWD-based travel planning system, the practical implementation requires careful consideration of technical aspects. This section has provided a comprehensive exploration of the foundational aspects of communication and collaboration within multi-agent systems guided by the CWD model. By adhering to well-defined communication protocols, establishing robust coordination mechanisms, and fostering effective knowledge sharing, such systems are equipped to handle complex, dynamic scenarios.

The next section transitions from these foundational concepts to a deeper exploration of practical methodologies. It focuses on implementing the CWD approach in generative AI systems, detailing advanced techniques such as state space management, environment modeling, memory systems, and handling LLM contexts to bring these theoretical concepts to life in real-world applications.

Implementing the CWD approach in generative AI systems

While we've explored how the CWD model maps to LLM-based agents and discussed role adaptations for our travel planning system, implementing this approach in generative AI systems requires careful attention to several technical considerations. The transition from traditional multi-agent systems to LLM-based implementations brings unique challenges and opportunities. LLMs, with their natural language understanding and generation capabilities, offer new ways to implement agent behaviors and interactions but also require specific architectural considerations to maintain the structured approach of the CWD model.

In traditional multi-agent systems, behaviors and interactions are typically programmed explicitly through code. However, in LLM-based implementations, these aspects are primarily controlled through carefully crafted prompts and interaction patterns. This fundamental difference requires us to adapt the CWD model's principles to work effectively with the nature of LLMs while maintaining the clear role boundaries and hierarchical structure we've discussed.

Before diving into the technical details that will be covered in the next chapter, let's examine three key implementation considerations that form the foundation of any LLM-based CWD system. These considerations – system prompts, instruction formatting, and interaction patterns – are essential for translating our theoretical model into a practical, functioning system.

System prompts and agent behavior

System prompts act as the fundamental configuration layer for LLM agents, defining their core characteristics and operational parameters. Unlike regular prompts that provide task-specific instructions, system prompts establish an agent's persistent traits, boundaries, and behavioral frameworks throughout its operational life cycle. In our travel planning system, each agent's system prompt must encompass the following:

- Role definition and scope of responsibilities
- Constraints and operational boundaries

- Communication protocols with other agents

- Decision-making frameworks specific to their role

For example, the flight booking worker's system prompt would include specific instructions about flight search parameters, pricing considerations, and airline partnerships, while the Coordinator's system prompt would focus on high-level planning and oversight capabilities.

We saw earlier how LLM agent frameworks such as CrewAI structure system prompts through `role` and `backstory` definitions. The `role` component defines the agent's functional boundaries and responsibilities, while `backstory` provides the context and expertise that shapes how the agent approaches these responsibilities. Together, they create a rich system prompt that guides the agent's behavior and decision-making process. For instance, an agent's role might be an *aviation booking specialist*, while its backstory as a *"former airline revenue management expert with deep knowledge of global aviation networks"* helps it make more nuanced decisions about routing and pricing options.

Instruction formatting

Clear and consistent instruction formatting ensures reliable agent performance and effective inter-agent communication. This becomes particularly crucial in LLM-based systems where instructions are interpreted through natural language understanding. Key aspects of instruction formatting include the following:

- **Input structuring**: Standardized formats for task assignments and requests. For example, the following structured input format ensures the flight booking worker receives unambiguous search parameters, with clear specifications for departure and destination locations along with desired travel dates:

```
{
  "task_type": "flight_search",
  "parameters": {
    "departure": "location",
    "destination": "location",
    "dates": "date_range"
  }
}
```

- **Output templates**: Consistent response structures that other agents can reliably parse. The standardized output format allows agents to quickly identify the task status and access relevant information. The `options` array might contain available flights, while `recommendations` could include preferred choices based on customer preferences:

```
{
  "status": "completed/failed",
  "result": {
```

```
            "options": [...],
            "recommendations": [...],
            "constraints": [...]
        }
    }
```

- **Communication protocols**: Clear formats for inter-agent messages and status updates. These protocols ensure transparent communication between agents, with clear identification of message type, sender, and recipient, along with structured content that can be easily processed:

```
    {
      "message_type": "update",
      "sender": "flight_booking_worker",
      "recipient": "coordinator",
      "content": {
        "progress": "in_progress",
        "completion": "60%",
        "pending_tasks": [...]
      }
    }
```

Interaction patterns

The success of a CWD-based system heavily depends on well-defined interaction patterns between agents. In an LLM-based implementation, these patterns must account for the unique characteristics of language model interactions. Essential interaction patterns include the following:

- **Message passing protocols**:

  - Structured formats for agent-to-agent communication

  - Clear handoff procedures between different processing stages

  - Error handling and recovery mechanisms

- **State management**:

  - How agents maintain awareness of their current task status

  - Methods for tracking progress through multi-step processes

  - Coordination of parallel activities

- **Feedback loops:**

  - How agents communicate success/failure

  - Methods for requesting clarification or additional information

  - Mechanisms for continuous improvement through interaction history

Summary

In this chapter, we explored the CWD model as a framework for designing effective multi-agent systems. Starting with the foundational concepts from early role-based research, we saw how these principles adapt perfectly to modern LLM-based agent architectures. We examined this through a practical travel planning system, where different agents – from flight bookers to activity planners – work together under a clear hierarchical organization. Key takeaways highlight the importance of well-defined roles and responsibilities within multi-agent systems, ensuring that each agent operates with clarity and purpose. They emphasize how specialized worker agents collaborate effectively under the oversight of coordinators, who align their efforts with overarching goals. Delegators play a crucial role in managing tasks and facilitating smooth workflow distribution. Additionally, the chapter underscored the significance of effective communication and collaboration patterns, which are essential for seamless information exchange and cooperative behavior among agents. Finally, implementation considerations such as designing system prompts and formatting instructions are critical for operational success, ensuring clarity and consistency in agent interactions.

This structured approach to agent design enables complex tasks to be broken down and executed efficiently while maintaining clear lines of communication and responsibility. Our travel planning example demonstrated how theoretical concepts translate into practical applications.

In the next chapter, we will dive deeper and explore how we can effectively design agents in real life.

Questions

1. Explain how the CWD model enhances the efficiency of multi-agent systems, using the travel planning system as an example.

2. What is the significance of "role" and "backstory" in LLM agent design, and how do they contribute to system prompts? Provide an example.

3. Compare and contrast the core travel workers with analysis and intelligence workers in the travel planning system. How do their functions complement each other?

4. Describe the key aspects of communication and collaboration in a CWD-based system, including protocols, coordination mechanisms, and knowledge sharing.

5. How does instruction formatting contribute to effective agent communication in an LLM-based system? Explain with examples of input and output structures.

Answers

1. The CWD model enhances efficiency by creating a clear hierarchical structure where the coordinator provides strategic oversight, the delegator manages task distribution, and specialized workers execute specific functions. In the travel planning system, this allows for parallel processing of tasks – while core travel workers handle bookings and arrangements, analysis workers simultaneously process data and search for opportunities. This structured approach ensures efficient task completion while maintaining clear lines of responsibility and communication.

2. Roles and backstories are crucial components in LLM agent design that form the system prompt. The role defines an agent's functional boundaries and responsibilities (for example, aviation booking specialist), while the backstory provides context and expertise that shapes decision-making (for example, *"former airline revenue management expert with deep knowledge of global aviation networks"*). Together, they create a rich system prompt that guides the agent's behavior and interaction patterns. For example, the flight booking worker's role and backstory enable it to make sophisticated decisions about routing and pricing based on its "experience" in airline operations.

3. Core travel workers (flight, hotel, activity, and transportation workers) handle the practical aspects of travel arrangements, making bookings, and confirming reservations. In contrast, analysis and intelligence workers (data analyst, experience reflector, and opportunity searcher) provide strategic support by analyzing trends, processing feedback, and identifying new opportunities. While core workers execute immediate tasks, analysis workers enhance the system's decision-making capabilities and future performance through data-driven insights and continuous improvement.

4. Communication and collaboration in CWD systems involve several key components: standardized communication protocols (such as FIPA ACL) ensure clear message exchange between agents; coordination mechanisms allow the coordinator to manage dependencies and timelines; negotiation strategies help resolve conflicts between agents (such as conflicting activity and transportation plans); and knowledge sharing enables continuous system improvement through shared insights and experiences. These elements work together to create a cohesive and efficient multi-agent system.

5. Instruction formatting in LLM-based systems ensures reliable agent communication through structured input/output patterns. This standardized formatting ensures unambiguous communication between agents, clear task specifications, and easily parseable results, contributing to the system's overall efficiency and reliability.

Subscribe to AI_Distilled, the go-to newsletter for AI professionals

To keep up with the latest developments in the fields of Generative AI and LLMs, subscribe to our weekly newsletter, AI_Distilled, at `https://packt.link/80z6Y`.

7

Effective Agentic System Design Techniques

In the previous chapter, we explored the **coordinator-worker-delegator** (**CWD**) model, a robust foundation for multi-agent system design that emphasizes cooperation and division of labor. We delved into the three distinct roles – coordinators, workers, and delegators – and discussed the intricate details of their interactions and contributions to effective task distribution.

This chapter begins by establishing the importance of system prompts and focused instructions as the foundation of agent behavior. It then explores the critical concepts of state space representation and environment modeling that agents operate within. The chapter proceeds to examine agent memory architectures and context management strategies, essential for maintaining coherent agent behavior across interactions. Finally, it covers advanced workflow patterns, including sequential and parallel processing approaches for LLM-based agent systems. This chapter is divided into four main sections:

- Focused system prompts and instructions for agents

- State spaces and environment modeling

- Agent memory architecture and context management

- Sequential and parallel processing in agentic workflows

By the end of this chapter, you will have gained a comprehensive understanding of how to design robust, scalable, and effective agentic systems that can handle complex tasks while maintaining consistent behavior and performance.

Technical requirements

You can find the code files for this chapter on GitHub at `https://github.com/PacktPublishing/Building-Agentic-AI-Systems`.

Focused system prompts and instructions for agents

Focused instruction plays a crucial role in directing the actions of an intelligent agent. It lays down the objective of the agent, its constraints, and the operating context. The clarity and explicitness of these instructions often significantly influence the agent's performance in achieving its intended goals.

Defining objectives

Defining clear objectives is a critical aspect of focused instruction for intelligent agents. Well-defined objectives serve as the foundation from which an agent's intended functions and behaviors are derived, guiding its actions and decision-making processes toward achieving specific goals.

To put this into perspective, let's continue our discussion with the example of our intelligent travel agent placed in a customer service role. The objective would be to maximize customer satisfaction by providing personalized travel solutions and resolving any queries or issues effectively. This overarching objective encompasses several key components:

- **Personalization**: The travel agent must tailor its recommendations and solutions to the unique preferences, budgets, and requirements of each individual customer. This involves gathering detailed information about the customer's travel goals, interests, and constraints and using this knowledge to craft customized itineraries and experiences.

- **Problem-solving**: In addition to planning travel arrangements, the agent should be equipped to address any queries, concerns, or issues that may arise throughout the customer's journey. This could involve resolving booking conflicts, providing guidance on travel advisories, or offering alternative solutions in case of disruptions or changes in plans.

- **Effective communication**: Maximizing customer satisfaction requires the travel agent to communicate clearly and effectively, ensuring that customers understand the proposed solutions, potential trade-offs, and any relevant details or recommendations. Clear communication also involves active listening and interpreting customer feedback or concerns accurately.

- **Continuous improvement**: By closely monitoring customer satisfaction levels and gathering feedback, the travel agent can iteratively refine its capabilities and approach. This feedback loop allows the agent to identify areas for improvement, adapt to changing customer preferences or industry trends, and continuously enhance the quality of its solutions and service.

Having well-defined objectives provides a clear benchmark against which the agent's performance can be evaluated. In the case of the intelligent travel agent, metrics such as customer satisfaction ratings, successful resolution of queries or issues, and the overall quality of personalized travel plans can be used to assess the agent's effectiveness in achieving its primary objective. Additionally, these objectives guide the agent's decision-making processes, prioritizing actions and solutions that align with maximizing customer satisfaction while adhering to constraints such as budget, time, or logistical limitations. A sample may look like the following:

Objective: Act as an expert travel agent to provide personalized travel solutions while maximizing customer satisfaction.

Core functions:

- Gather and analyze travel preferences, constraints, and budget

- Create personalized travel recommendations and itineraries

- Resolve travel-related issues and provide alternatives

- Communicate clearly and professionally

- Monitor customer satisfaction and adapt accordingly

Constraints:

- Stay within stated budget

- Prioritize customer safety

- Follow travel regulations

- Respect booking deadlines

Behavior:

- Use clear, professional language

- Show empathy and patience

- Anticipate customer needs

- Provide transparent pricing

- Present options with pros/cons

- Document key requirements and deadlines

Task specifications

Detailed task specifications help intelligent agents with a clear understanding of their duties and responsibilities. By detailing the specific steps to follow, expected outputs, and potential challenges associated with a particular task, task specifications enable agents to operate effectively and efficiently. Continuing our intelligent travel agent example, task specifications are essential for ensuring that the agent can successfully navigate the various aspects of the travel planning process.

Here are a couple of examples of how task specifications can be defined for different components of the travel agent's responsibilities:

- Customer interaction and inquiry handling (steps are as follows):

    I.   Greet the customer.

    II.   Gather relevant information (travel preferences, budget, dates, etc.).

    III. Identify the nature of the inquiry or request.

    IV.   Provide appropriate responses or solutions.

    V.   Confirm customer satisfaction.

    - **Expected outputs**: Clear and concise responses to customer inquiries, personalized travel recommendations or itineraries, booking confirmations or updates.

    - **Potential challenges**:

        - Ambiguous or incomplete customer requests

        - Language barriers

        - Conflicting preferences or constraints

        - Handling emotional or dissatisfied customers.

- Flight and accommodation booking:

    - **Steps**: Search for available flights and accommodations based on customer preferences, compare options based on factors such as price, duration, amenities, and customer ratings, present the top choices to the customer, and confirm and book the selected options.

    - **Expected outputs**: Confirmed flight and hotel bookings, itinerary with travel details, invoices, or payment receipts.

    - **Potential challenges**: Limited availability, fluctuating prices, handling changes or cancellations, managing groups or special accommodations.

Providing detailed task specifications helps the intelligent travel agent understand the specific steps involved in each aspect of the travel planning process, the expected outputs or deliverables, and the potential challenges that may arise. This knowledge equips the agent with the necessary guidance to handle various situations effectively, anticipate and mitigate potential issues, and, ultimately, deliver a seamless and personalized travel experience for customers.

A sample task specification for the flight inquiry may look like the following:

1. Initial query:

    - Capture departure/arrival locations

    - Get preferred dates and time ranges

    - Note any special requirements (class, layovers, airlines)

    - Confirm budget constraints

2. Search process:

    - Search available flights matching criteria

    - Filter by price range and preferences

    - Sort by best match (price/duration/stops)

    - Check seat availability

3. Presentation:

    - Show the top three flight options

    - Display price, duration, and layovers

    - Highlight unique features/restrictions

    - Note cancellation policies

- Outputs:

    - Flight comparison summary

    - Booking confirmation

    - Travel advisory notices

Contextual awareness

Contextual awareness forms the backbone of intelligent agent behavior, enabling them to operate effectively within their designated environments and adapt to changing situations. This awareness extends beyond simple task execution – it encompasses understanding the environment, user needs, and situational nuances that influence decision-making. At its core, contextual awareness is about understanding and responding to the full scope of circumstances that surround any given interaction or decision point.

For our intelligent travel agent, contextual awareness manifests in several critical dimensions. Consider how the agent must maintain awareness of both global and local contexts – from international travel restrictions and seasonal weather patterns to specific hotel policies and local transportation options. This multi-layered awareness allows the agent to make informed decisions and provide personalized recommendations that truly serve the customer's needs. The following figure demonstrates how the different layers of contextual awareness might be integrated within an agentic system.

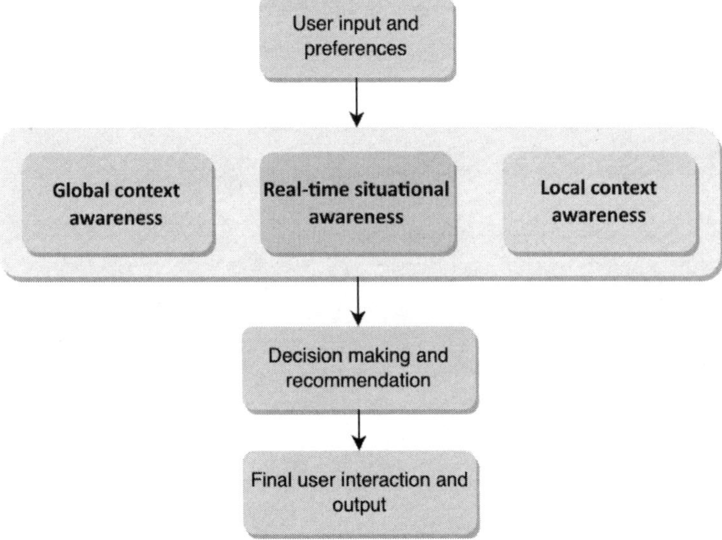

Figure 7.1 – Contextual awareness within an intelligent agentic system

The depth of contextual awareness can be illustrated through a few key examples from the travel domain:

- **Destination intelligence**: The agent maintains comprehensive knowledge of travel destinations, including peak seasons, local events, and cultural significance. When a customer expresses interest in visiting Japan, for instance, the agent doesn't just book flights – it considers cherry blossom seasons, major festivals, and regional weather patterns to suggest optimal travel dates and experiences.

- **Dynamic adaptation**: Contextual awareness enables real-time adaptation to changing circumstances. If a flight is canceled due to weather conditions, the agent doesn't simply relay this information – it immediately assesses alternative routes, considers the impact on subsequent bookings, and proposes solutions based on the customer's preferences and constraints.

- **Cultural competence**: Understanding cultural norms and local customs is crucial for providing meaningful travel recommendations. This might involve advising customers about appropriate dress codes for religious sites, suggesting restaurants that accommodate specific dietary restrictions, or recommending local customs that visitors should be aware of to ensure respectful interactions.

The agent can anticipate needs, avoid potential issues, and craft truly personalized travel experiences by integrating these aspects of contextual awareness. This goes beyond simple pattern matching – it requires a nuanced understanding of how different contextual elements interact and influence the overall travel experience. The true value of contextual awareness lies in its ability to transform standard service interactions into thoughtfully curated experiences. When an agent combines knowledge of destination specifics, customer preferences, and situational factors, it can deliver recommendations and solutions that feel both personal and practical.

State spaces and environment modeling

State spaces and environment modeling form the foundation of how intelligent agents perceive, understand, and interact with their operational context. This section explores the crucial aspects of designing and implementing effective state representations and environment models that enable agents to make informed decisions and maintain consistent behavior.

State space representation

State space representation defines how an agent maintains and updates its understanding of the current situation, available actions, and potential outcomes. A well-designed state space enables an agent to track relevant information while avoiding unnecessary complexity. For our intelligent travel agent example, the state space might include the following:

- **Customer profile state**:

    - Personal preferences and constraints

    - Travel history and feedback

    - Current interaction context

    - Budget parameters and flexibility

    - Special requirements or accommodations

- **Travel context state**:

    - Available flight options and pricing

    - Hotel availability and rates

    - Weather conditions and forecasts

    - Travel advisories and restrictions

    - Seasonal events and peak periods

- **Booking state**:

  - Reservation status and confirmations

  - Payment information and status

  - Cancellation policies and deadlines

  - Itinerary modifications and updates

  - Connection dependencies

The state space should be designed to capture both static and dynamic elements while maintaining efficiency. For instance, the agent might represent the flight booking state flight, hotel, and customer preferences as follows:

```
{
    "booking_id": "BK123456",
    "status": "confirmed",
    "components": {
        "flights": [{
            "status": "confirmed",
            "departure": "2024-05-15T10:00:00",
            "cancellation_deadline": "2024-05-01",
            "dependencies": ["hotel_check_in"]
        }],
        "hotels": [{
            "status": "pending",
            "check_in": "2024-05-15",
            "cancellation_policy": "48h_notice"
        }]
    },
    "customer_preferences": {
        "seat_type": "window",
        "meal_requirements": "vegetarian",
        "room_preferences": ["high_floor", "non_smoking"]
    }
}
```

The state consists of the status of the booking and the component of the itinerary such as flight status, hotel confirmation, as well as any other specific user preferences for the user.

While states provide the "moment in time" representation or knowledge about a specific task, the larger environment in which the environment operates is also critical. Such an environment often includes details of the tools the agent has access to, any specific policies or rules it needs to adhere to, and other details based on the specific use case. Let's discuss what environment modeling entails in the next section.

Environment modeling

Environment modeling is a critical component of intelligent agent design that involves creating a detailed representation of the world in which the agent operates. This representation serves as the agent's understanding of its operational context, encompassing everything from external systems it must interact with to real-world conditions that affect its decision-making. At its core, environment modeling addresses three fundamental questions:

- What systems and services can the agent interact with?
- What rules and constraints govern these interactions?
- What changing conditions must the agent monitor and respond to?

For instance, in our travel agent system, the environment model must represent the agent's connections to airline booking systems, hotel reservation platforms, and payment processors. It must also encode business rules about booking procedures and maintain awareness of dynamic factors such as price changes and availability. A well-designed environment model enables the agent to do the following:

- Make informed decisions based on current conditions
- Navigate complex systems and processes effectively
- Respond appropriately to changes in its operational context
- Maintain compliance with rules and regulations
- Optimize outcomes within given constraints

The environment model should capture both static rules that rarely change and dynamic elements that require constant monitoring. Let's understand the static and dynamic elements in detail:

- **Static environment elements**: Static elements represent the unchanging aspects of the environment that govern the agent's operation:

  - **Business rules and constraints**:

    - Booking policies and procedures
    - Payment processing requirements
    - Cancellation and modification rules
    - Service level agreements
    - Regulatory compliance requirements

- **System interfaces**:

  - API endpoints and specifications

  - Database schemas and relationships

  - Authentication mechanisms

  - Error handling protocols

  - Rate limits and quotas

- **Dynamic environment elements**: Dynamic elements represent the changing aspects of the environment that require real-time monitoring and adaptation:

  - **Resource availability**:

    - Real-time inventory levels

    - Pricing fluctuations

    - Service disruptions

    - Weather conditions

    - Local events and circumstances

  - **System performance**:

    - Response times and latency

    - Error rates and failures

    - Resource utilization

    - Queue lengths and processing times

    - System health indicators

The environment in which an agent operates dictates how effectively the agent can complete a given task. Careful consideration must be given while modeling an environment for an agent. Too many integration points and system interactions may create an overtly complex agentic system. A common way to mitigate this is to use a number of different purpose-built agents that are very good at completing one or two tasks effectively, and then have multiple agents coordinate to accomplish the final goal. This method will become more apparent when we discuss sequential and parallel workflows later in the chapter. Before we get there, let's discuss how these multiple agents may interact and integrate with each other.

Integration and interaction patterns

The success of state space and environment modeling relies heavily on effective integration patterns that enable smooth interaction between different components. Two critical patterns emerge in managing these interactions effectively:

- **Event-driven updates**: This pattern allows the agent to respond dynamically to changes in its environment. Rather than constantly polling for changes, the agent receives and processes events as they occur. For example, when an airline updates a flight status or a hotel room becomes unavailable, these events trigger immediate updates to the agent's state, enabling real-time responses to changing conditions. The following code demonstrates how an agent handles events that affect a travel booking's state. The `TravelAgentState` class contains a method that processes different types of events and updates the system accordingly. Example code for two of the possible events (flight change and weather alert) may look as follows:

```
class TravelAgentState:
    def update_booking_status(self, event):
        if event.type == "FLIGHT_CHANGE":
            self.check_dependencies()
            self.notify_customer()
        elif event.type == "WEATHER_ALERT":
            self.evaluate_alternatives()
            self.update_recommendations()
    ...
```

Let's look at an example of an airline changing a flight time from 10 AM to 2 PM:

I.   The system receives a `"FLIGHT_CHANGE"` event.

II.   The `update_booking_status` method processes this event.

III.   It checks whether the new flight time affects hotel bookings or transfers.

IV.   It automatically notifies the customer about the change.

Similarly, this example shows a severe weather alert issued for the destination:

I.   The system receives a `"WEATHER_ALERT"` event.

II.   The method evaluates whether the weather will affect travel plans.

III.   It identifies alternative dates or destinations if needed.

IV.   It updates the recommendations provided to the customer.

- **State validation and consistency**: This pattern ensures that the agent's understanding of its environment remains accurate and reliable. It involves checking that state transitions are valid, dependencies are maintained, and business rules are followed. For instance, before confirming a hotel booking, the agent must validate that the dates align with flight arrangements and that the booking complies with cancellation policies. The following code demonstrates how to implement robust state validation to ensure booking integrity and business rule compliance. This validation system acts as a gatekeeper, checking that all state changes are valid before they're applied:

```
def validate_state_transition(current_state, new_state):
    if not is_valid_transition(current_state, new_state):
        raise InvalidStateTransition("Invalid transition from
{current_state} to {new_state}")
    check_state_dependencies(new_state)
    validate_business_rules(new_state)
```

Here's how this validation works in practice:

1. Transition validation example:

   - Current state: `"on hold"` (for flight booking)

   - New state: `"confirmed"`

   - System checks the following:

     - Is payment received?

     - Are seats still available?

     - Is the price still valid?

2. Dependency checking example:

   - Booking includes flight and hotel

   - System verifies the following:

     - Hotel check-in time is after flight arrival

     - Transfer service availability matches flight time

     - Room type matches the number of travelers

3. Business rules example:

   - International booking is being made

   - System ensures the following:

     - Passport information is provided

     - Travel insurance is offered

     - Cancellation policy is acknowledged

If any validation step fails, the system prevents the state change and raises an appropriate error, maintaining the integrity of the booking system.

Monitoring and adaptation

Effective monitoring forms the cornerstone of maintaining robust state and environment models in intelligent agent systems. A comprehensive monitoring approach tracks key performance metrics that indicate the health and effectiveness of the system. These metrics include the latency of state updates, which directly impacts the agent's ability to respond to changes in real time, as well as the accuracy and precision of the model's predictions and decisions. Additionally, the system must monitor resource utilization patterns, track error rates and recovery times, and perhaps most importantly, measure customer satisfaction indicators that reflect the real-world impact of the agent's performance.

To maintain optimal performance, intelligent agents must employ sophisticated adaptation strategies that respond to insights gained through monitoring. This involves implementing dynamic resource allocation to handle varying workloads efficiently, while continuously refining and updating models based on new data and emerging patterns. The system should be capable of adjusting its rules and optimization parameters in response to changing conditions, such as seasonal travel patterns or shifts in customer preferences. Performance tuning and scaling mechanisms ensure the system can handle growing demands while maintaining responsiveness, and the incorporation of user feedback helps align the system's behavior with customer expectations and needs.

The ultimate success of an intelligent agent system hinges on its ability to effectively represent and manage its state space and environment model while adapting to changing conditions. Through careful design that considers both static and dynamic elements, implementation of robust integration patterns, and maintenance of effective monitoring and adaptation mechanisms, agents can achieve higher levels of performance and deliver superior service to users. This holistic approach to system design and maintenance ensures that the agent remains reliable, efficient, and responsive to user needs over time, even as the operational environment evolves and new challenges emerge.

Agent memory architecture and context management

Memory architecture and context management are fundamental components that enable intelligent agents to maintain coherent interactions and make informed decisions based on past experiences and current context. This section explores the design principles and implementation strategies for creating effective memory systems and managing contextual information in agent-based systems. Agent memory architectures typically incorporate three distinct types of memory, each serving different purposes in the agent's operation: short-term memory, long-term memory, and episodic memory. Let us discuss these memory architectures in detail.

Short-term memory (working memory)

Short-term memory, also known as **working memory**, serves as the agent's immediate cognitive workspace. It temporarily holds and manages information relevant to the current interaction or task being processed. This type of memory is particularly crucial for maintaining conversation context, handling multi-step processes, and managing active user sessions. In our travel agent system, short-term memory is essential for tracking ongoing search parameters, maintaining the current state of a booking process, and remembering context-specific details that might influence immediate decisions.

For example, when a customer is searching for flights, the short-term memory would maintain details such as their current search criteria, recently viewed options, and any temporary preferences they've expressed during the current session. This information doesn't need to be stored permanently but is critical for providing a coherent and personalized experience during active interaction. The temporary nature of this memory also helps in managing system resources efficiently, as the data is cleared once the session ends or the information becomes irrelevant.

For our travel agent system, a practical implementation of short-term memory might include the following Python class. This class defines the parameters required for an active real-time conversation such as `customer_id`, the session start timestamp, the current query in the conversation thread, and any specific preferences that are deduced from the user query. The `update_context` function is used to update the properties of `current_interaction` as the conversation progresses, keeping the short-term memory up to date with the current information. Since short-term memory is often ephemeral and session-specific, the `clear_session` function is used to remove and reset the state of `current_session` to prepare it for subsequent new sessions:

```python
class WorkingMemory:
    def __init__(self):
        self.current_interaction = {
            'customer_id': None,
            'session_start': None,
            'current_query': None,
            'active_searches': [],
            'temporary_preferences': {}
        }

    def update_context(self, new_information):
        # Update current interaction context
        self.current_interaction.update(new_information)

    def clear_session(self):
        # Reset temporary session data
        self.__init__()
```

While short-term memory helps provide sufficient context for the intelligent agent to perform its task, there is often additional persistent information, as opposed to ephemeral information, that is important for the intelligent agent to achieve its goal. Let us take a deeper look at what long-term memory, also known as the knowledge base, entails.

Long-term memory (knowledge base)

Long-term memory functions as the agent's persistent knowledge repository, storing information that remains relevant and valuable across multiple interactions and sessions. Unlike short-term memory, this type of storage is designed for data that needs to be preserved and accessed over extended periods. It serves as the foundation for the agent's accumulated knowledge, learned patterns, and established relationships with customers.

Long-term memory is particularly crucial for maintaining consistency in customer service and enabling personalized interactions based on historical data. For instance, in our travel agent system, this would include storing customer preferences discovered over multiple bookings, maintaining records of past travel arrangements, and preserving knowledge about destinations, seasonal patterns, and service provider relationships. This persistent storage allows the agent to make informed decisions based on historical patterns and provide personalized service without requiring customers to repeat their preferences in every interaction.

The implementation of long-term memory typically requires careful consideration of data organization, retrieval efficiency, and update mechanisms to ensure that the stored information remains accurate and accessible. In our travel agent system, this may include the following:

1. Customer profiles and preferences:

```python
class CustomerMemory:
    def __init__(self):
        self.profiles = {
            'preferences': {},
            'travel_history': [],
            'feedback_history': [],
            'special_requirements': {},
            'loyalty_status': None
        }

    def update_profile(self, customer_id, new_data):
        # Merge new information with existing profile
        self.profiles[customer_id] = {
            **self.profiles.get(customer_id, {}),
            **new_data
        }
```

2. Travel knowledge base:

```python
class TravelKnowledge:
    def __init__(self):
        self.destination_info = {}
        self.seasonal_patterns = {}
        self.service_providers = {}
        self.travel_regulations = {}

    def update_knowledge(self, category, key, value):
        # Update specific knowledge category
        getattr(self, category)[key] = value
```

Short-term and long-term memory serves as the important cornerstones of intelligent agentic systems. However, a third type of memory, known as episodic memory, has emerged, especially for conversational interfaces such as chatbots. This type of memory helps LLMs and intelligent agents further refine their actions and provide prescriptive outputs to the user.

Episodic memory (interaction history)

Episodic memory represents a specialized form of memory that captures and stores specific interactions, events, and their outcomes as discrete episodes. This type of memory enables the agent to learn from past experiences and use historical interactions to inform future decisions. Unlike general long-term memory, episodic memory focuses on the temporal sequence and context of events, making it particularly valuable for understanding patterns in customer behavior and service outcomes.

In the context of our travel agent system, episodic memory serves multiple critical functions. It helps identify successful booking patterns, understand common customer journey paths, and recognize situations that have led to either positive outcomes or challenges in the past. For example, if a customer previously encountered issues with layover times in specific airports, the agent can use this episodic information to avoid similar situations in future bookings. This memory type also enables the agent to provide more contextually relevant responses by referencing past interactions and their outcomes.

The implementation of episodic memory requires careful consideration of how to structure and store interaction records in a way that facilitates efficient retrieval and pattern recognition. For our travel agent system, this may include the following:

```python
class EpisodicMemory:
    def __init__(self):
        self.interaction_history = []

    def record_interaction(self, interaction_data):
        # Add timestamp and store interaction
        interaction_data['timestamp'] = datetime.now()
```

```python
        self.interaction_history.append(interaction_data)

def retrieve_relevant_episodes(self, context):
    # Find similar past interactions
    return [episode for episode in
            self.interaction_history
            if self._is_relevant(episode, context)]
```

Having established the core memory systems, we now turn our attention to how these different types of memory work together in practice. The agent needs sophisticated mechanisms to manage the flow of information between these memory systems and ensure that the right information is available at the right time. This brings us to two critical components: context management and decision-making integration.

Context management

Effective **context management** ensures that the agent maintains appropriate awareness of the current situation and relevant historical information. Imagine our travel booking agent assisting a customer with planning a multi-city business trip to Tokyo and Singapore. The agent must maintain awareness of various contextual elements: the customer's corporate travel policy limiting flight costs to $2,000, their preference for morning flights due to scheduled meetings, and the need to coordinate hotel bookings within walking distance of specific office locations. As the booking process unfolds, the agent continuously references and updates this information while navigating between flight searches, hotel availability, and meeting schedule constraints. This real-world scenario demonstrates why robust context management is essential for handling complex, multi-step travel arrangements. Effective context management ensures that the agent maintains appropriate awareness of the current situation and relevant historical information. This involves several key components:

- **Context hierarchy**: The context management system should maintain different levels of context:

  - **Global context**:

    - System-wide settings and constraints

    - Current operational status

    - Global travel alerts and advisories

  - **Session context**:

    - Current customer interaction state

    - Active searches and queries

    - Temporary preferences and constraints

- **Task context**:

  - Specific booking details

  - Current step in multi-step processes

  - Related bookings and dependencies

- **Context switching**: Context switching is a critical capability that allows the agent to smoothly transition between different operational contexts while maintaining coherence and continuity. This process involves several key aspects:

  - **Context preservation**:

    - Saving the current state before switching

    - Maintaining a history of context changes

    - Ensuring no critical information is lost during transitions

  - **Context restoration**:

    - Retrieving previous contexts when needed

    - Rebuilding the operational environment

    - Reestablishing relevant connections and states

  - **Context merging**:

    - Combining information from multiple contexts

    - Resolving conflicts between different contexts

    - Maintaining consistency across context changes

The sophisticated interplay between memory systems and context management ultimately serves one primary purpose: enabling intelligent decision-making. By maintaining awareness of both historical data and current context, the agent can make more informed and effective decisions. Let's examine how these components come together to support the agent's decision-making processes.

Integration with decision-making

The memory architecture and context management system must effectively support the agent's decision-making processes through several key mechanisms:

1. **Information retrieval**: The system must efficiently gather and synthesize relevant information from various memory components to support decision-making. This includes the following:

   - Accessing customer history and preferences

   - Retrieving similar past cases and their outcomes

   - Combining current context with historical data

   - Filtering and prioritizing relevant information

2. **Pattern recognition**: Pattern recognition capabilities enable the agent to identify relevant patterns and trends that can inform decisions:

   - Analyzing historical interaction patterns

   - Identifying successful booking patterns

   - Recognizing potential issues based on past experiences

   - Detecting seasonal trends and preferences

3. **Decision optimization**: The decision-making process should incorporate multiple factors and optimize outcomes based on the following:

   - Weighted evaluation of different options

   - Consideration of multiple constraints

   - Balance between customer preferences and system requirements

   - Risk assessment and mitigation strategies

The effective integration of memory architecture and context management systems enables agents to maintain coherent interactions, learn from past experiences, and make more informed decisions. By carefully designing these components and ensuring they work together seamlessly, agents can provide a more personalized and effective service while maintaining consistency across interactions.

Sequential and parallel processing in agentic workflows

The efficiency and effectiveness of an intelligent agent system often depend on how well it can manage multiple tasks and processes. This section explores two primary approaches to workflow management in agent systems: sequential and parallel processing.

Sequential processing

Sequential processing involves handling tasks in a defined order, where each step depends on the completion of previous steps. In our travel agent system, sequential processing is crucial for tasks that require strict ordering, such as the following:

1. Flight and hotel coordination:

    *   Confirming flight availability before booking hotels

    *   Ensuring transfer services align with arrival times

    *   Validating visa requirements before finalizing bookings

2. Payment processing:

    *   Verifying fund availability

    *   Processing the payment

    *   Confirming bookings

    *   Sending confirmation documents

The following figure shows a straightforward sequential processing workflow for our travel booking system:

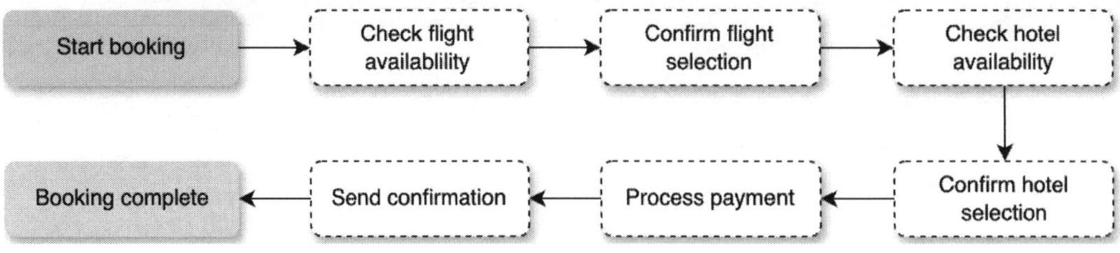

Figure 7.2 – Sequential processing

While sequential processing provides a clear and controlled workflow for dependent tasks, it can lead to inefficiencies when handling multiple independent operations. This limitation becomes particularly evident in complex use cases, for example, travel bookings where certain tasks could potentially be executed simultaneously. Understanding when to apply sequential versus parallel processing is crucial for optimizing the agent's performance and response time. Let's examine how parallel processing can enhance our system's efficiency.

Parallel processing

Parallel processing enables the agent to handle multiple independent tasks simultaneously, improving efficiency and response times. Key applications include the following:

1. Concurrent searches:

   - Querying multiple airline systems simultaneously

   - Checking availability across different hotel chains

   - Retrieving weather forecasts and travel advisories

2. Background processing:

   - Updating customer profiles

   - Processing feedback and reviews

   - Monitoring price changes

   - Updating travel advisories

The following figure shows a possible parallel processing workflow for our travel booking system:

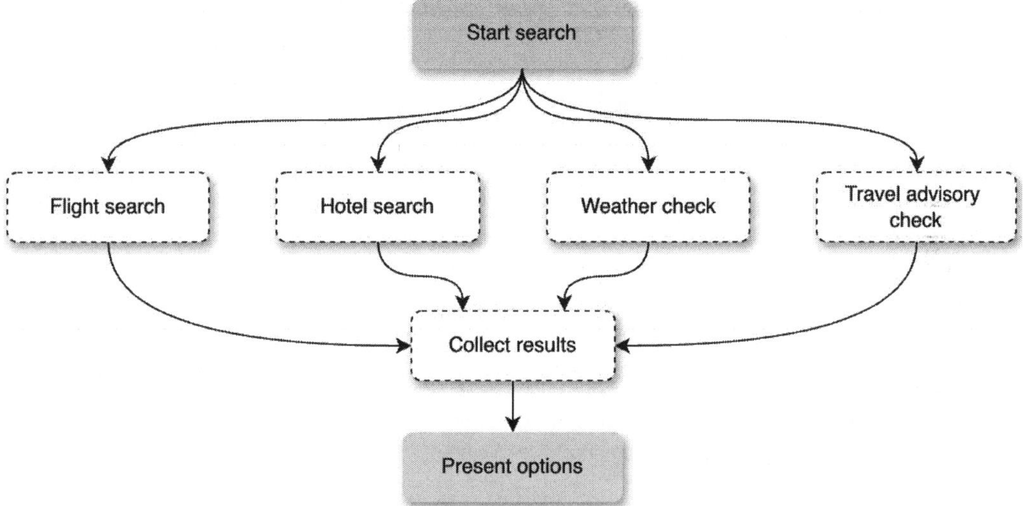

Figure 7.3 – Parallel processing

While both sequential and parallel processing approaches offer distinct advantages, the real challenge lies in determining when to use each approach and how to combine them effectively. An agent must be able to dynamically switch between these processing modes based on task requirements, system load, and time constraints. This necessitates a careful approach to workflow optimization.

Workflow optimization

Effective workflow optimization in agent systems requires a sophisticated approach to managing and coordinating different processing patterns. This involves not just choosing between sequential and parallel processing but also understanding how to combine them effectively while considering system resources, time constraints, and task dependencies. The following figure demonstrates a conceptual architecture of an optimal and dynamic workflow that may be designed:

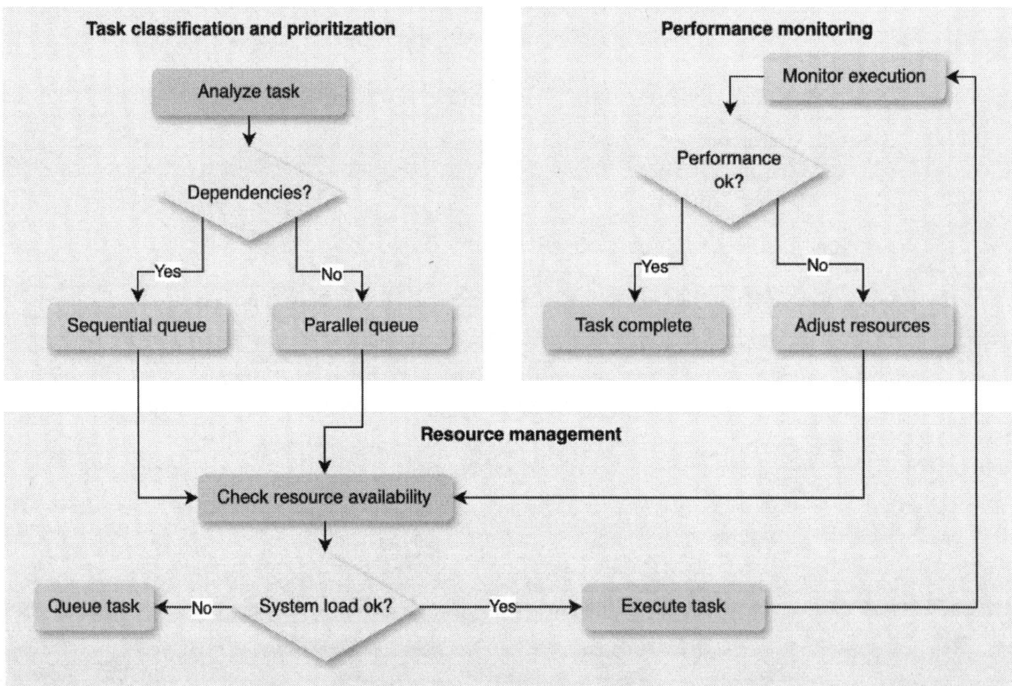

Figure 7.4 – Workflow optimization with dynamic workflows

Here is a detailed analysis of workflow optimization:

1. **Task classification and prioritization**: The first step in workflow optimization involves carefully analyzing and categorizing tasks:

    I.   Dependency analysis:

        *   Identifying critical path tasks that must be completed in sequence

        *   Mapping dependencies between different booking components

        *   Understanding data flow requirements between tasks

        *   Recognizing temporal constraints and deadlines

II.   Priority assignment:

- Evaluating task urgency and importance
- Considering customer SLAs and expectations
- Assessing the impact on the overall booking process
- Determining resource requirements

2. **Resource management**: Efficient allocation and utilization of resources is crucial for optimal workflow performance:

I.   System resource allocation:

- Monitoring and managing CPU and memory usage
- Balancing load across different system components
- Implementing throttling mechanisms when needed
- Optimizing database connections and caches

II.   External service management:

- Tracking API rate limits and quotas
- Managing concurrent external service requests
- Implementing retry strategies for failed operations
- Maintaining service provider priorities

3. **Dynamic workflow adjustment**: The system must be able to adapt its workflow patterns based on changing conditions:

I.   Load balancing:

- Adjusting parallel task execution based on system load
- Redistributing tasks during peak periods
- Managing queue depths and processing rates
- Implementing backpressure mechanisms

II.   Performance monitoring:

- Tracking task completion times and success rates
- Identifying bottlenecks and performance issues

- Measuring system throughput and latency

- Monitoring resource utilization patterns

By carefully implementing these optimization strategies, agent systems can achieve better performance while maintaining reliability. The key is to create workflows that are not just efficient but also resilient and adaptable to changing conditions. This balanced approach ensures that the agent can handle complex travel booking scenarios while providing consistent and responsive service to customers.

Summary

In this chapter, you learned about the essential components and techniques for designing effective agentic systems. We explored how focused system prompts guide agent behavior, how state space representations and environment models create a foundation for decision-making, and how different memory architectures – short-term, long-term, and episodic – work together with context management to enable coherent interactions and learning from past experiences.

Through our travel agent example, we demonstrated how the integration of sequential and parallel processing patterns, supported by intelligent workflow optimization strategies, enables agents to handle complex tasks efficiently while maintaining system reliability. These design techniques work together to create systems that can effectively manage real-world scenarios, adapt to changing conditions, and provide consistent, high-quality service to users. By implementing these practices thoughtfully, developers can create agent systems that not only meet current requirements but are also positioned to evolve with future needs. In the next chapter, we will explore the critical topic of building trust in generative AI systems, examining how to create transparent, reliable, and accountable AI solutions that users can confidently rely upon.

Questions

1. What are the three primary types of memory architecture in agent systems, and why are they important for maintaining effective agent behavior?

2. Explain the difference between sequential and parallel processing in agent workflows. When would you use each approach in a travel booking system?

3. How does context management contribute to effective agent operation, and what are the key levels of context that need to be maintained?

4. What role does the environment model play in agent design, and how does it differ from state space representation?

5. In workflow optimization, what factors should be considered when deciding between sequential and parallel processing approaches?

Answers

1. The three primary types of memory architecture are as follows:

   - **Short-term (working) memory**: Handles immediate interaction contexts and temporary information needed for current tasks – for example, maintaining active search parameters and current session state.

   - **Long-term (knowledge base) memory**: Stores persistent information valuable across multiple interactions, such as customer profiles, travel regulations, and destination information.

   - **Episodic memory**: Records specific interactions and their outcomes as discrete episodes, enabling learning from past experiences and pattern recognition in customer behavior. These are important because they enable the agent to maintain context, learn from experience, and make informed decisions based on both current and historical information.

2. Sequential processing involves handling tasks in a defined order where each step depends on the completion of previous steps (e.g., confirming flight availability before booking hotels and processing payments before sending confirmation). Parallel processing enables handling multiple independent tasks simultaneously (e.g., searching multiple airline systems, checking hotel availability, and retrieving weather forecasts concurrently). In a travel booking system, you would do the following:

   - Use sequential processing when tasks have dependencies (payment → confirmation)

   - Use parallel processing for independent tasks (multiple vendor searches)

3. Context management contributes to agent operation by ensuring appropriate awareness of the current situation and relevant historical information. The key levels are as follows:

   - **Global context**: System-wide settings, operational status, and global alerts

   - **Session context**: Current customer interaction state, active queries, and temporary preferences

   - **Task context**: Specific booking details and the current step in multi-step processes. This hierarchy enables the agent to maintain coherent interactions while efficiently managing information at different operational levels.

4. The environment model creates a comprehensive representation of the external factors and systems with which the agent interacts, including both static rules (business policies and system interfaces) and dynamic elements (resource availability and pricing changes). State space representation, in contrast, focuses on tracking the current situation, available actions, and potential outcomes. The environment model provides the broader operational context within which the state space exists.

5.   Key factors for workflow optimization include the following:

- **Task dependencies**: Whether tasks have prerequisites or can run independently

- **Resource availability**: System capacity and external service limitations

- **Time constraints**: Urgency of task completion and SLA requirements

- **System load**: Current processing capacity and queue depths

- **Performance requirements**: Throughput and latency expectations.

The decision should balance these factors while considering the specific requirements of each task and the overall system efficiency goals.

Get This Book's PDF Version and Exclusive Extras

Scan the QR code (or go to `packtpub.com/unlock`). Search for this book by name, confirm the edition, and then follow the steps on the page.

Note: Keep your invoice handly. Purchase made directly from packt don't require one.

Part 3: Trust, Safety, Ethics, and Applications

This part aims to provide you with a comprehensive understanding of building trustworthy, safe, and ethical generative AI systems while exploring real-world applications and future directions for the field.

This part contains the following chapters:

- *Chapter 8, Building Trust in Generative AI Systems*
- *Chapter 9, Managing Safety and Ethical Considerations*
- *Chapter 10, Common Use Cases and Applications*
- *Chapter 11, Conclusion and Future Outlook*

8
Building Trust in Generative AI Systems

In the previous chapter, we explored several design methods that can effectively guide intelligent agents toward desirable behavior while upholding ethical principles. Focused instruction, guardrails and constraints, and finding the right balance between autonomy and control are crucial strategies for aligning these agents with human values and mitigating potential risks.

Clear objectives, tasks, and operating contexts through focused instructions provide a well-defined framework for agents to operate within. Guardrails and constraints act as boundaries, preventing agents from wandering into unintended territory and minimizing the risks of adverse consequences. Meanwhile, a balanced approach that combines autonomous decision-making with human control allows agents to exercise independent judgment while remaining tethered to our values and principles.

However, beneath the successful adoption and acceptance of generative AI systems lies a critical component: trust. As these technologies become increasingly intertwined with various aspects of society, fostering user confidence and trust will be essential for their effective implementation.

In this chapter, we will delve into the importance of trust in AI and explore strategies for achieving it. This chapter underscores the importance of trust as a fundamental component for fostering user confidence and responsible implementation. It is divided into several sections, each addressing a different aspect of building trust. We will address two significant hurdles – uncertainty and biases – and emphasize the importance of transparency, explainability, and clear communication.

This chapter is divided into the following main sections:

- Importance of trust in AI

- Techniques for establishing trust

- Implementing transparency and explainability

- Handling uncertainty and biases

By the end of this chapter, you will know how to develop reliable generative AI systems that instill confidence in users and stakeholders, paving the way for their widespread and responsible adoption.

Technical requirements

You can find the code file for this chapter on GitHub at `https://github.com/PacktPublishing/Building-Agentic-AI-Systems`.

Importance of trust in AI

Trust constitutes a key ingredient for the successful adoption and acceptance of AI systems in general, including generative AI. If users lack confidence in the inner workings and decision-making processes of this new technology, it's highly doubtful that they will be willing to use or rely on its outputs. Building up trust in generative AI systems is an essential step toward gaining user confidence and ensuring that its use is widespread, responsible, and ethical.

Consider a scenario where a travel agency employs a generative AI system to assist customers in planning their vacations. The AI can suggest personalized itineraries, recommend accommodations, and provide travel tips based on the customer's preferences and historical data. However, if customers do not trust the AI's recommendations, they are unlikely to rely on its suggestions or share personal information necessary for tailoring the recommendations.

This means that trust in AI is multivariate, with factors relating to the reliability of the system, transparency, and correspondence with users' expectations and values. Users are more likely to interact with an AI system they perceive as trustworthy, including contributing feedback and sharing their data to further refine and enhance the performance and capability of the AI system.

In the travel agency example, customers may be more inclined to trust the AI's recommendations if the system is transparent about its decision-making process, explaining why specific destinations or activities were suggested based on their preferences and past travel histories. Additionally, if the AI's recommendations align with the customers' expectations and values, such as prioritizing eco-friendly or culturally immersive experiences, it will further reinforce trust in the system.

Where there is a deficiency in trust, it may lead to users being skeptical, resistive to its adoption, and, ultimately, abusing or misusing such technology. In the travel agency scenario, if customers do not trust the AI's recommendations, they may disregard its suggestions entirely or provide inaccurate information, resulting in suboptimal itineraries and a poor user experience.

Furthermore, a lack of trust can hinder the continuous improvement and advancement of the AI system. If customers are unwilling to share feedback or data due to mistrust, the AI's ability to learn and adapt to their evolving preferences and requirements will be limited.

To address these concerns, travel agencies and other organizations leveraging generative AI must prioritize building trust through various techniques, such as transparency in decision-making, addressing uncertainties and biases, effective communication of outputs, and ensuring ethical development practices. By fostering trust, businesses can unlock the full potential of generative AI, enabling seamless adoption, responsible use, and continuous improvement of these powerful technologies.

In the next section, we will explore some of the techniques for establishing trust.

Techniques for establishing trust

There are various techniques available to the developer and researcher community to help cultivate trust in generative AI systems, addressing user concerns and expectations. We will discuss the key techniques in the following subsections.

Transparency and explainability

Transparency into how an AI system arrives at its decisions and generates content forms the bedrock of building trust. Users need to understand the reasoning behind the AI's outputs and have confidence in its decision-making process. Without this transparency and explainability, users may perceive the AI as a black box, making it difficult to trust its recommendations or outputs fully. Transparency in AI operates on two levels: the **algorithmic level** and the **presentation level**. Algorithmic transparency involves openness about the model's architecture, training data, and potential biases, ensuring that developers and regulators can assess its reliability and fairness. Presentation transparency, or explainability, focuses on how the AI communicates its reasoning to users, helping them understand why a specific decision or recommendation was made. Both aspects are essential for trust – without algorithmic transparency, stakeholders may question the system's integrity, while a lack of explainability can leave users feeling uncertain about its outputs. A well-balanced approach strengthens confidence in AI-driven decisions.

Let's consider the travel agent scenario again. Imagine a customer planning a family vacation to Europe, and the AI system suggests visiting a particular city based on their preferences and travel history. The customer might be more inclined to trust the recommendation if the AI can explain its reasoning transparently. For instance, the system could highlight that the suggested city is known for its family-friendly attractions, rich cultural heritage, and affordable accommodations, aligning with the customer's preferences for educational and budget-friendly travel.

Explainable AI (XAI) techniques play a crucial role in achieving this transparency. In a content generation system such as GPT-4, users may want to know why certain phrases or sentences were chosen and how the AI factored in context, tone, and style preferences. XAI techniques, such as **attention visualization, saliency maps**, and **natural language explanations**, can provide insight into the model's inner workings, making it more interpretable and trustworthy.

The `chapter08_xai` notebook provides an example of how attention visualization, saliency maps, and natural language explanations can be generated simply using Python. The code demonstrates the use of a pre-trained BERT model to analyze text through attention visualization. It begins by importing the necessary libraries, including `torch` for tensor operations, `transformers` for loading the BERT model and tokenizer, and `matplotlib` and `seaborn` for visualizing the attention scores.

The model (`bert-base-uncased`) is used for sequence classification, and the tokenizer processes the input text into token IDs. The core functionality includes extracting attention scores from the model by enabling the `output_attentions=True` parameter, which provides insights into how different tokens within the input query relate to each other. The attention scores are then visualized using a heatmap, which shows the attention distribution across tokens in the last attention layer. This heatmap helps to understand which parts of the text the model focuses on when processing the query. By decoding the token IDs into readable tokens and plotting the attention scores, the code enables a detailed analysis of how BERT processes text, making it a valuable tool for XAI, where the goal is to improve model transparency and interpretability.

When asked *"What are the best family-friendly travel destinations in Europe?,"* the code snippet tokenizes the input text using the pre-trained tokenizer, converting it into a tensor format suitable for the model while applying truncation and padding as needed. It then defines a function to extract attention scores by passing the tokenized inputs to the model, providing insight into how different parts of the text attend to one another. Another function visualizes these attention scores using a heatmap, displaying the attention weights from the last layer with tokens labeled along both axes. Finally, the code retrieves the attention scores, decodes the token IDs into their corresponding tokens, and visualizes the attention weights to show the model's focus on the input text. *Figure 8.1* shows the attention visualization:

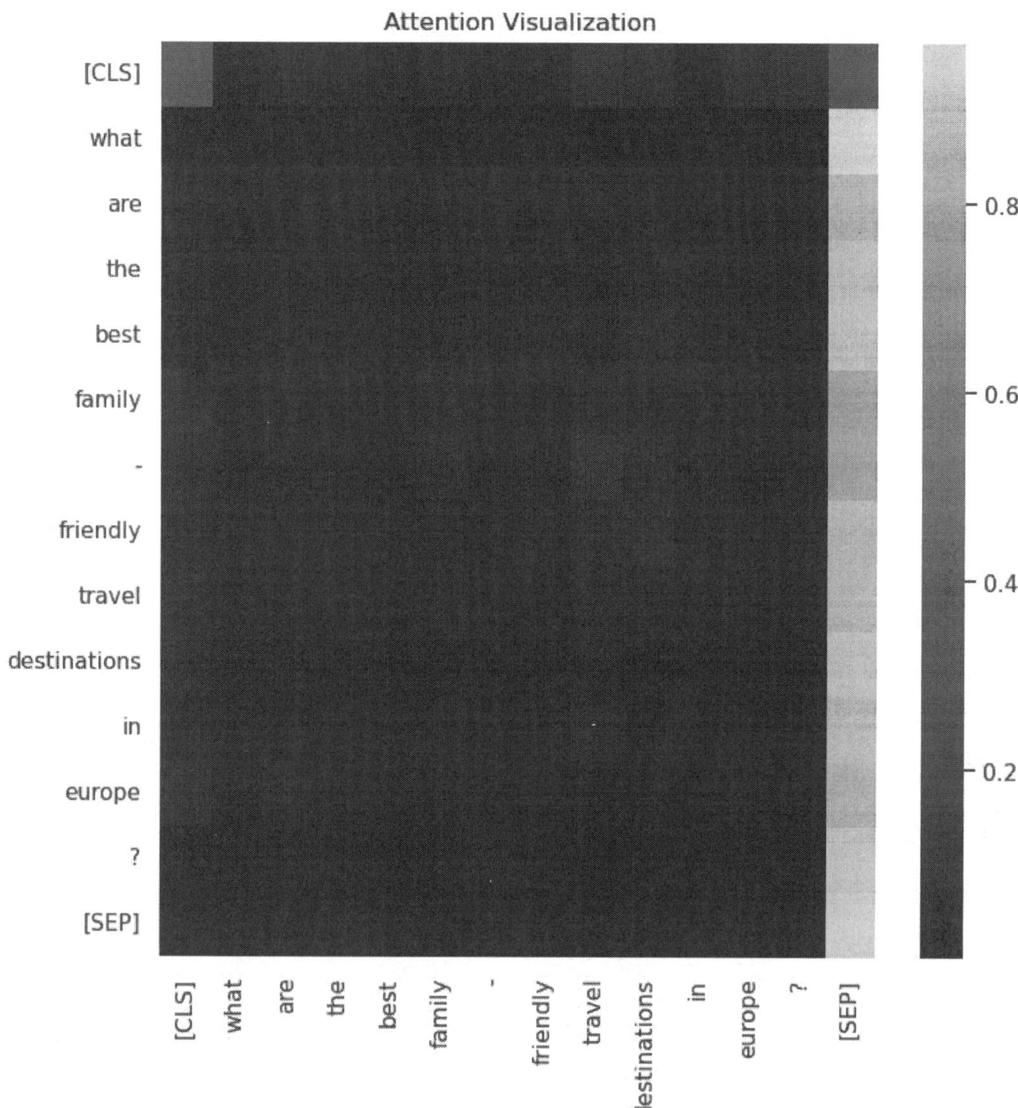

Figure 8.1 – Attention visualization

For example, an attention visualization could highlight the specific words or phrases from the user's prompt that the AI focused on while generating the content. This can help users understand how the AI interpreted their input and why certain creative choices were made. Similarly, *Figure 8.2* displays the saliency map for the same sentence:

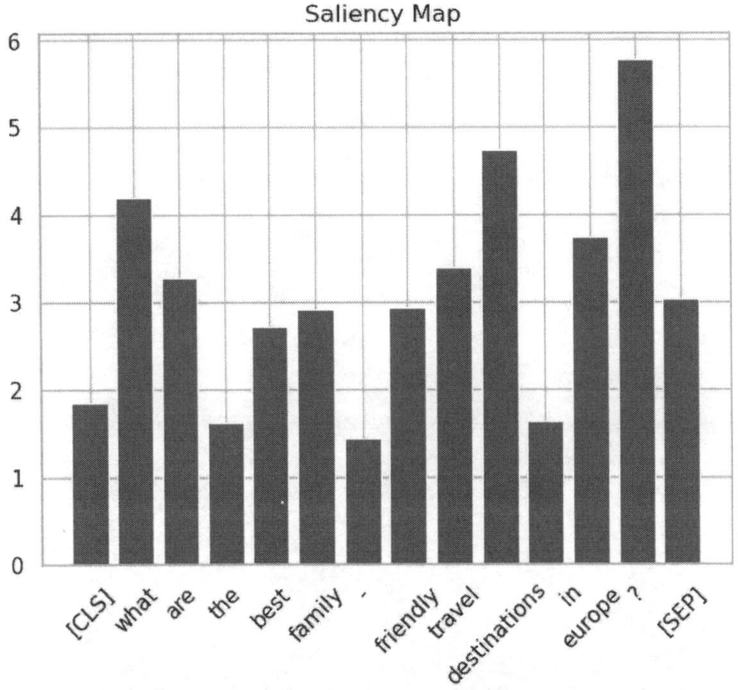

Figure 8.2 – Saliency map

The code (`chapter08_xai`) implements a saliency map visualization for the given sentence using a pre-trained BERT model. The process begins by tokenizing the input sentence into token IDs and attention masks, which are then passed through the model. The embeddings for the tokens are retrieved and tracked for gradients, allowing the saliency scores to be computed, indicating how much each token contributes to the model's prediction. A custom forward function is used to feed the embeddings into the model, and the saliency attribute method calculates the saliency scores. These scores are then aggregated across token embeddings, and the tokens are converted back to their readable form. Finally, a bar chart is generated to visually display the importance of each token, providing insights into which tokens had the most influence on the model's decision. This approach allows for better interpretability of the model's behavior by highlighting key tokens driving its output.

In some cases, natural language explanations can provide additional insight into the model. Natural language explanations in AI and machine learning are human-readable descriptions that help translate complex model outputs or decisions into understandable language. They are essential for improving interpretability and transparency, allowing users to comprehend the reasoning behind a model's behavior. For instance, when a model classifies an image, a natural language explanation might describe the features that led to the classification, such as "*This image was classified as a dog because it contains a tail and ears typical of dogs.*" These explanations bridge the gap between machine outputs and human understanding, fostering trust and collaboration between humans and AI. For an example, refer to *Figure 8.3*:

```
Explanation:
The question 'What are the best family-friendly travel destinations in Europe?' is significant for several reasons
in the context of travel:

1. **Diverse Needs of Families**: Families traveling with children have unique requirements compared to solo travel
ers or couples. This includes considerations for safety, availability of kid-friendly activities, and accommodation
s that cater to families. Identifying the best destinations helps families plan trips that meet these specific need
s.

2. **Quality Time and Bonding**: Family vacations provide essential opportunities for bonding and creating lasting
memories. Finding destinations that offer activities and experiences suitable for all ages can enhance family dynam
ics and improve relationships.

3. **Educational Opportunities**: Europe is rich in history, culture, and art. Family-friendly travel destinations
often incorporate educational components, allowing children to learn while having fun. This can enrich children's u
nderstanding of the world, making travel both enjoyable and informative.

4. **Health and Safety**: Choosing the right destination can also be crucial for health and safety. Certain locatio
ns may have better healthcare facilities, less crowded tourist areas, or environments that are more suitable for ch
ildren, thus easing parents' worries.

5. **Budget Considerations**: Families often travel on a budget. Knowing which destinations are family-friendly can
help parents find affordable options for accommodations, meals, and activities that provide good value for money.

6. **Cultural Exposure**: Traveling to Europe can expose families to different cultures, traditions, and languages.
Family-friendly destinations often facilitate these experiences in a manner that's engaging and accessible for chil
dren.

7. **Travel Logistics**: Family travel often involves more logistical planning, including transportation and access
ibility. Knowing which destinations are easier to navigate with children can simplify the travel experience and red
uce stress.

8. **Encouragement for Travel**: By highlighting family-friendly options, more families may be encouraged to trave
l. This can lead to increased cultural exchange and a broader appreciation for global diversity among younger gener
ations.

Overall, understanding the best family-friendly travel destinations in Europe allows families to make informed choi
ces that enhance their travel experiences, contributing positively to their overall well-being and enjoyment.
```

Figure 8.3 – Natural language explanation

We input the same text, "*What are the best family-friendly travel destinations in Europe?*," and can clearly observe why the model (GPT-4o-mini) identified it as encouraging. In high-stakes domains such as healthcare or finance, natural language explanations are crucial for ensuring the accountability and fairness of AI decisions. By providing clear insight into how models arrive at their conclusions, natural language explanations promote responsible and ethical AI deployment.

If we look at the healthcare industry, AI systems are increasingly being used for tasks such as disease diagnosis and treatment recommendation. Transparency and explainability become crucial in these high-stakes scenarios. Physicians and patients need to understand the reasoning behind an AI's diagnosis or treatment plan, particularly if it contradicts established medical knowledge or guidelines. XAI techniques such as feature importance and rule extraction can help explain the factors that influenced the AI's decision, allowing healthcare professionals to evaluate the recommendation's validity and build trust in the system.

Similarly, in the finance sector, AI models are used for tasks such as credit risk assessment, fraud detection, and investment portfolio optimization. XAI can help financial institutions understand the factors influencing an AI's decisions, ensuring compliance with regulations and building trust among customers and stakeholders.

Developers and researchers can leverage various XAI techniques based on the specific use case and model architecture. For instance, saliency maps can be useful for computer vision tasks, while natural language explanations may be more suitable for text generation or language understanding models.

By prioritizing transparency and explainability, organizations can create AI systems that are not just accurate but also trustworthy. Users can understand the reasoning behind the AI's outputs, evaluate its decisions, and, ultimately, develop confidence in the system's capabilities, paving the way for widespread and responsible adoption of these powerful technologies.

Dealing with uncertainty and biases

AI systems need to be designed to identify and mitigate uncertainties and biases that may have been introduced through their training data or algorithms. Quantifying and communicating uncertainty, as well as actively attempting to minimize biases, are crucial steps toward building trust between generative AI systems and their users.

In the travel agent scenario, consider a generative AI system that recommends personalized travel itineraries based on user preferences and historical data. If the user provides an ambiguous or vague prompt, such as *"I want to go on an adventure,"* the AI system should be able to acknowledge the uncertainty involved in interpreting such a broad request. It could convey this uncertainty by providing a range of potential itinerary options or highlighting the need for additional clarification from the user.

Additionally, the AI system might have inherent biases in its recommendations due to the training data it was exposed to. For instance, if the training data predominantly featured more affluent travelers or focused on specific regions, the AI's recommendations could be skewed toward luxury accommodations or popular tourist destinations, failing to capture the diversity of travel experiences. Addressing these biases is crucial for building trust and ensuring fair and inclusive recommendations.

Techniques such as debiasing algorithms, adversarial training, and human supervision can help reduce biases related to factors such as gender, race, age, or socioeconomic status. Debiasing algorithms aim to remove or mitigate biases by adjusting the model's parameters or modifying the training data. Adversarial training involves training the model to be robust against biased or adversarial inputs, while human supervision allows for manual intervention and correction of biased outputs. For instance, a text-to-image generation model should be able to acknowledge and convey the uncertainties involved in interpreting ambiguous prompts or generating complex scenes. If a user requests an *image of a magical forest*, the AI system could generate multiple variations and provide confidence scores or uncertainty estimates for each image, allowing the user to understand the model's interpretation and potential limitations.

In the healthcare domain, where AI systems are increasingly being used for tasks such as disease diagnosis and treatment recommendation, dealing with uncertainty and biases is of utmost importance. AI models should be able to quantify the uncertainty in their predictions, particularly in cases where the input data is incomplete or ambiguous. Additionally, addressing biases related to factors such as race, gender, or socioeconomic status is crucial to ensure fair and equitable healthcare outcomes. By implementing techniques to identify, quantify, and mitigate uncertainties and biases, developers and researchers can create AI systems that are not only accurate but also transparent and trustworthy. Users can better understand the limitations and potential biases of the system, leading to more informed decision-making and responsible use of these powerful technologies.

Effective output communication

How AI-generated content is framed and interpreted significantly impacts user trust. Developers should ensure that outputs are clearly labeled as AI-generated, provide context and attribution where appropriate, and suggest to users how they should interpret and utilize the content further.

In the travel agent scenario, consider a generative AI system that creates personalized travel blog posts or itinerary descriptions based on the user's preferences and destination. Effective output communication is crucial to ensure that users understand the nature and limitations of AI-generated content.

First, the AI-generated travel blog posts or itinerary descriptions should be clearly labeled as *AI-generated* or *AI-assisted* to set appropriate expectations and avoid any confusion or misrepresentation. Additionally, the AI system could provide context about the data sources and algorithms used in generating the content, such as the types of travel data, user reviews, and language models employed.

Furthermore, the AI system should transparently communicate any potential biases or limitations in the generated content. For instance, if the training data primarily focused on popular tourist destinations or mainstream travel experiences, the AI-generated content might lack representation of off-the-beaten-path or niche travel opportunities. By acknowledging these limitations, users can better understand the scope and potential blind spots of the AI-generated content.

Guidelines on how to interpret and utilize AI-generated content responsibly can also foster trust. For example, the AI system could suggest that users fact-check or verify specific details, such as opening hours, admission fees, or local customs, before relying solely on AI-generated information. Additionally, the system could recommend cross-referencing the content with other reliable sources or seeking local expertise when planning their travel itineraries.

In the news and journalism domain, where AI-generated content is becoming increasingly prevalent, effective output communication is paramount. AI-generated news articles should be clearly marked as such, with information about the data sources and any potential biases or limitations. For instance, if the AI system was trained on a specific set of news sources or time periods, it might have inherent biases in its reporting or framing of events.

Additionally, guidelines on fact-checking and verifying the information can help users engage with the AI-generated content responsibly. News organizations could provide resources or checklists for users to cross-reference the AI-generated articles with other credible sources, fact-check claims, and evaluate the article's objectivity and balance.

By implementing effective output communication strategies, developers and organizations can promote transparency, manage user expectations, and empower users to engage with AI-generated content critically and responsibly. This approach fosters trust, mitigates potential misunderstandings or misuse, and paves the way for the responsible adoption of generative AI technologies across various domains.

User control and consent

User control and consent refer to features that allow users to have more freedom in customizing and influencing the generative process, as well as soliciting explicit consent regarding data usage and content creation. This can help build trust and ensure user commitment.

In the travel agent scenario, consider a generative AI system that creates personalized travel itineraries or recommendations based on the user's preferences and historical data. Providing users with control over the generative process can help build trust and ensure that the AI-generated content aligns with their specific needs and expectations.

For instance, the AI system could allow users to adjust parameters such as travel style (e.g., adventure, relaxation, or culture), budget range, duration, or desired activities. By giving users the ability to fine-tune these parameters, they can better influence the AI's recommendations and have a sense of control over the generated output. This level of customization can increase user satisfaction and trust in the AI system, as they feel that their preferences are being accurately reflected in the recommendations.

Additionally, seeking explicit consent from users regarding the use of their personal data or travel histories can foster transparency and build trust. The AI system could present clear and easily understandable information about the data being collected, how it will be used, and any potential risks or limitations. Users could then provide informed consent, allowing the AI system to leverage their data while respecting their privacy and autonomy.

In the creative writing domain, an AI-powered writing assistant could allow users to adjust parameters such as tone (e.g., formal, casual, or humorous), style (e.g., descriptive, concise, or narrative), or content boundaries (e.g., family-friendly or explicit content). By giving users this level of control, they can better align the AI-generated content with their desired creative vision, fostering a sense of ownership and trust in the AI system.

Furthermore, seeking consent for using personal writing samples or data can promote transparency and build trust between users and the AI system. The AI system could clearly explain how the user's data will be utilized, such as for training or personalization purposes, and provide options for users to control the level of access or revoke consent at any time.

In the field of personalized healthcare, AI systems could allow users to adjust preferences related to treatment approaches (e.g., conventional, alternative, or integrative), risk tolerance, or specific dietary or lifestyle considerations. By giving users control over these parameters, the AI-generated treatment plans or recommendations can better align with their personal values and preferences, fostering trust and commitment to the AI system's recommendations.

By incorporating user control and consent features, developers and organizations can create AI systems that are not only accurate and efficient but also transparent, respectful of user autonomy, and responsive to individual preferences and needs. This approach can foster trust, user commitment, and responsible adoption of generative AI technologies across various domains.

Ethical development and responsibility

Fairness, privacy, and intellectual property rights are among the ethical considerations that should be heavily emphasized during the development and deployment process of generative AI systems to garner trust from users and other stakeholders. Developers should prioritize practices such as privacy-preserving techniques, responsible data handling, and respecting intellectual property rights. Ensuring that the AI system does not perpetuate harmful biases or discriminate against certain groups is also crucial for building trust and responsible adoption.

In the travel agent scenario, consider a generative AI system that creates personalized travel recommendations and itineraries. Ethical development and responsibility should be at the forefront to ensure that the AI system operates fairly, respects user privacy, and avoids infringing on intellectual property rights.

Fairness and non-discrimination are essential principles that should guide the development of such an AI system. The training data and algorithms used to generate recommendations should be carefully evaluated to identify and mitigate potential biases or discriminatory patterns. For example, if the training data predominantly features travel experiences catered to specific demographic groups or income levels, the AI system may inadvertently perpetuate biases in its recommendations, excluding or underrepresenting certain communities or travel preferences.

Developers should implement techniques such as debiasing algorithms, adversarial training, and diverse data collection strategies to ensure that the AI system generates fair and inclusive recommendations, regardless of factors such as race, gender, age, or socioeconomic status. By prioritizing fairness and non-discrimination, users can trust that the AI system treats them equally and does not reinforce harmful stereotypes or biases.

Privacy is another critical ethical consideration in the development of generative AI systems. Users may be hesitant to share personal data or travel histories if they lack confidence in the AI system's ability to protect their privacy. Developers should implement privacy-preserving techniques, such as differential privacy, secure multi-party computation, or encrypted data processing, to ensure that user data is handled responsibly and protected from unauthorized access or misuse.

Additionally, responsible data handling practices should be established to ensure that user data is collected, stored, and processed in compliance with relevant privacy laws and regulations. Transparent data policies and user consent mechanisms can further build trust by giving users control over how their data is used by the AI system.

Intellectual property rights are also a significant concern in the realm of generative AI systems. When creating travel content or recommendations, the AI system should respect copyrights, trademarks, and other intellectual property rights. Developers should implement techniques to detect and prevent the unauthorized use of copyrighted materials or the generation of content that infringes on existing intellectual property.

Furthermore, the AI system should provide proper attribution and credit when using or referencing third-party content or data sources. This not only respects intellectual property rights but also fosters transparency and trust among users, who can verify the sources and credibility of the information presented.

By prioritizing ethical development practices and addressing concerns related to fairness, privacy, and intellectual property rights, developers can create generative AI systems that are not only powerful and efficient but also trustworthy and socially responsible. Users and stakeholders can have confidence in the integrity of the AI system, promoting widespread adoption and responsible use of these technologies.

By implementing these techniques, developers and researchers can create generative AI systems that are transparent, accountable, and aligned with user expectations and ethical principles, fostering trust and enabling widespread responsible adoption of these powerful technologies.

Building on the foundation of fairness and accountability, let's explore, in the next couple of sections, how we can implement some of these practices in real life.

Implementing transparency and explainability

Transparency and explainability are cardinal characteristics of any trustworthy AI system. Indeed, explanations of how AI models arrive at their decisions in building content would provide insight for the users into the reasoning that led to such output, thereby fostering trust and confidence in the reliability of the system.

Consider the travel agent scenario, where a generative AI system recommends personalized travel itineraries based on user preferences and historical data. Transparency and explainability are crucial for building trust in such a system. Users may want to understand why certain destinations or activities were recommended over others, and how the AI factored in their preferences, budget constraints, and travel histories.

As we saw earlier, techniques such as saliency maps, feature importance, and natural language explanations are some of the XAI techniques that could be used to facilitate transparency and interpretability in an AI system. These methods provide insight into the input features or data points most valued in driving decisions derived from the AI and how changes in these features would affect the output.

For instance, saliency maps can highlight the specific aspects of a user's profile or preferences that were most influential in generating a particular travel recommendation. This visual representation can help users understand the reasoning behind the AI's decisions and ensure that the recommendations align with their true preferences.

Feature importance techniques can quantify the relative importance of different input features, such as travel history, budget, or desired activities, in shaping the AI's recommendations. This information can help users identify any potential biases or misalignments in the AI's decision-making process and provide feedback for further improvement.

Natural language explanations can provide textual justifications for the AI's recommendations, explaining the rationale behind suggesting specific destinations, accommodations, or activities. These explanations can be particularly valuable for non-technical users, making the AI's decision-making process more accessible and understandable.

Another facet of transparency is the disclosure of limitations and potential risks relevant to generative AI systems. In other words, users should be cognizant of the fact that as powerful as this technology is, it is not perfect and is subject to uncertainties and biases.

For example, a travel recommendation AI system may have limitations in understanding nuanced or context-specific preferences, or it may be biased toward popular destinations due to the nature of its training data. Developers should set realistic expectations and provide clear guidelines on how the technology should be used, acknowledging its strengths and limitations.

In the healthcare domain, transparency and explainability are particularly crucial when AI systems are used for tasks such as diagnosis or treatment recommendations. Physicians and patients need to understand the reasoning behind the AI's decisions, especially when they contradict established medical knowledge or guidelines. XAI techniques can help explain the factors that influenced the AI's decision, allowing healthcare professionals to evaluate the recommendation's validity and build trust in the system.

Handling uncertainty and biases

Uncertainty and biases are inherent in AI systems, including generative AI models. Uncertainty might arise due to various reasons, such as incompleteness or ambiguity in data, inherently unpredictable events, or limitations in the model's knowledge or training process.

In the travel agent scenario, consider a generative AI system that recommends personalized travel itineraries based on user preferences and historical data. Uncertainty can arise from ambiguous or vague user inputs, incomplete or outdated travel information in the training data, or unforeseen events such as weather disruptions or local conflicts.

To handle uncertainty, developers could consider probabilistic modeling, Bayesian inference, and uncertainty quantification approaches in generative AI systems. These techniques allow the models to yield probabilities or confidence intervals instead of deterministic outputs, update beliefs as new data arrives, and estimate uncertainties associated with their predictions.

For example, when a user provides a broad prompt such as *"I want a romantic trip,"* the AI system could present multiple potential itinerary options with associated confidence scores or uncertainty estimates, allowing the user to understand the model's level of confidence and make informed decisions.

Biases, on the other hand, can manifest in AI systems due to various factors, including the training data, algorithmic design, or societal biases. These biases can lead to unfair or discriminatory outcomes, perpetuating historical inequities and undermining trust in the system.

In the travel agent scenario, biases could arise if the training data predominantly features travel experiences catered to specific demographic groups, income levels, or cultural perspectives. As a result, the AI system's recommendations might inadvertently exclude or underrepresent certain communities, travel preferences, or destinations.

Addressing bias in AI systems requires a multilayered approach, including the use of representative and diverse training data, frequent monitoring and evaluation of model performance, and incorporating feedback from a diverse range of stakeholders. This helps identify and mitigate potential biases, ensuring that the AI system generates fair and inclusive recommendations.

For instance, in the travel recommendation system, developers could implement debiasing algorithms to reduce biases related to factors such as race, gender, or socioeconomic status. Additionally, they could incorporate human supervision, where travel experts or diverse user groups review and provide feedback on the AI's recommendations, helping to identify and correct any biases or oversights.

By addressing the issues of uncertainty and bias, generative AI systems can earn the trust of users and ensure that the technology is used responsibly and ethically. Users can have confidence in the reliability and fairness of the AI-generated outputs, promoting widespread adoption and positive impact across various domains.

Summary

To conclude, trust is the bedrock of generative AI's successful adoption and responsible use. Transparency and explainability empower users to comprehend the rationale behind AI decisions, fostering confidence and reliability. Advanced techniques, such as saliency maps, feature importance analysis, and natural language explanations, enhance interpretability while addressing uncertainties and biases ensure robust and equitable outcomes.

Clear communication, supported by labeling, context, and guidance, equips users to engage with AI outputs responsibly. A comprehensive approach to mitigating bias, ethical development practices, and user-centric features such as control and consent mechanisms further solidify trust.

By embracing these principles, developers can unlock the transformative potential of generative AI, driving meaningful innovation and societal progress. As this technology evolves, maintaining a steadfast focus on user trust will pave the way for harmonious collaboration between humans and AI, shaping a future built on accountability, fairness, and shared success.

As we delve deeper into the complexities of generative AI, the next chapter explores critical topics including potential risks and challenges, strategies for ensuring safe and responsible AI, ethical guidelines and frameworks, and the vital need to address privacy and security concerns.

Questions

1. Why is trust crucial for the adoption of Generative AI systems?

2. What role does transparency and explainability play in building trust in AI?

3. How do uncertainty and bias affect generative AI systems?

4. How can AI developers foster trust through ethical development practices?

5. What steps can organizations take to improve user trust in AI-generated outputs?

Answers

1. Trust is essential for the widespread and responsible adoption of generative AI. If users lack confidence in the system's decision-making process, they will be reluctant to rely on its outputs. Trust influences how users interact with AI, whether they share feedback, provide data, or even adopt the technology in the first place. A lack of trust can lead to skepticism, resistance, and even misuse of AI systems.

2. Transparency and explainability help users understand how an AI system arrives at its decisions, making it more trustworthy. Transparency operates at two levels:

    -   **Algorithmic transparency** – Openness about the model's architecture, training data, and biases ensures that AI systems can be assessed for reliability and fairness.

    -   **Presentation transparency (explainability)** – AI should clearly communicate its reasoning so users can interpret and trust the output. Techniques like attention visualization, saliency maps, and natural language explanations help users understand AI-generated decisions.

3. Uncertainty and bias can significantly impact the fairness and reliability of generative AI:

    -   Uncertainty arises when AI lacks sufficient data, receives vague inputs, or encounters unpredictable scenarios. Addressing it requires probabilistic modeling and confidence scoring to communicate uncertainty effectively.

    -   Bias can be introduced through training data, algorithm design, or societal influences. If not mitigated, biases can lead to unfair or discriminatory outcomes, excluding certain groups or perspectives. Techniques like debiasing algorithms, adversarial training, and diverse data collection help reduce bias and improve fairness.

4. Ethical AI development requires fairness, privacy, and intellectual property protection:

- **Fairness**: AI models should be trained on diverse and representative data to avoid biases.

- **Privacy**: User data should be handled responsibly, following privacy-preserving techniques like differential privacy and encryption.

- **Intellectual property protection**: AI-generated content should respect copyrights and provide proper attribution.

By implementing these principles, developers can build AI systems that users trust and adopt responsibly.

5. Organizations can enhance trust by clearly communicating AI-generated outputs, ensuring users understand their limitations and how to interpret them. Key strategies include:

- Labeling AI-generated content to set clear expectations.

- Providing explanations for recommendations or decisions, ensuring users understand why an output was generated.

- Allowing user control and consent so they can customize AI behavior and influence its decision-making.

Subscribe to AI_Distilled, the go-to newsletter for AI professionals

To keep up with the latest developments in the fields of Generative AI and LLMs, subscribe to our weekly newsletter, AI_Distilled, at `https://packt.link/8Oz6Y`.

9

Managing Safety and Ethical Considerations

In the previous chapter, we explored the pivotal role of trust in facilitating the successful adoption and acceptance of generative AI systems. We examined ways to foster trust, highlighting the role of transparency, explainability, addressing biases and uncertainties, and clear communication of AI outputs to improve user understanding and confidence. As generative AI technologies rapidly advance, fueled by immense interest and excitement across diverse domains from creative industries to healthcare, a sense of urgency has arisen to address the safety and ethical implications of these powerful systems. The discussion now turns to potential risks and challenges associated with generative AI, strategies for safe and responsible deployment, ethical guidelines, and considerations regarding privacy and security.

The remarkable capabilities of generative AI systems have sparked both awe and concern, highlighting the need for a proactive approach to mitigating potential risks and ensuring responsible development and deployment. While these technologies hold immense potential for driving innovation and positive change, their misuse or unintended consequences could have far-reaching implications. This chapter is divided into the following main sections:

- Understanding potential risks and challenges

- Ensuring safe and responsible AI

- Exploring ethical guidelines and frameworks

- Addressing privacy and security concerns

By the end of this chapter, you will understand the key risks and challenges of generative AI, including misinformation and bias concerns, know strategies for safe deployment, and have gained insight into crucial ethical considerations around privacy and data protection. You will also discover frameworks and guidelines for responsible AI development that balance innovation with societal well-being.

Understanding potential risks and challenges

The landscape of AI has evolved significantly with the emergence of **large language models (LLMs)** that power both generative AI and agentic systems. While generative AI focuses primarily on creating content based on prompts and patterns, agentic systems built on these same LLMs take this capability further by incorporating decision-making, planning, and goal-oriented behavior. This combination of generative capabilities with agency creates a powerful but potentially risky synergy.

Agentic systems leverage the generative capabilities of LLMs to not just produce content but also to actively analyze situations, formulate strategies, and take action toward specific objectives. This means that any inherent risks in generative AI systems – such as biases, hallucinations, or the generation of misleading information – become particularly critical when the system is empowered to act autonomously or semi-autonomously based on this generated content.

Generative AI systems are powered by massive language models, which, while incredibly powerful, also exhibit a range of vulnerabilities and risks. These risks can be broadly classified into the following key areas.

Adversarial attacks

One of the significant risks associated with generative AI systems is their susceptibility to adversarial attacks. Malicious individuals can exploit flaws in these systems by crafting carefully designed inputs or perturbations that corrupt the data in a way that leads to harmful outputs or extracts confidential information. These adversarial attacks can have serious consequences, such as data breaches, unauthorized access to sensitive information, or the generation of malicious or misleading content.

When these vulnerabilities extend to agentic systems, the risks become even more pronounced as these systems not only generate responses but also execute actions based on their understanding. An adversarial attack on an agentic system could potentially manipulate its decision-making process, causing it to take harmful actions or make dangerous choices autonomously. For instance, an agentic system managing supply chain operations could be tricked into making catastrophic inventory decisions, or a trading agent could be manipulated into executing harmful financial transactions.

In the travel industry, consider a scenario where an agentic AI system is used by a travel agency to not only provide personalized travel recommendations but also to automatically book flights, hotels, and activities. An adversarial attack on such a system could potentially lead to disastrous consequences. Beyond just recommending unsafe destinations, the system could actively make bookings in dangerous areas, confirm reservations with fraudulent providers, or execute financial transactions that compromise clients' security.

Additionally, adversarial attacks could be used to extract sensitive information, such as customer travel histories, credit card details, or personal preferences, from the system. This risk is amplified in agentic systems because they often have broader access to execute transactions and make decisions, potentially exposing more sensitive data and control points to attackers.

Real-world examples of adversarial attacks on AI systems have already been documented. In 2017, researchers demonstrated how minor perturbations to images could fool state-of-the-art computer vision models into misclassifying objects, such as a stop sign being recognized as a speed limit sign. Similarly, in the natural language processing domain, researchers have shown how carefully crafted input sequences can cause language models to generate harmful or inappropriate content. When these vulnerabilities are exploited in agentic systems, the impact could extend beyond content generation to actual real-world actions and decisions.

Similarly, in a medical context, an adversarial attack on an agentic AI system used for diagnosis or treatment recommendations could potentially lead to life-threatening errors or data leaks. Imagine a scenario where an adversarial input causes the AI to not only misdiagnose a condition but also automatically schedule incorrect treatments, order wrong medications, or make dangerous adjustments to medical devices under its control.

These examples highlight the severe consequences that adversarial attacks can have on both generative and agentic AI systems, underscoring the importance of robust security measures and ongoing research into defense mechanisms against such attacks. Techniques such as adversarial training, input sanitization, and anomaly detection can help mitigate the risks, but it is an ongoing challenge that requires vigilance and collaboration within the AI community. For agentic systems, additional safeguards such as action verification, decision auditing, and multi-step authentication processes become crucial to prevent malicious exploitation of their autonomous capabilities.

Bias and discrimination

We are aware that generative AI models are trained on vast datasets that may carry inherent biases and historical prejudices. When these models form the foundation for agentic systems, the implications of bias become even more critical as these systems not only generate content but also make autonomous decisions that can directly impact people's lives.

The issue of bias in AI systems has been a long-standing concern, and both generative AI models and the agentic systems built upon them are susceptible to this challenge. These models learn from their training data, and if that data contains biases or reflects societal prejudices, the AI will inevitably absorb and perpetuate those biases not just in its outputs but in its decision-making processes and actions too.

For instance, consider an agentic AI system used not just for screening job candidates but also for making autonomous hiring decisions, scheduling interviews, and managing employee assignments. If biased, such a system could systematically discriminate against certain demographic groups throughout the entire employment life cycle, from initial screening to promotion decisions. This automated perpetuation of bias could be particularly harmful as it operates at scale and may be harder to detect than human bias.

In the travel industry, bias in agentic AI systems could manifest beyond mere recommendations to actual booking decisions and resource allocations. An autonomous travel management system might systematically direct certain demographic groups to specific neighborhoods or price ranges, effectively implementing digital redlining. It might also autonomously negotiate different rates or terms for different users based on biased assumptions, creating a form of algorithmic discrimination in pricing and service delivery.

In 2018, researchers found that commercial facial recognition systems exhibited higher error rates for identifying women and people with darker skin tones. When such biased systems are integrated into agentic AI that controls access to buildings, financial services, or healthcare resources, these technical shortcomings transform into systemic barriers that actively restrict opportunities and services for certain groups.

Addressing bias in agentic AI systems requires an expanded approach beyond what's needed for traditional generative AI. While diverse training data and debiasing algorithms remain important, additional measures are needed to ensure fairness in autonomous decision-making. This includes implementing decision auditing systems, creating accountability frameworks for autonomous actions, and developing real-time bias detection mechanisms that can intervene before discriminatory actions are taken.

Moreover, involving diverse stakeholders becomes even more crucial when developing agentic systems, as these stakeholders can help identify potential negative impacts across the full range of autonomous actions the system might take. Regular audits of not just the system's outputs but also its decision-making patterns and action histories are essential for detecting and correcting systematic biases.

By proactively addressing biases in both generative and agentic AI systems, organizations can ensure these technologies serve as tools for promoting equity rather than reinforcing discrimination. This is particularly critical for agentic systems, as their ability to autonomously act on biased assumptions can multiply the harmful effects of discrimination and create self-reinforcing cycles of inequity.

Misinformation and hallucinations

Generative AI systems have a tendency to produce information that may be factually incorrect or inconsistent with reality, a phenomenon known as **hallucination**. When these systems are integrated into autonomous agents, the implications become even more serious, as hallucinated information can directly influence real-world decisions and actions taken by the agent. The hallucination problem in both generative and agentic AI systems stems from their underlying architecture. While incredibly powerful, these models lack a true understanding of the world and cannot reliably distinguish between factual information and fabricated content. In agentic systems, this limitation is particularly concerning because the agent may act upon hallucinated information without human verification, potentially causing cascading errors or harmful decisions.

In the realm of autonomous decision-making, an agentic system that hallucinates could take actions based on non-existent information or false assumptions. For instance, an autonomous trading agent might execute large financial transactions based on hallucinated market trends, or a healthcare management agent might schedule treatments based on incorrectly generated medical histories. These scenarios are far more dangerous than simple content generation errors, as they involve direct real-world consequences.

For example, consider an agentic AI system deployed in emergency response management. If the system hallucinates information about the severity or location of an emergency, it could autonomously dispatch resources to the wrong location or make inappropriate response decisions, potentially putting lives at risk. Unlike a generative system that merely produces incorrect text, an agentic system's hallucinations can lead to immediate, real-world actions with serious consequences.

In the travel industry, hallucinations in agentic AI systems could go beyond just providing incorrect information – they could result in actual bookings being made based on non-existent flights or hotels, autonomous rerouting of travelers based on hallucinated weather conditions, or emergency evacuations triggered by fabricated security threats.

Real-world examples of hallucinations in AI systems have been documented across various domains. In 2022, researchers found that large language models such as GPT-3 can produce *hallucinated* scientific claims that sound plausible but are entirely fabricated. For agentic systems built on these models, such hallucinations could lead to automated decisions in research resource allocation, experimental design, or data analysis that could compromise scientific integrity.

Addressing hallucinations in agentic AI systems requires additional safeguards beyond those used for generative AI. While fact-checking and knowledge grounding remain important, agentic systems also need real-time verification mechanisms, action validation protocols, and fallback procedures for cases where information reliability is uncertain. Moreover, implementing *uncertainty-aware* decision-making processes that can appropriately handle cases where the agent is not confident about its information is crucial.

When deploying agentic systems, organizations must implement robust monitoring systems that can detect and prevent actions based on hallucinated information before they occur. This might include multi-step verification processes for critical decisions, confidence thresholds for autonomous actions, and human oversight mechanisms for high-stakes situations. By proactively addressing hallucinations in agentic AI systems, organizations can better ensure that autonomous agents make decisions based on reliable information. This is particularly critical as these systems become more prevalent in domains where incorrect actions could have significant consequences for safety, security, or business operations.

Data privacy violations

Generative AI models are trained on vast amounts of data, which may inadvertently include **personally identifiable information** (**PII**) or sensitive data. In agentic systems, this risk is compounded because these systems not only process and generate information but also actively access, manipulate, and make decisions about personal data as part of their autonomous operations.

The sheer volume of data required to train and operate these systems increases the likelihood of privacy violations. For agentic systems, this risk extends beyond training data to include operational data that they actively collect and use, such as user interactions, transaction histories, and real-time behavioral data that helps them make decisions.

For example, an agentic AI system in healthcare might not only have access to historical medical records for training but also actively manage patient scheduling, treatment plans, and medical device settings. If such a system mishandles private information, it could autonomously share sensitive medical details with unauthorized parties, schedule appointments that reveal confidential conditions, or make treatment decisions that inadvertently expose protected health information.

In the travel industry, privacy violations could occur when agentic systems go beyond simple data exposure to actively making privacy-compromising decisions. An autonomous travel assistant might not just leak travel itineraries but could also make bookings that reveal sensitive personal information, automatically share location data with third parties, or create patterns of behavior that expose confidential business travel or personal relationships. The risks became evident in 2019 when OpenAI's language model was found to have memorized and reproduced portions of its training data such as personal information like emails, home addresses, and phone numbers. For agentic systems, similar issues could lead to automated decisions being made based on memorized private information, potentially causing systematic privacy violations at scale.

Addressing data privacy violations in agentic AI systems requires an enhanced approach beyond traditional generative AI safeguards. While robust data governance and sanitization remain crucial, agentic systems also need real-time privacy monitoring, decision auditing systems, and automatic privacy-preserving mechanisms that prevent unauthorized data access or sharing during autonomous operations. Additionally, techniques such as differential privacy must be adapted for dynamic decision-making scenarios. Organizations need to implement privacy-aware decision protocols that ensure autonomous actions don't inadvertently reveal sensitive information through patterns of behavior or chains of decisions, even when individual actions appear privacy-compliant.

To safeguard privacy in these systems, new frameworks must extend beyond traditional data protection measures. Teams deploying agentic AI need to scrutinize how autonomous decisions could compromise privacy across time – watching for subtle patterns that might reveal sensitive information through a series of seemingly innocent actions. This means rethinking privacy from the ground up: privacy isn't just about protecting data anymore, but about understanding how chains of autonomous decisions could inadvertently reveal what should stay hidden.

The most successful deployments of agentic AI will likely be those that make privacy an integral part of their system's "nervous system" rather than an afterthought. This means building systems that instinctively protect privacy at every decision point, much like how humans naturally modulate their behavior to protect sensitive information in different contexts. When privacy becomes part of the agent's core decision-making process rather than just a compliance checkbox, we can better ensure these powerful systems enhance rather than endanger our privacy rights in an increasingly automated world.

Intellectual property risks

The integration of generative AI capabilities into agentic systems introduces complex intellectual property challenges that go far beyond traditional content generation concerns. When autonomous agents are empowered to not only create content but also make decisions about how to use, modify, and deploy intellectual property, the stakes become significantly higher.

The increasing use of autonomous agents in content generation raises significant concerns about **intellectual property (IP)** infringement, necessitating robust detection and mitigation strategies. AI-generated content tracking systems such as *Copyleaks* for plagiarism detection, Google's *SynthID* for watermarking AI-generated images, and *Truepic* for verifying digital authenticity help identify unauthorized use of copyrighted material. Dataset auditing tools such as Hugging Face's *Dataset Card Standard*, LAION's transparency efforts, and Adobe's **Content Authenticity Initiative (CAI)** ensure that datasets used by autonomous agents comply with licensing and provenance requirements. Automated copyright violation detection services, including Microsoft's *Azure Content Moderator*, *Amazon Rekognition* for identifying copyrighted images and logos, and Meta's *Rights Manager* for monitoring IP violations across social platforms, further enhance compliance efforts. Additionally, legal and policy compliance frameworks, such as *WIPO PROOF* for timestamping IP ownership (now discontinued), IBM's *AI Governance Toolkit* for assessing infringement risks, and OpenAI's licensing agreements that impose API-level restrictions, provide structured safeguards against IP violations. By integrating these methodologies, organizations can ensure that autonomous agents operate within ethical and legal boundaries, minimizing the risks associated with unauthorized content generation and distribution.

The fundamental challenge stems from both the training and operational aspects of these systems. During training, agentic AI systems, like their generative counterparts, ingest vast amounts of potentially copyrighted material – from code and design files to creative works and proprietary business processes. But unlike purely generative systems, agents can actively implement this learned information in ways that could systematically violate intellectual property rights at scale and at machine speed.

Consider an autonomous software development agent that doesn't just suggest code snippets but actively writes and deploys applications. Such a system might inadvertently incorporate proprietary algorithms or protected code patterns across thousands of projects before any violation is detected. Similarly, in creative industries, an agentic system managing content production could autonomously remix and repurpose copyrighted materials in ways that create complex chains of derivative works, each with its own potential infringement issues.

The real-world implications are already emerging. The 2022 lawsuit against Stability AI's Stable Diffusion image generator highlighted concerns about training data usage (`https://jipel.law.nyu.edu/andersen-v-stability-ai-the-landmark-case-unpacking-the-copyright-risks-of-ai-image-generators/`), but agentic systems raise even thornier questions. What happens when an AI agent autonomously creates and executes marketing campaigns using style elements it learned from copyrighted works? Or when it modifies and redistributes protected content based on its understanding of fair use?

Addressing these challenges requires a radical rethinking of intellectual property protection in an age of autonomous systems. Organizations must develop new frameworks that can anticipate and prevent potential IP violations before they occur, rather than just detecting them after the fact. This means implementing real-time monitoring systems that can track the provenance of agent-generated content and decision trees that can evaluate IP implications before autonomous actions are taken.

Technical innovation will play a crucial role in this evolution. We're seeing the emergence of new approaches such as blockchain-based content tracking, automated license verification systems, and AI agents specifically designed to audit other agents for potential IP violations. These tools, combined with traditional legal safeguards, form the foundation of a new approach to IP protection in the age of autonomous systems.

As we navigate this complex landscape, flexibility and adaptation will be key. The legal frameworks governing intellectual property were designed for a world of human creators and human decision-makers. As agentic AI systems become more prevalent, these frameworks will need to evolve – not just to protect existing rights but also to foster innovation in a world where machines are increasingly active participants in the creative process.

Ensuring safe and responsible AI

The deployment of LLM-based agentic systems introduces unique safety and responsibility challenges that go beyond those of traditional generative AI. While generative AI primarily focuses on content creation, agentic systems can autonomously plan, decide, and act, making their safe deployment significantly more complex and critical. Core safety considerations for agentic systems include the following:

- **Action boundaries**: Defining strict action boundaries is critical to ensuring that agentic systems operate within safe and ethical constraints. These boundaries can be enforced using policy-based governance frameworks such as OpenAI's Function Calling API and Amazon Bedrock Guardrails, which allow agents to interact with external systems while adhering to predefined operational limits. Additionally, **role-based access control** (**RBAC**) and context-aware permissions can be implemented to restrict agents from taking unauthorized actions, particularly in high-risk domains such as finance and healthcare.

- **Decision verification**: Agentic systems must incorporate multi-step validation processes for critical decisions, ensuring robustness and alignment with human oversight. This can be achieved using neural-symbolic reasoning, constraint satisfaction models, and logical verification techniques that validate each decision against predefined ethical and operational constraints before execution. Techniques such as tree search algorithms and Monte Carlo simulations can be applied to evaluate multiple possible outcomes and ensure optimal decision-making in real time.

- **Rollback capabilities**: The ability to undo or reverse autonomous actions is essential for mitigating unintended consequences. This can be implemented through event sourcing and state management frameworks such as Apache Kafka and Temporal.io, which maintain an immutable log of agent actions, enabling controlled rollbacks. Version control for decision states, combined with checkpointing mechanisms, can allow systems to revert to a stable state when anomalies or failures are detected.

- **Real-time monitoring**: Continuous monitoring of agent behavior is crucial for detecting deviations and preventing harmful actions. Anomaly detection models such as Facebook's AI Anomaly Detection Pipeline and Amazon CloudWatch anomaly detection use machine learning-based pattern recognition to track behavioral shifts in real time. Additionally, drift detection algorithms can identify when an agent's behavior diverges from expected patterns, triggering alerts or initiating corrective actions. **Explainable AI (XAI)** techniques further enhance monitoring by providing human-readable insights into why an agent made a particular decision.

- **Reinforcement learning feedback loops**: Incorporating human-in-the-loop oversight through **reinforcement learning from human feedback (RLHF)** helps fine-tune agentic decision-making. By continuously integrating feedback from human reviewers, agents can improve their behavior over time while maintaining safety and ethical alignment. In high-stakes environments, hybrid AI-human workflows can be used to escalate decisions that require human judgment.

- **Performance metrics**: Evaluating agentic systems requires more than just output quality; it must also assess decision consistency, ethical alignment, risk assessment, and adaptability. AI auditing tools such as IBM's AI Fairness 360 and Google's Explainable AI provide comprehensive evaluation frameworks that measure not only accuracy but also transparency, robustness, and fairness. Additionally, causal inference models can help quantify the impact of agent decisions, ensuring alignment with ethical and regulatory standards.

By integrating these technologies and methodologies, organizations can deploy agentic systems that are *safe, transparent,* and *aligned with regulatory and ethical considerations*, reducing the risks associated with autonomous decision-making while maintaining operational efficiency.

Let's examine how these safety measures manifest in practical deployments. Consider an agentic system managing a corporate travel program – beyond just generating recommendations, it actively books flights, adjusts schedules, and manages expenses. A system like this demands layered safety protocols that address both its generative and autonomous aspects, as highlighted here:

- Action boundaries might include financial limits on booking changes without approval, restrictions on booking destinations flagged as high risk, and rules about when schedule changes can be made autonomously

- Decision verification could involve multi-step checks before finalizing expensive bookings – perhaps requiring human approval for transactions above certain thresholds or automated cross-verification with company travel policies

- The system's rollback capabilities would need to account for real-world constraints, such as airline cancellation policies or hotel booking deadlines, ensuring that autonomous actions don't incur unnecessary penalties

- Real-time monitoring in this context would track patterns of bookings and expenses, flagging unusual activities such as multiple booking changes in short succession or deviations from typical corporate travel patterns

- Performance metrics would go beyond simple measures such as successful bookings to evaluate decision quality – for instance, assessing whether the system consistently makes cost-effective choices while respecting traveler preferences and company policies

This travel management example demonstrates how safety measures must be carefully tailored to both protect against potential risks and ensure efficient operation. The system needs to balance autonomy (such as automatically rebooking disrupted flights) with appropriate caution (such as requiring approval for significant itinerary changes), all while maintaining clear audit trails and explanation capabilities for its decisions. *Figure 9.1* shows the safety measures for this agentic travel management system:

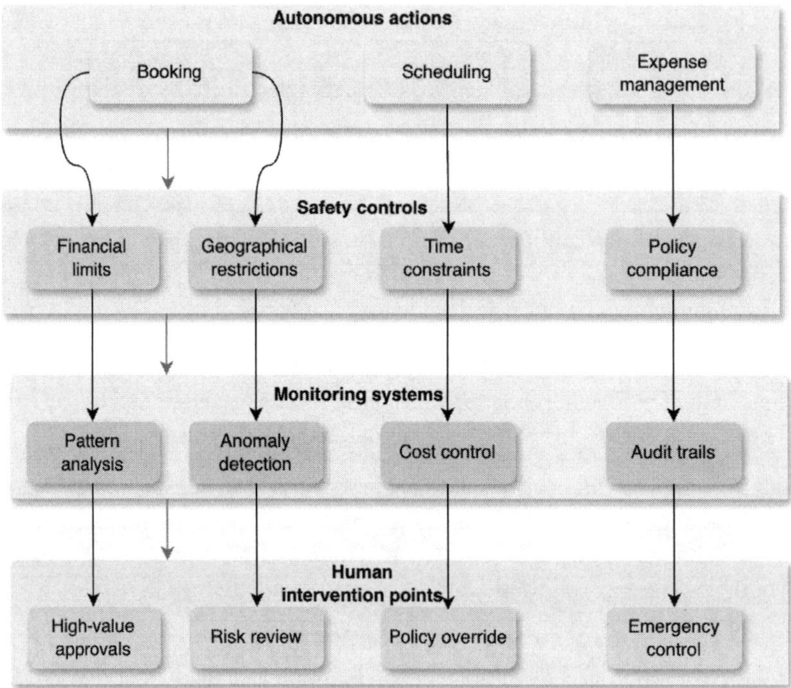

Figure 9.1 – Safety measures for agentic travel management system

Testing for agentic systems must be more comprehensive than traditional generative AI testing. While generative AI testing focuses on output quality, agentic system testing must evaluate entire decision chains and action sequences. This includes simulating complex scenarios where the agent must make interconnected decisions, handle unexpected situations, and maintain safety constraints across multiple actions.

Human oversight takes on new dimensions with agentic systems. Rather than simply reviewing generated content, humans must monitor decision patterns, intervene in complex situations, and help refine the system's understanding of acceptable actions. This creates a need for new oversight tools and frameworks that can track and evaluate autonomous behavior in real time.

The concept of *safe learning* becomes crucial for agentic systems. These systems must be able to learn from experience without compromising safety during operation. This might involve creating sandboxed environments where agents can safely explore new strategies or implementing gradual automation where human oversight is reduced as the system proves its reliability. Critical implementation strategies include the following:

- **Progressive autonomy**: Starting with heavily restricted action capabilities and gradually expanding them based on demonstrated reliability

- **Contextual safety bounds**: Implementing different safety protocols based on the risk level of specific actions

- **Continuous validation**: Regular assessment of decision patterns to identify potential safety risks

- **Emergency protocols**: Clear procedures for rapid human intervention when needed

Trust building with agentic systems requires more than just transparency – it needs demonstrable reliability in autonomous operation. Organizations must develop clear frameworks for communicating both the capabilities and limitations of their agentic systems, helping stakeholders understand when and how to rely on autonomous decisions.

The ethical deployment of agentic systems also requires careful consideration of societal impact. These systems must be designed to respect not just individual privacy and rights but also broader social values and norms. Implementing explicit ethical constraints in the decision-making process involves encoding predefined ethical rules, fairness constraints, and compliance policies into the system's logic using techniques such as constraint programming, rule-based ethics engines, and reinforcement learning with ethical reward models. For example, symbolic AI approaches can integrate formal ethics rules (e.g., Asimov's laws of robotics and GDPR privacy requirements) directly into decision-making pipelines, ensuring that agents adhere to predefined ethical boundaries. Additionally, differential privacy mechanisms and bias mitigation algorithms (such as IBM's AI Fairness 360) can enforce fairness and privacy compliance at runtime.

To ensure ethical adaptability, organizations can implement community feedback loops using **human-in-the-loop** (**HITL**) systems, where flagged decisions are reviewed and incorporated into future model refinements. Additionally, governance frameworks should include periodic ethical audits, the establishment of red-teaming exercises to stress-test decision-making under edge cases, and mechanisms for incorporating stakeholder feedback into system improvements. As agentic systems become more prevalent, these comprehensive governance measures will be critical in balancing automation with ethical responsibility, ensuring that AI-driven decisions align with societal expectations and regulatory requirements.

By understanding and addressing these unique challenges of agentic systems, organizations can work toward deployments that not only leverage the power of autonomous operation but do so in a way that prioritizes safety, responsibility, and ethical considerations throughout the system's life cycle.

Exploring ethical guidelines and frameworks

As generative AI systems become increasingly sophisticated and integrated into various aspects of society, it is crucial to establish robust ethical guidelines and frameworks to ensure their responsible development and deployment. A sound ethical framework should encompass a range of principles and guidelines that prioritize human well-being, accountability, privacy protection, and inclusive governance.

Human-centric design

At the core of ethical AI development lies the principle of human-centric design. Generative AI systems should be designed with a focus on enhancing human well-being and delivering positive experiences. This requires developing intuitive, accessible, and inclusive solutions that are aligned with human values, such as fairness, dignity, and respect for individual autonomy.

For example, in the context of a travel agency, a human-centric generative AI system would prioritize personalized recommendations that cater to diverse preferences, cultural sensitivities, and accessibility needs, ensuring that all users can benefit from the technology in a meaningful and respectful manner.

Accountability and responsibility

Organizations developing and deploying generative AI systems must be held accountable for the outputs and potential impacts of these technologies. This involves establishing clear lines of responsibility, comprehensive documentation of decision-making processes, and mechanisms for reviewing and addressing ethical implications.

Implementing review boards or advisory committees comprising interdisciplinary experts, including ethicists, legal professionals, and representatives from potentially affected communities, can help organizations navigate complex ethical challenges and ensure responsible decision-making.

Privacy and data protection

User privacy and data protection should be embedded as foundational principles in the development of generative AI systems. Organizations must adopt a **privacy-by-design** approach, practicing data minimization, anonymizing sensitive data, and ensuring that data handling practices comply with relevant privacy laws and regulations. A privacy-by-design approach ensures that AI systems embed privacy protections at every stage, minimizing risks while complying with laws such as **General Data Protection Regulation (GDPR)**, **California Consumer Privacy Act (CCPA)**, and **Health Insurance Portability and Accountability Act (HIPAA)**. This includes data minimization (collecting only essential information), anonymization (using techniques such as k-anonymity and pseudonymization), and **privacy-preserving machine learning** (PPML) methods such as federated learning, homomorphic encryption, and **secure multi-party computation (SMPC)**. For example, in a healthcare AI assistant, patient data can be encrypted and processed locally using federated learning, while **role-based access control (RBAC)** ensures that only authorized personnel can access sensitive data. Additionally, automated audit logs and explainability tools track decisions for accountability. These techniques help organizations deploy AI responsibly, ensuring privacy without sacrificing functionality.

In the travel industry, this could involve implementing robust data governance frameworks, obtaining explicit consent from users for data collection and usage, and implementing secure data storage and processing mechanisms to protect sensitive information such as travel histories, preferences, and payment details.

Involvement of diverse stakeholders

Ethical AI development requires the involvement of diverse stakeholders, including ethicists, technologists, policymakers, and representatives from potentially affected communities. This collaborative approach fosters inclusive dialogue, identifies potential blind spots or unintended consequences, and promotes more equitable and socially responsible approaches to AI governance.

For instance, in the development of a generative AI system for travel recommendations, engaging with stakeholders from diverse cultural backgrounds, disability rights advocates, and environmental organizations could help identify potential biases, accessibility barriers, or sustainability concerns, leading to more inclusive and responsible solutions.

By adhering to these ethical guidelines and frameworks, organizations can foster trust, accountability, and responsible innovation in the development and deployment of generative AI technologies. This approach not only mitigates potential risks and unintended consequences but also unlocks the full potential of these powerful technologies to drive positive societal impact while upholding fundamental human rights and values.

Addressing privacy and security concerns

As generative AI systems become increasingly prevalent across various domains, addressing privacy and security concerns is of utmost importance. Organizations must take proactive measures to safeguard sensitive data, protect against potential breaches, and ensure the resilience of their AI systems against malicious attacks.

In the context of a travel agency employing a generative AI system for personalized recommendations and itinerary planning, implementing a comprehensive data governance framework is crucial. This framework should outline data handling practices, access controls, and compliance measures to protect private information within the organization, such as customer travel histories, preferences, and payment details.

Access controls and role-based permissions can help ensure that only authorized personnel can access and modify sensitive data used for training or generating recommendations. Additionally, adhering to relevant data protection laws and industry-specific regulations, such as the GDPR or the **Payment Card Industry Data Security Standard** (**PCI DSS**), is essential to maintain compliance and avoid potential legal liabilities.

Incorporating security considerations into the AI development life cycle is also vital. This includes conducting regular security risk assessments to identify potential vulnerabilities, implementing secure coding standards to mitigate coding errors or vulnerabilities, and performing regular testing and audits to detect and address any security weaknesses in the AI system. For example, the travel agency could employ penetration testing techniques to simulate potential attack scenarios and assess the resilience of their generative AI system against adversarial attacks or data breaches. This proactive approach can help identify and address security gaps before they are exploited by malicious actors.

Educating users about the potential risks associated with generative AI and providing training on safe usage practices can empower them to make informed decisions and recognize potential threats. In the travel agency scenario, this could involve educating customers about the importance of safeguarding their personal information, recognizing phishing attempts or suspicious communications, and reporting any concerns or incidents promptly.

Organizations should also establish robust incident response plans to deal with potential security breaches or data leaks effectively. These plans should outline clear protocols for rapid response, containment, investigation, and mitigation strategies to limit the damage and protect affected individuals or entities.

In the event of a data breach involving customer information, the travel agency should be prepared to swiftly notify affected individuals, regulatory authorities, and stakeholders, while implementing measures to secure the compromised systems and prevent further data loss.

Additionally, techniques such as adversarial training and anomaly detection can help improve the resilience of generative AI systems against adversarial attacks specifically. Adversarial training involves exposing the AI model to carefully crafted adversarial examples during the training process, enhancing its ability to recognize and defend against such attacks. Anomaly detection algorithms can identify and flag suspicious or anomalous inputs or outputs, enabling timely intervention and mitigation efforts. By prioritizing privacy and security considerations throughout the AI development and deployment life cycle, organizations can foster trust and confidence in their generative AI systems, while ensuring compliance with relevant regulations and safeguarding sensitive data and intellectual property.

Summary

In this chapter, we discovered that while advanced intelligent agentic systems hold immense potential to drive innovation, enhance creativity, and revolutionize various industries, their deployment and development must be approached with utmost care and responsibility. Armed with awareness of the potential risks and challenges associated with generative AI, organizations and stakeholders can proactively implement measures to ensure safety, uphold ethical principles, and address privacy and security concerns. By doing so, they can harness the transformative power of these technologies in a trustworthy and accountable manner, fostering confidence among users and stakeholders. Embracing a proactive and responsible approach to generative AI development involves implementing robust testing and monitoring frameworks, adhering to ethical guidelines and frameworks that prioritize human well-being, accountability, and inclusive governance, and establishing comprehensive data governance and security protocols to safeguard sensitive information and intellectual property.

It is crucial to address the uncertainties and biases in AI systems. By employing techniques such as probabilistic modeling, uncertainty quantification, and debiasing algorithms, developers can improve the reliability and fairness of generative AI models, fostering trust and responsible adoption. Collaboration among stakeholders, including developers, researchers, policymakers, and ethicists, is essential for navigating the challenges and ethical implications of generative AI. An inclusive, multidisciplinary approach helps identify blind spots, mitigate unintended consequences, and align solutions with human values. Agentic systems heighten AI risks by autonomously acting on biased or compromised information, making robust safety measures, including action boundaries, decision verification, and real-time monitoring, critical. Effective deployment requires balancing autonomy with appropriate human oversight, especially for high-stake decisions. Privacy protection must extend beyond data safeguards to account for the potential exposure of sensitive information through autonomous decisions. Additionally, intellectual property frameworks must evolve to handle AI agents as active creators, with real-time monitoring and verification systems in place.

In the next chapter, we will explore some of the common use cases and applications of LLM-based intelligent agents using various patterns and techniques that we've learned so far.

Questions

1. How do the risks of hallucination differ between generative AI and agentic systems? Why are hallucinations potentially more dangerous in agentic systems?

2. What are the core safety considerations that need to be implemented when deploying LLM-based agentic systems, and how do they manifest in a practical example such as a travel management system?

3. How does bias in agentic AI systems differ from bias in traditional generative AI systems, and what additional measures are needed to address it?

4. What unique challenges do agentic systems pose for data privacy compared to traditional generative AI systems, and how should organizations address these challenges?

5. How do intellectual property risks evolve when moving from generative AI to agentic systems, and what new approaches are needed to address these risks?

Answers

1. In generative AI, hallucinations primarily result in incorrect content generation, but in agentic systems, hallucinated information can directly influence real-world decisions and actions. For example, while a generative AI might simply produce incorrect text, an agentic system might execute financial transactions based on hallucinated market trends or make medical decisions based on fabricated patient histories. This is more dangerous because it leads to immediate real-world consequences without human verification.

2. Core safety considerations include action boundaries, decision verification, rollback capabilities, real-time monitoring, and performance metrics. In a travel management system, they manifest as financial limits on booking changes, multi-step checks for expensive bookings, mechanisms to handle cancellation policies, tracking of booking patterns for anomalies, and evaluation of decision quality against company policies and traveler preferences. These measures ensure both protection against risks and efficient operation.

3. Bias in agentic systems goes beyond generating biased content to actively making biased decisions that affect people's lives. For example, while a generative AI might produce biased text, an agentic system could systematically discriminate in hiring decisions or resource allocations. Additional measures needed include decision auditing systems, accountability frameworks for autonomous actions, real-time bias detection mechanisms, and regular audits of decision-making patterns and action histories.

4. Agentic systems not only process and generate information but actively access, manipulate, and make decisions about personal data during operations. They need enhanced safeguards including real-time privacy monitoring, decision auditing systems, and privacy-aware decision protocols. Organizations must scrutinize how chains of autonomous decisions could reveal sensitive information over time, even when individual actions appear privacy-compliant, and make privacy an integral part of the system's decision-making process.

5. Agentic systems can actively implement learned information and make decisions about intellectual property use at machine speed and scale. For example, they might autonomously incorporate proprietary code across thousands of projects or create complex chains of derivative works. New approaches needed include real-time monitoring systems for content provenance, decision trees for evaluating IP implications before actions, blockchain-based content tracking, and automated license verification systems. Legal frameworks need to evolve to handle machines as active participants in the creative process.

10

Common Use Cases and Applications

Building upon our previous examination of risks and challenges in LLM-based agent systems, from adversarial attacks to ethical concerns, we now turn our attention to their practical applications. This chapter explores how agentic systems are transforming various domains by combining LLMs with goal-directed behavior and autonomous decision-making capabilities. We'll see how these agents can understand context, formulate plans, and take action to achieve specific objectives while maintaining meaningful interactions with humans.

As we explore these applications, we will focus on how agents leverage LLMs not just as language processors but also as core reasoning engines that enable sophisticated planning and execution across different domains. This represents a fundamental shift from traditional AI systems, as these agents can now adapt their behavior, learn from interactions, and operate with increasing levels of autonomy while maintaining alignment with human intentions. The chapter begins by exploring the transformative impact of LLM-based agents in creative and artistic domains, followed by their advancements in natural language processing and conversational systems. It then delves into the integration of these agents within robotics and autonomous systems, culminating in their role in decision support and optimization.

 The chapter is structured into four main sections:

- Creative and artistic applications

- Natural language processing and conversational agents

- Robotics and autonomous systems

- Decision support and optimization

By the end of this chapter, you will understand how LLM-based agents are reshaping our approach to automation and human-AI collaboration across different domains. This knowledge will help you identify opportunities for deploying agentic systems in your own fields while maintaining awareness of the unique capabilities and considerations that come with these more autonomous and interactive AI systems.

Creative and artistic applications

The integration of LLM-based agents in creative fields marks a significant evolution beyond simple generative AI tools. This section explores how agentic systems are transforming creative workflows through their ability to understand context, maintain creative direction, and actively collaborate with human artists. Unlike traditional AI tools that simply generate content, these agents can engage in sustained creative dialogues, adapt to changing requirements, and balance multiple artistic and technical constraints simultaneously.

Evolution of creative and artistic agents

The development of creative and artistic agents represents a paradigm shift in how AI systems contribute to the creative process. Early generative AI tools focused primarily on producing static outputs based on predefined prompts, offering limited interaction and adaptability. Modern agentic systems, however, have evolved to actively participate in dynamic and iterative creative processes. They leverage advanced capabilities such as context retention, adaptive learning, and multi-modal integration to function as true collaborators rather than passive tools. These agents not only generate content but also understand artistic intent, refine outputs based on feedback, and align with human collaborators' vision. This evolution underscores a broader trend in AI development, moving from static generation to interactive, context-aware, and adaptive systems that complement and enhance human creativity in unprecedented ways. Key areas where agentic systems are making an impact include the following:

- **Artistic collaboration**: Agents that can assist artists by maintaining a consistent style, artistic intent, and thematic coherence across multiple iterations, enabling seamless integration of human creativity with AI-generated enhancements

- **Music composition**: Systems that are designed to understand and apply musical theory, adapt to different genres, and collaborate in real time with performers or composers to create harmonious and innovative compositions

- **Writing and narrative development**: Agents that can co-create with authors by maintaining character consistency, plot coherence, and narrative flow, offering creative suggestions while preserving the author's unique voice and storytelling style

Real-world applications

The practical implementation of agentic systems in creative fields has already begun to show promising results. Adobe's Firefly agent system demonstrates how multiple specialized agents can maintain creative consistency across complex projects. In this system, different agents work in concert: one maintains brand identity and style guidelines, another ensures consistent asset representation across various media, and a third handles technical specifications and format requirements. This represents a significant evolution from simple generative tools to a collaborative system that maintains creative context and adapts to user feedback in real time.

Similarly, Universal Music Group's AI-powered music production system showcases how agentic systems can maintain creative coherence in musical composition. The system employs specialized agents for different aspects of music creation: melody agents that understand musical themes and motifs, harmony agents that maintain tonal consistency, and orchestration agents that handle instrumental arrangement. These agents work together while preserving the composer's creative intent and style preferences throughout the production process, demonstrating how multiple agents can collaborate on complex creative tasks while maintaining artistic vision.

To better understand how agentic systems can transform complex creative workflows, let's examine a detailed use case from the film industry. This example demonstrates how multiple agents can collaborate to bridge the gap between creative vision and technical execution, a challenge that has long plagued the pre-visualization process in film production.

Problem statement

Film directors and storyboard artists spend considerable time iterating on pre-visualization sequences, requiring constant communication between multiple departments to align creative vision with technical feasibility. Traditional tools lack the ability to understand and adapt to creative intent while considering technical constraints. The goal is to create a multi-agent system that assists in translating the director's creative vision into technically feasible pre-visualization sequences while maintaining artistic coherence and production constraints.

The agentic system approach is as follows:

- **Director agent**:

    - Processes natural language descriptions of scenes

    - Maintains overall creative vision and style consistency

    - Communicates artistic intent to other agents

- **Technical supervisor agent**:

  - Evaluates technical feasibility

  - Considers budget and resource constraints

  - Proposes alternative solutions when needed

- **Visualization agent**:

  - Generates initial storyboards and 3D previews

  - Adapts output based on feedback from other agents

  - Maintains visual consistency across scenes

The agents work together through the following means:

- Shared context understanding via LLM capabilities

- Continuous feedback loops between creative and technical requirements

- Real-time adaptation to changes in either creative direction or technical constraints

Environment and external systems

The multi-agent system operates within a production environment that includes the following:

- **Asset management database**: Stores 3D models, textures, and previous storyboards

- **Production management system**: Tracks budgets, schedules, and resource allocation

- **Rendering farm API**: Manages compute resources for 3D visualization

- **Camera and equipment database**: Technical specifications and availability

- **Reference library**: Archive of past productions, style guides, and mood boards

- **Version control system**: Maintains history of iterations and changes

- **Collaboration platform**: Enables real-time feedback from team members

Why this is better

Current pre-visualization tools operate in isolation, requiring human intermediaries to translate between creative and technical requirements. An agentic system approach provides several advantages:

- Continuous alignment between creative vision and technical feasibility

- Reduced iteration cycles through real-time collaboration

- Ability to maintain creative consistency while adapting to constraints

- More efficient resource utilization through automated technical validation

This approach highlights how agentic systems go beyond simple content generation to actively contribute to creative decision-making processes, addressing multiple constraints and objectives with nuanced understanding. Their success in pre-visualization underscores their broader applicability in creative domains that require complex collaboration, iterative refinement, and the ability to adapt to evolving artistic visions. By retaining context, understanding intent, and balancing competing priorities, these systems are emerging as indispensable creative partners rather than mere tools.

Having explored their transformative impact on creative workflows, we now shift our focus to one of the most groundbreaking applications of agentic systems: natural language processing and conversational interfaces. These systems excel at understanding nuanced language, maintaining context in complex dialogues, and executing tasks effectively, making them essential for fostering meaningful human-AI interactions – a topic we'll delve into in the next section.

Natural language processing and conversational agents

Building on our exploration of creative applications, we now turn to perhaps the most natural domain for LLM-based agents: language understanding and conversation. While traditional language models can process and generate text, agentic systems add crucial capabilities: maintaining context over long interactions, executing complex tasks through dialogue, and adapting their responses based on user needs and feedback.

Evolution of language agents

Today's conversational agents represent a significant leap beyond simple chatbots or virtual assistants. These systems can maintain complex dialogues, understand nuanced contexts, and execute sophisticated tasks through natural conversation. For example, Anthropic's Claude and OpenAI's ChatGPT can engage in detailed technical discussions while maintaining consistency across multiple turns, adapting responses based on the user's level of expertise and previous interactions. Key capabilities that distinguish modern language agents from traditional chatbots are as follows:

- **Context retention**: Modern language agents excel at maintaining coherent and meaningful discussions, even as conversations evolve across multiple topics and sessions. This ability to remember prior exchanges allows them to provide more personalized and contextually relevant responses over time.

- **Task execution**: These agents go beyond simple Q&A functionality by translating natural language instructions into actionable steps, enabling seamless task completion in areas such as scheduling, data retrieval, or system configuration. This capability bridges the gap between communication and execution.

- **Adaptive interaction**: Modern agents dynamically adjust their communication style, tone, and complexity to suit user preferences, expertise levels, or situational needs, fostering more engaging and accessible interactions for diverse audiences.

- **Multi-modal understanding**: Unlike traditional chatbots, modern agents can process and respond to combinations of text, images, code, and structured data, enabling them to tackle more complex queries and integrate diverse forms of information for a richer, more nuanced understanding of user requests.

Real-world applications

Current implementations demonstrate the versatility of language agents across different domains. For instance, Salesforce's Agentforce (formerly the Einstein virtual assistant) helps customer service representatives by maintaining context across multiple customer interactions while accessing relevant database information in real time. Similarly, GitHub's Copilot Chat can maintain technical discussions about code while executing relevant development tasks. Let's take a look at a use case involving an enterprise knowledge management system.

Problem statement

Large organizations struggle with knowledge fragmentation across departments, making it difficult for employees to access and utilize institutional knowledge effectively. Traditional search systems and documentation fail to capture context and connections between different pieces of information.

To solve the problem, create a multi-agent system that can understand, organize, and retrieve corporate knowledge while maintaining context and handling complex queries that span multiple domains and documents.

Here's the agentic system approach:

- **Query understanding agent**:

    - Processes natural language questions

    - Identifies implicit context and requirements

    - Breaks down complex queries into subtasks

- **Knowledge navigation agent**:

    - Maps relationships between different knowledge sources

    - Maintains context across multiple documents

    - Tracks information provenance

- **Response synthesis agent**:

    - Combines information from multiple sources

    - Adapts response detail level to user role

    - Maintains consistency across multiple interactions

The agents collaborate through the following means:

- A shared understanding of organizational context

- Continuous learning from user interactions

- Dynamic adaptation to different user roles and needs

Environment and external systems

The knowledge management system interfaces with multiple corporate systems and data sources:

- **Internal systems**:

  - **Document management system**: SharePoint, Confluence, and internal wikis

  - **Communication platforms**: Slack and MS Teams

  - **Project management tools**: Jira and Asana project documentation

  - **Email servers**: Archived email threads and attachments

  - **Code repositories**: GitHub and GitLab documentation and discussions

  - **HR systems**: Training materials and policy documents

  - **Customer relationship management**: Customer interaction histories and support tickets

- **External APIs and services**:

  - **Industry news APIs**: Bloomberg or Reuters for market updates

  - **Research databases**: Academic papers and patent databases

  - **Regulatory databases**: Compliance documentation and legal updates

  - **Cloud storage**: Google Drive or OneDrive for shared documents

  - **Translation services**: For multilingual document processing

  - **Web monitoring**: Social media and competitor websites

- **Access control layer**:

  - Role-based access management system

  - Security classification database

  - User authentication service

  - Audit logging system

  - Compliance monitoring tools

Why this is better

Traditional knowledge management systems rely on exact keyword matches and predefined categories. An agentic approach offers several advantages:

- Natural language understanding of complex queries

- Context-aware information retrieval

- Dynamic connection of related information

- Personalized responses based on user role and expertise

This approach to knowledge management demonstrates how agentic systems can transform information access and utilization within organizations, making institutional knowledge more accessible and actionable. As we've seen how language agents can revolutionize information access and communication, we now turn our attention to their physical world applications in robotics and autonomous systems. The ability to combine language understanding with physical control creates new possibilities for human-robot interaction, which we'll explore in the next section.

Robotics and autonomous systems

Moving from language-based interactions to physical world applications, we now explore how LLM-based agents are transforming robotics and autonomous systems. While traditional robots rely on pre-programmed behaviors and rigid control systems, agentic systems enable robots to understand natural language instructions, reason about their environment, and adapt their behavior dynamically. This integration of language models with physical control systems represents a fundamental shift in how robots interact with both humans and their environment.

Evolution of robotic agents

The marriage of LLMs with robotics has created systems that can bridge the gap between human intent and physical action. Unlike traditional robotic systems that operate on fixed rules, modern robotic agents can understand context, learn from experience, and make autonomous decisions while maintaining alignment with human objectives. Here are the key capabilities that distinguish modern robotic agents:

- Natural language understanding for physical tasks

- Contextual reasoning about environmental constraints

- Real-time adaptation to changing conditions

- Learning from demonstration and feedback

- Multi-modal integration of vision, language, and control

Real-world applications

Current implementations showcase the versatility of agentic systems across various domains. At Boston Dynamics, robots such as Atlas demonstrate how language-based instruction can be translated into complex physical movements. Similarly, UC Berkeley's robotic systems show how generative models enable real-time adaptation to cluttered environments, while MIT's RoboBrain system illustrates how agents can creatively solve physical manipulation tasks by drawing on vast knowledge bases. Let's consider a real use case and evaluate how an agentic system may help implement such a system.

Problem statement

Traditional manufacturing cells struggle with product variation and unexpected disruptions. Current systems require extensive reprogramming for new products and can't effectively handle unexpected situations such as equipment failures or supply chain disruptions. Human operators must constantly intervene to manage changes and optimize workflows. The goal is to create a multi-agent system that orchestrates a flexible manufacturing cell, capable of adapting to product variations, handling disruptions, and optimizing processes while maintaining quality standards and safety protocols.

Let's look at the agentic system approach:

- **Planning and coordination agent**:

  - Understands natural language production requirements

  - Develops and adapts manufacturing sequences

  - Coordinates between different robotic systems

  - Maintains overall production goals

- **Robot control agent**:

  - Translates high-level instructions into motion primitives

  - Manages real-time sensor feedback

  - Adapts movements based on environmental changes

  - Ensures safe human-robot interaction

- **Quality and optimization agent**:

  - Monitors production quality in real time

  - Suggests process improvements

  - Predicts maintenance needs

  - Optimizes resource utilization

- **Exception handling agent**:

    - Detects anomalies and disruptions

    - Generates recovery strategies

    - Manages unexpected human interventions

    - Maintains safety protocols during exceptions

The agents collaborate through the following means:

- A shared understanding of the manufacturing context

- Real-time sensor data integration

- Continuous feedback loops for process optimization

- Dynamic task reallocation during disruptions

Environment and external systems

The manufacturing system interfaces with several systems:

- **Manufacturing infrastructure**:

    - **Robotic arms and end effectors**: Multiple robot types with different capabilities

    - **Vision systems**: Cameras and 3D sensors for part recognition and quality control

    - **PLC systems: Programmable logic controllers** (PLCs) for equipment control

    - **Material handling systems**: Conveyors, **automated guided vehicles (AGVs)**, and storage systems

- **Information systems**:

    - **Manufacturing execution system (MES)**: Production scheduling and tracking

    - **Enterprise resource planning (ERP)**: Resource and inventory management

    - **Quality management system (QMS)**: Quality data and specifications

    - **Digital twin platform**: Real-time simulation and prediction

    - **Maintenance management system**: Equipment health monitoring

- **External interfaces**:

  - **Supply chain management system**: Material availability and logistics

  - **Customer order system**: Product specifications and requirements

  - **Compliance database**: Safety standards and regulatory requirements

  - **Knowledge base**: Historical production data and best practices

Why this is better

Traditional robotic manufacturing systems rely on rigid programming and require extensive human intervention for adaptations. An agentic system approach offers several transformative advantages:

- Natural language interaction for production changes and problem-solving

- Real-time adaptation to product variations without reprogramming

- Autonomous handling of disruptions and exceptions

- Continuous optimization based on historical and real-time data

- Seamless integration of human expertise when needed

- Proactive quality control and maintenance prediction

This approach fundamentally transforms manufacturing flexibility by enabling robots to understand context, adapt to changes, and make autonomous decisions while maintaining alignment with production goals and safety requirements. The success of agentic systems in manufacturing demonstrates their potential in complex physical environments where multiple systems must coordinate while adapting to changing conditions. By combining language understanding with physical control and real-time optimization, these systems are evolving from simple automation tools to intelligent collaborators in the manufacturing process.

As we conclude our exploration of robotics and autonomous systems, we turn our attention to how agentic systems are transforming business operations through decision support and optimization. The ability to process complex data streams while maintaining business context makes these systems particularly valuable for strategic decision-making, which we'll examine in the next section.

Decision support and optimization

Having explored the physical world applications of agentic systems, we now turn to their role in augmenting human decision-making and solving complex optimization problems. While traditional decision support systems rely on fixed rules and static analysis, LLM-based agents can understand context, reason about trade-offs, and provide adaptive recommendations while maintaining alignment with business objectives and constraints.

Evolution of decision support agents

The integration of LLMs with decision support systems has transformed how organizations process information and make strategic choices. Modern decision agents can analyze multiple data streams, understand complex business contexts, and generate actionable insights while maintaining awareness of organizational goals and constraints. Key capabilities that distinguish modern decision support agents are as follows:

- Multi-modal data analysis and synthesis

- Context-aware recommendation generation

- Real-time adaptation to changing conditions

- Explanation of reasoning and trade-offs

- Integration of domain expertise with data-driven insights

Real-world applications

Current implementations demonstrate the versatility of agentic systems across various domains:

- **Financial sector**:

  - JPMorgan Chase's LOXM system analyzes market data, news, and social media to identify investment opportunities

  - Two Sigma's Venn system combines market analysis with reinforcement learning for investment strategies

- **Healthcare**:

  - University of Michigan's HealthPal provides personalized treatment recommendations by analyzing medical records and genetic data

  - Stanford's DeepPill system optimizes drug therapies based on patient profiles and medical history

- **Industrial applications**:

  - Siemens' MindSphere optimizes manufacturing processes through real-time analysis and adaptation

  - ExxonMobil's Energy Outlook uses predictive modeling for long-term resource planning

The complexity of modern supply chains offers a compelling example of how agentic systems can transform traditional business processes. Let's examine a real-world implementation where multiple agents work together to orchestrate a global supply chain network, demonstrating how these systems can handle complex, multi-stakeholder environments while maintaining business objectives.

Problem statement

Global supply chains face unprecedented complexity with multiple stakeholders, variable lead times, and frequent disruptions. Traditional optimization tools struggle to handle the dynamic nature of modern supply chains and can't effectively balance competing objectives such as cost, speed, and sustainability. Human planners are overwhelmed by the volume of data and the speed of required decisions. Here, we aim to create a multi-agent system that orchestrates end-to-end supply chain optimization, capable of real-time decision-making while balancing multiple objectives and adapting to disruptions.

The agentic system approach is as follows:

- **Strategic planning agent**:

    - Analyzes market trends and demand patterns

    - Develops long-term sourcing strategies

    - Balances cost, risk, and sustainability goals

    - Maintains alignment with business objectives

- **Operational optimization agent**:

    - Manages day-to-day logistics operations

    - Optimizes routing and resource allocation

    - Handles real-time scheduling adjustments

    - Coordinates with multiple carriers and warehouses

- **Risk management agent**:

    - Monitors global events and disruptions

    - Assesses impact on supply chain operations

    - Generates contingency plans

    - Provides early warning signals

- **Sustainability optimization agent**:

    - Tracks environmental impact metrics

    - Optimizes for carbon footprint reduction

    - Suggests alternative routing and sourcing

    - Ensures compliance with environmental regulations

The agents collaborate through the following means:

- A shared understanding of the supply chain context

- Real-time data integration and analysis

- Continuous scenario planning and risk assessment

- Dynamic re-optimization based on changing conditions

Environment and external systems

The supply chain system interfaces with multiple corporate systems and data sources:

- **Core infrastructure**:

  - **ERP systems**:

    - SAP and Oracle for business operations data

    - Inventory management systems

    - Production planning systems

  - **Transportation management systems (TMSs)**:

    - Real-time fleet tracking

    - Carrier management platforms

    - Route optimization engines

  - **Warehouse management systems (WMSs)**:

    - Inventory tracking and optimization

    - Labor management

    - Order fulfillment systems

- **External data sources**:

  - **Market intelligence platforms**:

    - Bloomberg or Reuters for market data

    - Industry-specific news feeds

    - Social media monitoring systems

- **Weather and environmental systems**:

  - Global weather forecasting

  - Natural disaster tracking

  - Environmental impact monitoring

- **Supplier networks**:

  - Supplier performance databases

  - Capacity and capability tracking

  - Risk assessment platforms

- **Integration layer**:

  - API management system

  - Real-time data streaming platform

  - Event processing engine

  - Document management system

  - Blockchain network for traceability

Why this is better

Traditional supply chain optimization systems operate with limited context and struggle to adapt to rapid changes. An agentic system approach provides several transformative advantages:

- Natural language interaction for strategy development and problem-solving

- Real-time adaptation to multiple changing variables

- Proactive risk identification and mitigation

- Balanced optimization across multiple competing objectives

- Integration of human expertise at strategic decision points

- Continuous learning and improvement from historical decisions

This approach fundamentally transforms supply chain management by enabling intelligent, context-aware decision-making that considers multiple stakeholders and objectives while maintaining alignment with business goals and sustainability requirements.

The success of agentic systems in supply chain optimization demonstrates their potential in complex business environments where multiple factors must be balanced while adapting to constant change. By combining language understanding with advanced optimization techniques and real-time adaptation, these systems are evolving from simple decision-support tools to trusted strategic advisors.

Summary

It is now time to conclude our deep dive into the applications of agentic systems powered by LLMs. In this chapter, we witnessed their transformative impact across diverse domains. These systems represent more than just technological advancement – they mark a fundamental shift in how AI can understand, reason about, and participate in complex human endeavors.

Throughout this chapter, we explored four key domains where agentic systems are reshaping possibilities: creative applications, natural language processing, robotics, and decision support. While these domains showcase significant developments, they represent only a fraction of the areas in which agentic systems are making an impact. From education and scientific research to healthcare and environmental protection, these systems are finding novel applications across numerous fields not covered in this chapter.

The real-world applications we've explored – from collaborative film pre-visualization to manufacturing cell orchestration, and from enterprise knowledge management to supply chain optimization – demonstrate how agentic systems are becoming valuable partners rather than just tools. They show us that the future of AI lies not in replacing human capabilities but in augmenting them through intelligent collaboration.

In the final chapter, we'll review key concepts of agentic systems, explore emerging tools and research, and discuss the possibilities and challenges of artificial general intelligence and artificial superintelligence, concluding with the challenges and opportunities ahead as these technologies evolve.

Questions

1. How do agentic systems in creative applications differ from traditional generative AI tools? Discuss with an example from the chapter.

2. In the context of manufacturing cell orchestration, explain how multiple agents work together and why this approach is more effective than traditional automation systems.

3. Compare and contrast the role of agentic systems in robotics versus decision support systems. How do their approaches to maintaining context differ?

4. Using the enterprise knowledge management use case from the chapter, explain how different agents collaborate to solve complex information retrieval problems.

5. The chapter discussed the supply chain optimization network as a use case. What are the key advantages of using an agentic system approach in this context, and how do the different agents complement each other?

Answers

1. Agentic systems in creative applications maintain context and creative vision across multiple iterations, unlike traditional tools that simply generate content. For example, in the film pre-visualization use case, the director agent maintains creative vision while collaborating with the technical supervisor and visualization agents to ensure both artistic integrity and technical feasibility. This enables continuous alignment between creative goals and practical constraints, something traditional generative tools cannot achieve.

2. In manufacturing cell orchestration, four specialized agents (planning and coordination, robot control, quality and optimization, and exception handling) work together through shared context understanding and continuous feedback loops. This approach is more effective because it enables real-time adaptation to product variations and disruptions while maintaining quality standards. Traditional automation systems lack this flexibility and require human intervention for changes or unexpected situations.

3. In robotics, agentic systems focus on translating language understanding into physical actions while maintaining safety and operational constraints. For example, the robot control agent translates high-level instructions into motion primitives while ensuring safe human-robot interaction. **Motion primitives** are fundamental movement patterns in robotics, such as grasping or turning, used as building blocks for complex actions. A **robot control agent** translates high-level commands into these primitives to ensure safe and efficient execution while maintaining operational constraints.

    In decision support systems, agents focus on processing multiple information streams while maintaining business context and strategic objectives. While both maintain context, robotics agents must bridge the physical-digital divide, while decision support agents must balance multiple competing objectives.

4. In the enterprise knowledge management system, three agents collaborate:

    * The query-understanding agent processes natural language questions and identifies the implicit context

    * The knowledge navigation agent maps relationships between different information sources

    * The response synthesis agent combines information while adapting to user roles

    These agents share organizational context and learn from user interactions, enabling them to handle complex queries that span multiple domains and documents more effectively than traditional search systems.

5. The supply chain optimization network demonstrates the advantages of agentic systems through four specialized agents (strategic planning, operational optimization, risk management, and sustainability optimization) that work together to balance multiple objectives. Key advantages include natural language interaction for strategy development, real-time adaptation to changes, proactive risk identification, and balanced optimization across competing objectives. The agents complement each other by maintaining different aspects of the supply chain context – from long-term strategy to day-to-day operations, risk management, and sustainability goals.

Subscribe to AI_Distilled, the go-to newsletter for AI professionals

To keep up with the latest developments in the fields of Generative AI and LLMs, subscribe to our weekly newsletter, AI_Distilled, at `https://packt.link/8Oz6Y`.

11

Conclusion and Future Outlook

This final chapter brings together everything we've learned in this book about AI-powered systems that can act on their own (agentic systems). We will start by going over the main ideas we've covered, making sure you have a solid understanding of how these systems work. We will then look at what's new and exciting in this field, exploring fresh ideas and research that could change how we think about and use these technologies.

We will also talk about **artificial general intelligence** (**AGI**) – the idea of creating AI that can think and learn like humans across many different tasks. While AGI remains a concept with no practical implementation yet, current AI systems are **narrow AI**, meaning they excel at specific tasks but lack general reasoning abilities. Despite significant advancements in deep learning and large language models, *true AGI requires breakthroughs in reasoning, adaptability, and self-learning beyond predefined tasks*. We'll explore recent progress, the challenges that make AGI difficult to achieve, and what future developments might bring us closer to this vision.

But with great progress come important questions. We'll discuss real challenges such as making these systems work at a larger scale, understanding how they make decisions, and how they might affect society. By looking at both the problems and opportunities, you'll be better prepared to work with and think about these technologies. This chapter is structured into four main sections:

- Recap of key concepts

- Emerging trends and research directions

- Artificial general intelligence

- Challenges and opportunities

By the end of this chapter, you'll have a clear picture of where AI systems are today and where they're heading. You'll understand both their potential and their limitations, helping you be part of the conversation about how to develop these technologies responsibly.

Recap of key concepts

Our journey through the world of AI agents started with the building blocks of generative AI. We learned how these systems can create new content, from images to text, using different approaches such as **Generative Adversarial Networks** (**GANs**) and autoregressive models. This foundation helped us understand not just how these AI systems work but also their current limitations.

We then explored what makes an AI system *agentic* – meaning it can act on its own. These systems need three key abilities: they must react to their environment, take initiative to reach goals, and work well with other agents. Think of it like teaching a computer to be both independent and a good team player.

The book then showed us how these agents think and make decisions. They need ways to store knowledge, learn from experience, and plan their actions. Just like humans use their memory and past experiences to make choices, AI agents need similar capabilities to work effectively.

One of the most interesting aspects we covered was how agents can think about their own actions – what we call reflection and introspection. This self-awareness helps them improve over time and make better decisions. We also learned how agents can use tools and make plans, much like how humans use calculators or make to-do lists to solve problems more efficiently.

A key practical framework we introduced was the Coordinator-Worker-Delegator model. This approach splits tasks between different types of agents:

- Coordinators who manage the overall process

- Workers who handle specific tasks

- Delegators who decide who should do what

We spent time understanding how to build these systems responsibly, focusing on trust and safety. This included making sure AI systems can explain their decisions, protect privacy, and follow ethical guidelines. These considerations are crucial as AI becomes more integrated into our daily lives.

Finally, we explored real-world applications across different fields – from creative tasks such as art and music to practical uses in robotics and decision-making systems. These examples showed how AI agents are already making a difference in various industries.

In the next section, we'll explore what's new in this field and where it's heading. We'll look at exciting developments that could shape the future of AI agents and how they might change the way we work and live.

This recap gives you a strong foundation for understanding what's next. By knowing these basics, you will be better prepared to understand the cutting-edge developments we'll discuss in the coming sections.

Emerging trends and research directions

Let's explore the latest developments that are shaping the future of AI agents and generative systems. We'll look at three main areas where exciting progress is happening: how AI understands multiple types of input, improvements in language understanding, and new ways AI learns from experience, before ending the section with a review of their practical implications.

Multi-modal intelligence – integrating diverse inputs

AI systems are increasingly capable of processing and integrating multiple forms of data—text, images, audio, and video—simultaneously. This multi-modal approach mirrors human perception, allowing for more comprehensive understanding and interaction. For instance, models such as OpenAI's GPT-4o can process and generate text, images, and audio, enabling functionalities such as the following:

- **Visual interpretation**: Analyzing images to provide detailed descriptions

- **Image generation**: Creating visuals from textual prompts

- **Speech processing**: Understanding voice commands and responding appropriately

- **Interactive responses**: Combining visual and textual information to generate contextually relevant outputs

These capabilities enhance user interaction, making AI more intuitive and versatile.

Advanced language comprehension

Language models have achieved remarkable progress, leading to more nuanced and context-aware AI interactions. Key advancements include the following:

- **Few-shot learning**: Enabling models to learn and adapt from minimal examples, improving efficiency in handling new tasks

- **Enhanced contextual understanding**: Allowing AI to maintain coherence over extended conversations, providing more relevant and accurate responses

- **Domain expertise**: Developing specialized models tailored to specific fields, such as medicine or law, to offer expert-level insights

- **Natural conversational abilities**: Incorporating elements such as humor and subtle nuances to make interactions more human-like

For example, **OpenAI's o1 model** focuses on enhanced reasoning capabilities, outperforming previous models in complex tasks that require step-by-step logical processes. Unlike earlier AI systems that often relied on pattern matching and statistical inference, o1 incorporates structured reasoning techniques to break down problems, analyze multiple possibilities, and arrive at more accurate and coherent conclusions. This improvement brings AI closer to advanced problem-solving, but it still falls short of true AGI, as it lacks human-like adaptability, intuition, and self-directed learning across diverse domains.

Experiential learning – reinforcement learning innovations

Advancements in **reinforcement learning (RL)** are transforming how AI systems learn from interactions and experiences. Notable developments include the following:

- **Autonomous skill enhancement**: AI agents independently practicing tasks to achieve proficiency without human intervention

- **Adaptive learning**: Modifying strategies based on past errors to improve future performance

- **Real-world applications**:

  - **Robotics**: Training robots to perform intricate physical tasks through trial and error, enhancing adaptability in dynamic environments

  - **Gaming**: Developing AI that devises novel strategies, surpassing traditional human approaches

- **Improved decision-making**:

  - **Uncertainty management**: Handling incomplete or ambiguous information to make informed choices

  - **Transparent reasoning**: Providing explanations for decisions to build trust and facilitate understanding

For instance, Google's DeepMind has developed AI models such as RoboCat, capable of controlling robotic arms and adapting to new tasks and hardware with minimal human intervention.

Practical implications across industries

These AI advancements are driving innovation and efficiency in various sectors:

- **Healthcare**: AI systems analyzing medical data to assist in diagnostics and treatment planning

- **Finance**: Predicting market trends and managing risks through sophisticated data analysis

- **Entertainment**: Creating more immersive and responsive gaming experiences with AI-driven characters

- **Creative arts**: Assisting in the creation of art, music, and design, expanding the boundaries of creative expression

For example, as we discussed in the previous chapter, AI-generated music and art are becoming increasingly prevalent, with models capable of producing original compositions and artworks based on minimal input. The convergence of multi-modal intelligence, advanced language comprehension, and experiential learning is propelling AI toward more sophisticated and human-like capabilities, with profound implications for technology and society.

Artificial general intelligence

Let's break down what AGI means and why it matters to the future of intelligent systems.

What makes AGI different

Today's AI is like a collection of very specialized tools – great at specific jobs but unable to adapt to new situations. AGI aims to create something different: machines that can think, learn, and solve problems the way humans do. Imagine an AI that could write a symphony one day and solve complex engineering problems the next, all while understanding the deeper meaning behind both tasks.

The big challenge

Building AGI is challenging because we still don't fully understand how human intelligence works. Unlike AI models, humans don't just process information – they reason, adapt, and transfer knowledge seamlessly across domains. Think about how a child learns: they can quickly pick up new skills, grasp cause and effect, and apply lessons from one situation to a completely different one. Replicating this in machines requires solving some major challenges:

Learning to learn

To build AGI, we need AI systems that go beyond memorization and truly generalize knowledge across tasks. This involves the following:

- **Understanding abstract concepts**: Recognizing deeper meanings, analogies, and high-level reasoning

- **Applying knowledge to new situations**: Adapting learned principles to unfamiliar tasks without retraining

- **Developing common sense reasoning**: Making intuitive judgments based on everyday experiences

- **Building on previous experiences**: Retaining and refining knowledge over time, rather than starting from scratch for each task

Real-world understanding

Human intelligence is deeply connected to **perception**, **context**, and **adaptability** – qualities that are difficult for AI to replicate. Key challenges include the following:

- **Processing information like humans do**: Integrating multiple sensory inputs and reasoning beyond structured data

- **Making sense of messy, real-world data**: Handling incomplete, contradictory, or ambiguous information

- **Understanding context and nuance**: Interpreting meaning based on cultural, emotional, and situational cues

- **Dealing with unexpected situations**: Responding flexibly to novel problems that were never explicitly programmed

Overcoming these hurdles requires breakthroughs in areas such as causal reasoning, self-supervised learning, and embodied AI – moving beyond pattern recognition to develop truly adaptive, self-improving systems. While current AI models excel at narrow tasks, true AGI remains a distant goal, requiring a fundamental shift in how machines learn, reason, and interact with the world.

When we combine AGI with autonomous agents, we create something truly revolutionary – systems that can think deeply while acting independently in the world. These combined systems would make complex decisions on their own, understanding not just the technical aspects but also the social and ethical implications of their choices. They would learn continuously from every interaction, whether with humans or other systems, growing more capable over time. Most importantly, they would work as true partners with humans, understanding our goals and values while bringing their own unique capabilities to help solve problems.

The impact of combining AGI with agentic systems could transform how we approach major challenges. Imagine scientists working with AI partners that truly grasp the nuances of research goals, offering novel insights and spotting connections humans might miss. In medicine, these systems could revolutionize diagnosis by connecting seemingly unrelated symptoms with rare conditions, drawing on a vast knowledge base while considering each patient's unique circumstances. For environmental challenges, they could develop comprehensive solutions that balance complex global factors, from economic impacts to ecosystem effects. In education, they could create truly personalized learning experiences, understanding each student's needs, learning style, and interests to deliver exactly the right content at the right time.

The journey toward combining AGI with agentic systems brings up crucial questions about safety, control, and ethics. We need to ensure these powerful systems align with human values and operate within appropriate bounds. This isn't just science fiction anymore – serious researchers and organizations are making real progress toward these goals. The key lies in understanding both the enormous potential and the very real limitations of these systems as we work toward this ambitious vision.

In the next section, we'll dive into these challenges and opportunities, exploring how we can develop these transformative systems responsibly while maximizing their benefits for humanity.

Challenges and opportunities

As we look to the future of AI agents and generative systems, we face both exciting possibilities and important challenges to solve. One of the biggest challenges is making learning systems that can handle massive amounts of complex data efficiently. With data growing exponentially, our current learning methods are starting to show their limits. To solve this, researchers are developing new approaches such as meta-learning, transfer learning, and few-shot learning.

Meta-learning is particularly interesting because it teaches AI systems how to learn better. Instead of just learning specific tasks, these systems learn the process of learning itself. This means they can pick up new skills much faster with less training data. A good example is the **model-agnostic meta-learning (MAML)** system, which works across different types of tasks from image recognition to language processing.

Transfer learning is like teaching AI to apply what it learns in one area to solve problems in another. Think of how a person who learns to play piano might find it easier to learn guitar – the basic music knowledge transfers over. In AI, we see this when models trained on huge image datasets can quickly adapt to specific tasks such as medical imaging.

Few-shot learning addresses another critical limitation: the need for extensive labeled datasets. Unlike traditional methods, few-shot learning aims to train models using only a handful of examples. This approach is invaluable in scenarios where collecting vast amounts of labeled data is impractical, such as rare disease diagnoses or highly specialized industrial applications. By mimicking human-like learning from minimal examples, few-shot learning pushes the boundaries of what AI can achieve.

These advanced learning paradigms come with both challenges and opportunities. They require innovative architectures, computational efficiency, and careful consideration of generalization and bias. However, their potential to enable more adaptable, resource-efficient, and impactful AI systems positions them as pivotal elements in the future of generative AI and autonomous agents.

Another major challenge is making AI systems that can explain their decisions clearly. As these systems get more complex, it becomes harder to understand how they reach their conclusions. This lack of transparency can make people hesitant to trust AI, especially in important areas such as healthcare or financial decisions. To address this, we're developing new ways to visualize and understand how AI makes decisions, such as attention maps that show which parts of an input the AI focuses on most.

Making AI systems reliable and secure in the real world is also crucial. They need to work well even when faced with unexpected situations or attempts to trick them. This means building safeguards and constantly monitoring how they perform.

But there are also huge opportunities ahead. One of the most exciting is creating AI that interacts with humans more naturally. Think about how virtual assistants such as Siri and Alexa have already changed how we interact with technology. Future systems could be even better, understanding not just our words but also our gestures, expressions, and the context of our conversations.

We could also see personalized AI tutors that adapt perfectly to each person's learning style. Imagine a teaching assistant that knows exactly how to explain complex ideas in a way that makes sense to you, using examples from topics you're interested in.

The key to moving forward is finding the right balance between pushing innovation and developing these systems responsibly. We need to solve the technical challenges while making sure these technologies help rather than harm society. By focusing on making AI systems that are scalable, understandable, reliable, and human-friendly, we can unlock their potential to improve our lives in meaningful ways.

Summary

As we wrap up our journey through the world of AI-powered systems that can think and act on their own, we find ourselves at an exciting turning point in technology. What we've explored in this book isn't just about new software or algorithms – it's about creating intelligent systems that could fundamentally change how we solve problems and interact with technology.

Throughout this book, we covered the building blocks of these systems: how they learn, how they make decisions, and how they can work together. We saw how they can look at their own actions and improve, use tools to solve problems, and work in teams with different agents handling different parts of complex tasks. We also tackled the crucial questions of trust and safety, making sure these powerful tools help rather than harm.

The future ahead is both challenging and thrilling. Yes, we need to solve tough problems such as making these systems work with huge amounts of data, helping them explain their decisions clearly, and keeping them secure. But the opportunities are incredible – imagine AI assistants that truly understand us, educational tools that adapt perfectly to how each person learns, and systems that can help us tackle global challenges such as climate change and disease.

The idea of AGI – AI that can think and learn as humans do – might seem like a distant dream. But the work we're doing today in building these autonomous systems that can reason, learn, and adapt is laying the groundwork for that future. Each breakthrough in how AI agents learn from experience, work together, and understand the world brings us closer to that goal.

But perhaps most importantly, we learned that creating these systems isn't just a technical challenge – it's a human one. We need to build them thoughtfully, making sure they align with our values and serve the greater good. The future of AI isn't about replacing human intelligence but about creating tools that enhance our own capabilities and help us solve problems in new ways.

As you close this book, remember that you're now part of this journey. Whether you're a developer, researcher, or someone interested in where technology is heading, you have the knowledge to help shape how these systems develop and how they're used to benefit society. The field of AI and autonomous systems is moving quickly, but the principles we've covered – about how these systems learn, how they should be designed responsibly, and how they can work alongside humans – will remain relevant as the technology evolves. The future isn't just about what these systems can do – it's about what we choose to do with them.

Looking ahead, the possibilities are boundless. We're not just building better software; we're working toward a future where artificial intelligence can help us tackle our biggest challenges and open up new opportunities we haven't even imagined yet. That's the real promise of AI agents – not just smarter machines but better solutions to human problems.

Get This Book's PDF Version and Exclusive Extras

Scan the QR code (or go to `packtpub.com/unlock`). Search for this book by name, confirm the edition, and then follow the steps on the page.

Note: Keep your invoice handly. Purchase made directly from packt don't require one.

12
Unlock Your Exclusive Benefits

Your copy of this book includes the following exclusive benefit:

- ⟳ Next-gen Packt Reader
- 📄 DRM-free PDF/ePub downloads

Follow the guide below to unlock them. The process takes only a few minutes and needs to be completed once.

Unlock this Book's Free Benefits in 3 Easy Steps

Step 1

Keep your purchase invoice ready for *Step 3*. If you have a physical copy, scan it using your phone and save it as a PDF, JPG, or PNG.

For more help on finding your invoice, visit `https://www.packtpub.com/unlock-benefits/help`.

> **Note**
>
> If you bought this book directly from Packt, no invoice is required. After *Step 2*, you can access your exclusive content right away.

Step 2

Scan the QR code or go to `packtpub.com/unlock`.

On the page that opens (similar to *Figure 12.1* on desktop), search for this book by name and select the correct edition.

Discover and unlock your book's exclusive benefits

Bought a Packt book? Your purchase may come with free bonus benefits designed to maximise your learning. Discover and unlock them here

Discover Benefits   Sign Up/In   Upload Invoice

Need Help?

1. Discover your book's exclusive benefits

Search by title or ISBN

CONTINUE TO STEP 2

2. Login or sign up for free

3. Upload your invoice and unlock

Figure 12.1: Packt unlock landing page on desktop

Step 3

After selecting your book, sign in to your Packt account or create one for free. Then upload your invoice (PDF, PNG, or JPG, up to 10 MB). Follow the on-screen instructions to finish the process.

Need help?

If you get stuck and need help, visit
`https://www.packtpub.com/unlock-benefits/help`
for a detailed FAQ on how to find your invoices and more. This QR code will take you to the help page.

> **Note**
>
> If you are still facing issues, reach out to `customercare@packt.com`.

Index

I

intelligent agent

characteristics 35, 36

reviewing 35, 36

intelligent agent, key attributes

proactiveness 35

reactivity 35

social ability 35

inductive reasoning 58, 59

applications 59

input structuring 155

instruction formatting 155

input structuring 155

integrated development environments (IDEs) 18

integration and interaction patterns

event-driven updates 171

state validation and consistency 171, 173

integration tools 113

intellectual property (IP) 211

intelligent agents

decision-making 62

introspection 82

knowledge representation 52

planning 62

reasoning 56

interaction patterns 156

feedback loops 157

message passing protocols 156

state management 156

introspection

in intelligent agents 82

K

key performance indicators (KPIs) 99

knowledge-based architectures 36

knowledge representation approaches, in intelligent agents

frames 54, 55

logic-based representations 55, 56

semantic works 52, 53

L

LangGraph

implementing 132, 133

versus AutoGen 134

versus CrewAI 134

large language models (LLMs) 9, 206

large language models (LLMs) types

autoregressive LLMs 10

domain-specific LLMs 11

encoder-decoder LLMs 10

encoder-only LLMs 10

instruction-tuned LLMs 10

multimodal LLMs 10

learning mechanisms, adaptive agents

reinforcement learning 62

supervised learning 61

transfer learning 62

unsupervised learning 61

less practical planning algorithms 117

A* planning 118

GraphPlan 118

MCTS 118

STRIPS 117

LLM-based planning 117, 120-122

LLMFastForward class

create_relaxed_plan 119

select_next_action 119

LLM-powered AI agents 11-17

logic-based representations

in real-world applications 56

U

V

W

Z

packtpub.com

Subscribe to our online digital library for full access to over 7,000 books and videos, as well as industry leading tools to help you plan your personal development and advance your career. For more information, please visit our website.

Why subscribe?

- Spend less time learning and more time coding with practical eBooks and Videos from over 4,000 industry professionals

- Improve your learning with Skill Plans built especially for you

- Get a free eBook or video every month

- Fully searchable for easy access to vital information

- Copy and paste, print, and bookmark content

Did you know that Packt offers eBook versions of every book published, with PDF and ePub files available? You can upgrade to the eBook version at packtpub.com and as a print book customer, you are entitled to a discount on the eBook copy. Get in touch with us at customercare@packtpub.com for more details.

At www.packtpub.com, you can also read a collection of free technical articles, sign up for a range of free newsletters, and receive exclusive discounts and offers on Packt books and eBooks.

Other Books You May Enjoy

If you enjoyed this book, you may be interested in these other books by Packt:

Generative AI on Google Cloud with LangChain

Leonid Kuligin, Jorge Zaldívar, Maximilian Tschochohei

ISBN: 978-1-83588-932-9

- Build enterprise-ready applications with LangChain and Google Cloud
- Navigate and select the right Google Cloud generative AI tools
- Apply modern design patterns for generative AI applications
- Plan and execute proof-of-concepts for enterprise AI solutions
- Gain hands-on experience with LangChain's and Google Cloud's AI products
- Implement advanced techniques for text generation and summarization
- Leverage Vertex AI Search and other tools for scalable AI solutions

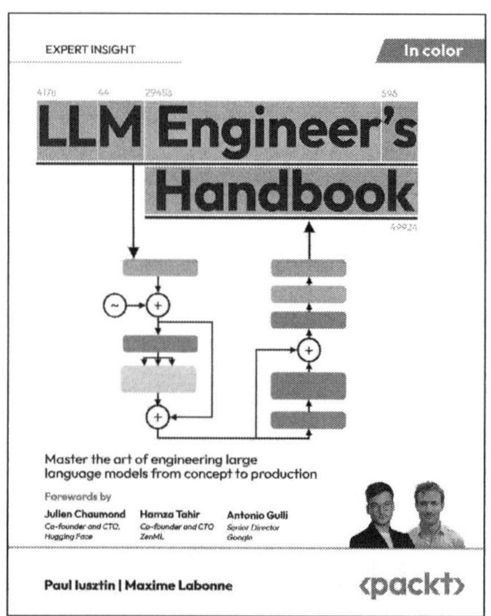

LLM Engineer's Handbook

Paul Iusztin, Maxime Labonne

ISBN: 978-1-83620-007-9

- Implement robust data pipelines and manage LLM training cycles

- Create your own LLM and refine it with the help of hands-on examples

- Get started with LLMOps by diving into core MLOps principles such as orchestrators and prompt monitoring

- Perform supervised fine-tuning and LLM evaluation

- Deploy end-to-end LLM solutions using AWS and other tools

- Design scalable and modularLLM systems

- Learn about RAG applications by building a feature and inference pipeline

Packt is searching for authors like you

If you're interested in becoming an author for Packt, please visit `authors.packtpub.com` and apply today. We have worked with thousands of developers and tech professionals, just like you, to help them share their insight with the global tech community. You can make a general application, apply for a specific hot topic that we are recruiting an author for, or submit your own idea.

Share Your Thoughts

Now you've finished *Building Agentic AI Systems*, we'd love to hear your thoughts! Scan the QR code below to go straight to the Amazon review page for this book and share your feedback or leave a review on the site that you purchased it from.

`https://packt.link/r/1803238755`

Your review is important to us and the tech community and will help us make sure we're delivering excellent quality content.

Join our community on Discord

Have questions about the book or want to contribute to discussions on Generative AI and LLMs? Join our Discord server at `https://packt.link/z8ivB`.

Subscribe to AI_Distilled, the go-to newsletter for AI professionals

To keep up with the latest developments in the fields of Generative AI and LLMs, subscribe to our weekly newsletter, AI_Distilled, at `https://packt.link/8Oz6Y`.

Made in the USA
Monee, IL
02 July 2026